William Whewell, James Mackintosh

On the Progress of ethical Philosophy

Chiefly during the XVIIth & XVIIIth Centuries. Fourth Edition

William Whewell, James Mackintosh

On the Progress of ethical Philosophy
Chiefly during the XVIIth & XVIIIth Centuries. Fourth Edition

ISBN/EAN: 9783337076566

Printed in Europe, USA, Canada, Australia, Japan

Cover: Foto ©ninafisch / pixelio.de

More available books at **www.hansebooks.com**

ON THE PROGRESS

OF

ETHICAL PHILOSOPHY

CHIEFLY DURING THE XVIITH & XVIIITH CENTURIES

BY

SIR JAMES MACKINTOSH

LL.D., F.R.S.

EDITED BY WILLIAM WHEWELL, D.D.

LATE MASTER OF TRINITY COLLEGE, CAMBRIDGE
CORRESPONDING MEMBER OF THE INSTITUTE OF FRANCE

FOURTH EDITION

EDINBURGH
ADAM AND CHARLES BLACK
1872

[*All rights reserved.*]

NOTICE.

This Edition is simply a reprint, in an altered form, of the previous edition in demy octavo, edited by the late Professor Whewell in 1862. At the same time, while passing through the press, the opportunity has been taken to correct a few typographical errors which had inadvertently crept in, and to add to the work a General Index.

EDINBURGH, *January* 1872.

CONTENTS.

	PAGE
ADVERTISEMENT (Biographical)	vii
NOTE TO THE EDITION OF 1862	x
EDITOR'S PREFACE	xiii
I. The Affections are not Selfish	xv
II. Existence and Supremacy of the Moral Faculty	xxii
III. The Sentiments are formed by Association	xxxix
IV. Mackintosh's Theory of Conscience	xlii
V. Moral Faculty and greatest Happiness agree	xliv
VI. Relation of Morality and Religion	xlv
VII. Moral Explanation of Free-will	xlvi

THE DISSERTATION.

INTRODUCTION	1
Section 1. Preliminary Observations	8
2. Retrospect of Ancient Ethics	16
3. Retrospect of Scholastic Ethics	33
4. Modern Ethics	52
GROTIUS	52
HOBBES	54
Remarks	62

CONTENTS.

	PAGE
Section 5. Controversies concerning the Moral Faculties and the Social Affections	70
CUMBERLAND	70
CUDWORTH	73
CLARKE	78
Remarks	81
SHAFTESBURY	88
FÉNELON—BOSSUET	96
LEIBNITZ	100
Remarks	102
MALEBRANCHE	105
EDWARDS	107
BUFFIER	110
6. Foundations of a more just Theory of Ethics	112
BUTLER	113
Remarks	118
HUTCHESON	124
BERKELEY	128
HUME	133
SMITH	146
Remarks	150
PRICE	155
HARTLEY	156
TUCKER	174
PALEY	179
BENTHAM	187
STEWART	210
BROWN	227
7. General Remarks	241
NOTES AND ILLUSTRATIONS	279
INDEX	305

ADVERTISEMENT.

THE following Dissertation forms one of a series of similar Pieces, intended to exhibit a view of the History of the Sciences, and which compose the first or introductory volume of the eighth edition of the *Encyclopædia Britannica*. In presenting it to the world detached from that work, the proprietors have complied with a wish very frequently expressed for its separate publication; and they think themselves fortunate in being enabled to accompany it with a Preface which presents a succinct and comprehensive view of its leading objects and doctrines. As allusion is there made to the "irregular and interrupted manner" in which it was written, and to the want of any notice of the recent Ethical speculations of the Continental Philosophers, it may be proper, in justice to the very eminent author, to lay before the reader the following history of its composition, as given in the interesting Memoirs of his Life, published by his Son.

"The late Mr. Dugald Stewart and Mr. Playfair had agreed to furnish Dissertations, the one on the history of Metaphysical, Ethical, and Political Philosophy, the other on the history of Mathematical and Physical Science, to be prefixed to the *Supplement* to the *Encyclo-*

pædia Britannica. The design was not completed by either of those illustrious writers. Both died before their respective portions of it were finished. The history of the mathematical and physical sciences, by the latter, was brought down to the period marked by the discoveries of Newton and Leibnitz; and the history of metaphysical philosophy was, by the former, brought down to the close of the last century. In treating this great branch of his subject, Mr. Stewart has occasionally adverted to the kindred branches of ethics and politics; but there was wanting to the completion of his design a full view of the progress of opinion in those sciences, particularly during the eighteenth century. In 1828, a new and improved edition of the *Encyclopædia*, being the seventh, was projected, and it was a part of the Editor's plan for the improvement of this edition, to continue the magnificent historical Dissertations that had been published with the *Supplement*, and to prefix the whole, in their completed form, to this edition of the principal work. A proposal to write a Dissertation in continuation of that of Mr. Stewart upon the Ethical and Political Philosophy of the last century, was, in August 1828, accordingly made to Sir James, by the Editor, Mr. Macvey Napier. Having already resolved to devote the remainder of his labours to British history, he had considerable difficulty in acceding to the proposal. But his love of the subject, his natural wish to preserve some of his early reading and reflections, and the entreaties of Mr. Napier, who had a few years before been introduced to him by Mr. Stewart, and with whom he was in the habit of corresponding, prevailed over his scruples, and an agreement in consequence took place for the execution of an historical Dissertation, embracing this object, and extending over the period that had been left untouched by his predecessor. It had originally been agreed, as above stated, that the Dissertation should include political as well as ethical philosophy, but the author's uncertain health, and the parliamentary duties of an interesting crisis, occasioned the abandonment of this part of the plan, and even obliged him to omit the history of the ethical philosophy of the Continent.

"In a letter to Mr. Napier, dated in January 1829, he says, 'I am now reconciled to my labour by a new rising hope, that it may enable me to make some of the contributions to Ethics which, in more ambitious days, I presumed to expect would have been more extensive.' And in another letter, written about the same time, he thus expresses himself : 'You will see I have made some (I hope useful) additions to one of the sections, and I would have made more, if I could have afforded the time. But alas! I have none to spare; otherwise, I like this sort of work much better than any other.' Speaking of his progress, a little afterwards, he says, 'I begin to hope well of my discourse, which I endeavour to make a development of ethical principles, as they historically arose—a new attempt in our language.'

"Again, he thus adverts to the section on Bishop Butler then just finished :—'The part in which I think I have done most service is that in which I have endeavoured to slip in a foundation under Butler's doctrine of the supremacy of conscience, which he left baseless.'—When he came, in April 1829, to fear that it would be necessary to abandon all notice, not only of the progress of political philosophy, but also of the ethical philosophy of the Continent, he expressed great regret at the probable omission of this last section. 'I shall be quite sorry,' he said, 'if time should require the omission of the continental part, which would be the newest of the whole.'

"No one could be more thoroughly aware than himself of the imperfections that must attach to a work on such a subject, written by snatches, and amidst such frequent and sometimes distressing interruptions; and he accordingly mentions that it was very earnestly his wish 'to leave an edition of it, with such improvements as time, criticism, conversation, and reflection might suggest.' This very natural wish he unfortunately did not live long enough to have an opportunity afforded him of carrying into execution."

NOTE TO THIS EDITION.

The Dissertation of Sir James Mackintosh was circulated among his friends before it was regularly published in the *Encyclopædia*. Mr. James Mill hereupon wrote some remarks upon it, which he says were written "with that severity of reprehension which the first feelings of indignation against an evil-doer inspire." From unavoidable circumstances the publication of these Remarks was delayed till the death of Sir James. They were then published (in 1835) with the title "*A Fragment on Mackintosh:*" this title being imitated from Bentham's first work, *A Fragment on Government*, which was a severe critique on the early part of Blackstone's *Commentaries*, then recently published. The remarks on Mackintosh's Dissertation appeared to me erroneous in their principles; but more especially worthy of blame as an attempt to lower the reputation of the author by captiousness, contumely, and buffoonery. This view of the nature of the attack led me to wish to say something in defence of Mackintosh; and it was therefore that I proposed to the editors to publish a separate edition of the Dissertation with remarks of mine. To this proposal they agreed; and the Dissertation was published in 1836, with the following Preface. W. W.

CAMBRIDGE, 1862.

PREFACE.

THE publication of Sir James Mackintosh's "Dissertation on the Progress of Ethical Philosophy," detached from the voluminous work of which it originally appeared as part,* will probably be acceptable to a large portion of the English public. The author's extensive acquaintance with the literature of the subject, his comprehensive and philosophical views, his sagacity as a critic, and his skill as a writer, have long been generally acknowledged. The work now before the reader afforded a favourable field for the exercise of his talents, and cannot fail to attract attention from all who feel any interest in him or his subject.

A History of the Philosophy of Morals may, for many purposes, be considered as forming a large portion of the Philosophy itself; and probably, to most readers, the portion which is by far the most agreeable. The writer of such a history, if it be worthy the name, must present all that has been done by the moralists of preceding times as steps in a progress; and must thus be led to point out the ultimate position which the subject has in his own day assumed.

The history of ethical speculations which the following Dissertation contains, has, however, not only the merit of exhibiting the present condition of ethical philosophy, but has also a peculiar advantage in the point

* The *Encyclopædia Britannica*.

of view from which the subject is regarded; since the author's opinions were, in the main, those to which the most moderate and popular writers of his own country had generally been led, and which had therefore most influenced general literature and common reasonings. A view of Moral Philosophy written in such a spirit escapes, and may in some measure correct, the exaggerations and paradoxes of new and immature theories.

Some of Mackintosh's views were peculiarly his own, but much of his system of opinions was adopted from the doctrines of the great philosophers whom he here reviews. Perhaps some light may be thrown on the following Dissertation, by stating the main points of both kinds, as they may be collected from the work itself; and this will be in some measure done in the present preface. Also, as the ethical system embraced by Mackintosh included some tenets which have in our own time been the subject of much controversy, and on which it appears to me that errors have been widely prevalent, I have ventured to make a few remarks, such as I thought most fitted to put the doctrines in their proper point of view. I may add, that as my author's survey is in a great measure restricted to British writers, I have not thought myself called on to take note of the direction which ethical speculations have recently assumed in France and Germany, or of the indications which have appeared in the literature of our own country of the influence of these foreign impulses.

The views which Mackintosh entertained, and which were peculiarly the result of his own reasonings, are delivered in various parts of the Dissertation, but will perhaps become more intelligible by being stated as they are to be collected from the whole. The work was written in an irregular and interrupted manner; a circumstance which introduced many repetitions, and a mixture of the didactic with the historical portions, which may have given rise to some confusion.

I. The first main point in Mackintosh's view of ethics, is his opinion, that those which are usually termed the benevolent affections (as, for example, parental love and compassion) are properly described as *disinterested*. This doctrine he notices as one of the valuable truths which Butler brought clearly into view (p. 116); and he attaches to it so much consequence, that, in concluding his Dissertation (p. 277), he declares himself ready to relinquish his theory, if it be proved to be at variance with the reality of the social affections, which he there speaks of as the most indisputable and the most important part of human nature.

Opinions opposite to this have been asserted in various forms; some, for instance, have said, that the affections are all merely forms of self-love; or that they are selfish; or that they really regard self; or have professed to deduce them from some selfish principle, as Hobbes from the love of power. A few remarks may here suffice on each of these modifications of the selfish system.

(1.) Butler, and after him other writers, as well as Mackintosh, wish, for the sake of clearness, to confine the application of the term *self-love* to that cool and prudential regard to our own welfare which weighs and estimates the chances and means of happiness; and which is thus distinct from the passions and affections which impel us to action immediately, without intervening reflection or calculation of consequences. It will probably be universally allowed, that gratitude or pity, friendship or filial love, are clearly distinct from self-love, *in this sense*. The term self-love has been objected to altogether by some persons, and Mackintosh himself appears to be dissatisfied with it. Yet it seems to be not inapt to describe that state of mind in which we regard ourselves as external and detached objects of solicitude, and provide for our own well-being, as we would do for that of a friend whose passions we can resist, and whose future and permanent good we try to secure, without losing our calmness of feeling and clearness of view. The self-love which aims at our own welfare in such a temper may make us do kind actions; but it is, in itself, broadly distinguished from kindness and love of other persons.

But further, it is argued by Butler and Mackintosh, that not only the benevolent affections, but the *appetites* also are clearly distinguishable from *this* self-love. A man may, as Butler says, eat from self-love, out of a regard to his health; he may also eat from the appetite of hunger; but the grounds of action are plainly different in the two cases. The gratification which results from the act does not make it an act of self-love. And just as little, they urge, does the gratification which accompanies the exercise of the domestic, or any other benevolent affections, justify us in ascribing them to such self-love as we have described.

(2.) As the object of the appetites is something different from ourselves and our own feelings, the object of the benevolent desires is so too. As food is the object of hunger, the gratification or the well-being of the child is the object of parental affection. The pleasure which results when the object is attained is not the aim of the agent, for it does not enter into his contemplation; nor could we derive pleasure from the attainment of such objects except the desire had previously existed (p. 119). In conformity with this view, it is maintained by the writers of this school, that neither the appetites nor the desires can properly be called *selfish*. (Stewart, *Outlines of Moral Philosophy*, p. 86.)

The term *selfish*, which is, I think, not used by Butler in the part of his works now referred to, is, however, that about which the controversy on this subject has generally raged most hotly. In opposition to the opinion just stated, it has often been said, that the desire of power, of wealth, of superiority, of esteem, are selfish principles.

If it be contended that these desires (and the benevolent affections for the same reason) are selfish because they are felt *by* self, Mackintosh answers (p. 119), that acts of the understanding, and processes of reasoning, might be called selfish on the same ground. But it is easily seen that something different from this is usually meant by the assertion. When it is popularly contended that the love of fame, for instance, is a selfish principle of action, it is generally implied that this affection is more selfish than to common eyes it appears. The assertor gives himself credit for having analysed the motive in question into elements not immediately obvious;—for discerning that a feeling, which at first appears to have an elevated and exterior aim, has in fact, latently, a reflex view and a lower object. The disposition which men have to be pleased with such attempts at the dissection of motives into baser elements, is widely prevalent: it is this disposition, for instance, which has given to the Maxims of La Rochefoucauld their charm and their popularity.

But the flashes of the epigrammatist, whatever applause they may excite, are not likely to be of much use as a light to the philosophical reasoner; and the question, What motives can properly be called *selfish?* as a point of moral philosophy, must be decided in a very different spirit. Now, the popular disposition to detect selfishness in human motives is obviously accompanied by a depreciating estimate of the feelings in which this taint is perceived. But this disapproval, in spite of the conceit and ill-nature in which it may originate, manifestly implies a belief that men's feelings may be, and ought to be, other than selfish; for how can we contemn a person for having selfish feelings only, if human nature admits of no others? The common application of the term *selfish*, implies a moral disapprobation as well as a metaphysical analysis. We endeavour in vain to dissolve this association; and yet, so long as it subsists, it is plain that the condemnation which we pronounce in some cases, implies the possibility of cases in which it is not deserved. If we despise the love of fame as a selfish motive, we reserve our admiration for motives of a different class. The emphasis with which we apply the term, implies that it is not universally applicable. But when we assert, as a universal philosophical truth, that all our affections are selfish, we employ the word in a technical manner, distinct from its common use. Now, where is the advantage to philosophy of telling us that our love of parents and friends, that our gratitude and compassion, are selfish feelings, if the assertion be true only when the word is used in a sense different from the common one? The paradox startles us; when explained, it ceases to shock; but why incur the necessity of such an explanation? It must be allowed that such affections as I have just mentioned deserve and attract our love and approbation as much as any feelings can do; why, then, use terms which seem fitted only to direct towards them our disapproval and aversion?

We may add, with Brown (*Lectures*, vol. iv. p. 63), that if the benevolent and virtuous affections are to be called selfish, it will be necessary to form two divisions of selfish actions;—one containing those selfish actions in which self is the direct object; the other containing those very different selfish actions which are usually called disinterested. Till it is seen what advantage would be gained by this new nomenclature, it is surely better to use terms in their usual sense.

It is not easy to fix precise limits to the use of the term selfish, which thus denotes, not a positive philosophical attribute, but a comparative quality, to which some blame inevitably clings. Mackintosh says well that "The weakness of the social affections, and the strength of the private desires, properly constitute selfishness." And Stewart (*Outlines*, p. 114) gives nearly the same account of this word, which he illustrates by saying, "Though we apply the epithet selfish to avarice, and to low and private sensuality, we never apply it to the desire of knowledge, or to the pursuits of virtue, which are certainly sources of more exquisite pleasures than riches or sensuality can bestow."

(3.) That the benevolent affections, in their usual form, have not self for their immediate *object*, is so evident that it needs hardly to be insisted on. In what sense can the mother who unhesitatingly exposes her life to save that of her child, be said to regard herself, of whom she never once thinks? In what way does Desdemona act from self-regard, when, in the very article of death, she endeavours to shelter the reputation of the husband who murders her?* To speak of self as the object of the regard or contemplation of the person acting in such instances, or in any instances in which the action proceeds directly from the benevolent affections, is to deprive words and phrases of all distinct and intelligible meaning and use.

(4.) When any particular theory is propounded, by which the results of the benevolent affections are traced to some remote interested principle, a refutation of the theory is readily suggested by a consideration of the common characteristic circumstances of the affections. Thus, with regard to Hobbes' system—that the affections have their origin in the love of power—Butler

---

* *Desdemona.* A guiltless death I die.
    Emilie.   O who hath done
        This deed?
    Desdemona.   Nobody; I myself; farewell;
        Commend me to my kind lord; O farewell.—(*Dies.*)

answers briefly, but satisfactorily, that such an hypothesis does not lead us to anything at all resembling the known state of the case ;—that we wish good to others quite independently of our being ourselves the authors of it ;—that we make distinctions among the objects of our good-will, where the love of power would make no difference ;—that the love of power would be gratified by doing harm as well as good, and that thus cruelty and benevolence would be the same affection. (Sermon I., Note ; and the following Dissertation, p. 116.) And if it were proposed to reduce the benevolent affections to any other system of original principles and associations of thought, it might be answered that if these supposed original principles involve the desire of any besides physical pleasures (as the desire of wealth, power, dignity), they themselves require analysis, at least as much as the affections. It is, at least, as possible to love a father as it is to desire his estate ; and the greatest good that the estate can procure us can hardly consist of anything more intelligible than filial love. Nor would such an hypothesis avail us ; for the affections are, in the greater number of cases, far stronger than any aggregation of such supposed elements would make them. To what purpose do we associate ideas with the desire of wealth, power, and dignity, in order to form the family affections, if we are compelled to allow that the whole feeling thus produced is greater than the sum of all its parts ? To claim philosophical merit for such an analysis of the disinterested emotions into the effects of association of ideas, is to deprive the terms Association and Analysis of all meaning. Or how are our benevolent affections accounted for by the need we have of our friends as means, if this regard to the means be both much stronger and much more distinctly intelligible than the regard to the ends can ever become? Does not this show that, in fact, the hypothetical end is not *our* end?

On such grounds, Mackintosh and other writers appear to do well in arranging the benevolent affections as a class of principles of action distinct from the desire of power, superiority, and the like. Those are not capable of being analysed into these, and we are sensible of an unsurmountable incongruity when the two classes are brought into comparison. If the love of a parent be a compound of love, of power, and similar ingredients, will it not follow, that if we expect to gain power by sacrificing a parent rather than by serving him, it is *consistent with the nature* of our best affections that we should do so? And is not this a conclusion too monstrous to be accepted by any moralist? The benevolent and family affections, and the desire of power, appear, then, to differ in some other way than in being modifications of the same elements; and, even if we choose (unphilosophically as it has appeared) to call the latter class of principles selfish, the former must be arranged in a different group, which we cannot designate better than by calling them disinterested.

II. The next leading principles of Mackintosh's philosophy are, the independent *existence* and the *supremacy* of the conscience or moral faculty. Here also he ascribes to Butler the merit of having first brought these doctrines into a clear light (p. 122); though Hutcheson, who had somewhat of a steadier view of this faculty, gave it the name of the *moral sense*.

The question of the moral sense has been much discussed since Butler's time. It is not necessary here to go fully into this controversy, but I may be allowed to make a few remarks on some of the arguments connected with the following Dissertation.

(1.) In the first place, as to the *existence* of the moral faculty. It is allowed on all sides that we have a conception of moral obligation; and the question is, Whether this conception can be resolved into some operation of the intellectual faculties, as the perception of general utility; or whether, on the contrary, it is incapable of being thus resolved, and must properly be ascribed to a separate faculty?

It will readily appear that the discussion of this question must be attended by great difficulties, for we cannot easily find a test to determine, or terms to express, the identity or the difference of our perceptions of the useful and the right. These internal perceptions can only be described by means of analogical and metaphorical language; and this must discharge its office very imperfectly. Even with respect to external senses, where the meaning of our terms is naturally much more clear and palpable, an exact treatment of such questions is far from easy. We cannot, by mere language, convey a conception of the difference of sights and sounds. Is the perception of form a different faculty from the perception of colour? This question has been found extremely perplexing; we may therefore be certain that the question of the distinct existence of the moral faculty will require great clearness and steadiness of thought for its solution.

But still the question does not seem to be incapable of answer. Do we mean the same thing when we say that an action is right, and when we say that it is, on the whole, and taken in all its consequences, useful? It must be observed, that the question is not, Whether right actions *are*, on the whole, useful? for that we will suppose to be granted; but it is, Whether, by describing them as right, *we mean* nothing more than that we believe them to be useful? If by *right*, and by equivalent words, we intend some quality and attribute which *useful* and similar terms do not express, we must have the faculty of conceiving such a quality; and this faculty is the moral sense. Such a faculty Butler, and after him many modern writers, including Mackintosh, hold to be part of human nature. The following are some of the grounds for his opinion :—

(2.) The words which express what is morally right, and the related ideas, cannot be replaced by any different set of terms. Right, duty, what we ought to do, are not expressed to the satisfaction of any one by any phraseology borrowed from the consideration of consequences. They are as untranslatable into the language which contemplates utility alone, as the names of colours are incapable of being expressed by those denoting the properties of space. When I say that an act is my duty, that it is right, I give an entire assent to the rule which commands me to do it, whatever be the consequences.* It may be true that all

---

* Whewell's *Elements of Morality*, Art. 73. (2d Edition.)

acts of duty are, taken in all their consequences, useful; but assuredly this is not what we mean, this is not the quality we ascribe to them, by the use of such terms.

Perhaps the most distinctive of these terms is the word *ought*, and the corresponding words which occur in all languages. It is universally felt that when we say, in a moral sense, that we ought to do any action, we mean something different from saying it is advantageous in its consequences. This word *ought*, which, as Mackintosh says, "most perfectly denotes duty," appears to be the simplest and most universal expression of the moral sense.

(3.) The impossibility of wresting this word, *ought*, to the side of the utilitarian theory, may, I think, be inferred from the amusing vehemence with which Mr. Bentham endeavours to expel it from his territory. "The talisman of arrogance, indolence, and ignorance, is to be found in a single word, an authoritative imposture, which in these pages it will be frequently necessary to unveil. It is the word 'ought,' 'ought or ought not,' as circumstances may be. In deciding you ought to do this, you ought not to do it, is not every question of morals set at rest?

"If the use of the word be admissible at all, it 'ought' to be banished from the vocabulary of morals." (*Deontology*, vol. i. p. 32.)*

Till this is done, he proposes to neutralise this obnoxious term by the use of another potent word— "why?"

* The title of this book is "Deontology, etc., from the MSS. of Jeremy Bentham;" but recently I have been blamed in a Review for citing it as his. (1862.)

It is clear that the reason why the word so frequently occurs to excite Mr. Bentham's displeasure is, that it refers to a universal and unavoidable aspect of actions, which men constantly recognise, and cannot help expressing in the words they familiarly employ. And Mr. Bentham's "why" involves an assumption no less dogmatical than that of which he complains; for by it he intends to prescribe that the answer shall be in no other language than that of the utilitarian theory.

(4.) The unavoidable occurrence of the conception implied in the word *ought*, notwithstanding that it resists the attempt at analysis of which we have just spoken, may be inferred from its use by those whose theoretical views would lead them to reject it; as, for example, Mr. Bentham himself. He supposes a controversy between an ancient and a modern moralist. (*Deont.*, vol. i. p. 72.) "The modern, as probably he will keep neither his principles nor his temper, says to the ancient, 'Your moral sense is nothing to the purpose; yours is corrupt, abominable, detestable; all nations cry out against you.' 'No such thing,' replies the ancient; 'and if they did, it would be nothing to the purpose: our business was to inquire, not what people *think*, but what they *ought to think*.'" And this "ought" of the ancients is supposed to terminate the controversy, so far as dialogue is concerned.*

---

* Perhaps the reader may be amused by Mr. Bentham's mode of winding up the scene :—"Thereupon the modern kicks the ancient, or spits in his face; or, if he is strong enough, throws him behind the fire. One can think of no other method that is at once natural and consistent, of continuing the debate." It is satisfactory to see that Mr. Bentham does not seem to have thought the use of the word *ought* by the one party, though very provoking, justified the extreme measures which he describes on the other side.

(5.) It is, indeed, expressly allowed by Mr. Bentham himself, that the word *utility*, and its conjugates, do not express our judgment in cases of moral conduct. "The mind will not be satisfied," he says (vol. i. p. 35), "with such phrases as—'it is useless to commit murder,' or 'it would be useful to prevent it.'" Surely we may be allowed to say that the reason why men are not *satisfied* with such phrases is, that they do not express their meaning. The repugnance and indignation with which we regard crimes and vices is something distinct from the perception of their results; and no word which expresses the transgression of utility satisfies us, except it also express the transgression of rectitude. Murder is harmful to society, but it is also wicked. The former expression states the view of our understanding as to the consequences of the act; the latter expression conveys the feeling of our moral nature as to its moral quality; the utilitarian scheme of Mr. Bentham appears to aim at confounding these assertions.

(6.) But the same recognition of the difference of duty and usefulness in common apprehension, which Mr. Bentham has made in the passage just quoted, appears also in other circumstances; as, for instance, in the title of the work already quoted, *Deontology*, and in the reasons assigned for coining such a name. This term is professedly chosen because "utilitarianism offers too vague and undefined an impression to the mind." (Vol. i. p. 34.) If the word from which Deontology is derived had borrowed its meaning from the notion of utility alone, it is not likely that it would have become more intelligible by being translated out of Latin into Greek. But the term Deontology expresses Moral Science (and expresses it well), precisely because it signifies the *Science of Duty*, and contains no reference to utility. It is a term well chosen, to describe a system of ethics founded on any other than Mr. Bentham's principle. Mackintosh, who held that τὸ δέον,—what men *ought* to do,—was the fundamental notion of morality, might very properly have termed the science Deontology. The system of which Mr. Bentham is the representative—that of those who make morality dependent on the production of happiness, has long being designated in Germany by the term *Eudemonism*, derived from the Greek word for happiness (εὐδαιμονία). If we were to adopt this term we should have to oppose the Deontological to the Eudemonist school; and we must necessarily place those who hold a peculiar moral faculty—Butler, Stewart, Brown, Mackintosh—in the former, and those who are usually called utilitarian philosophers in the latter class.

(7.) The irrelevancy of Paley's mode of treating the question of the moral sense is so generally allowed at present that we need not dwell on it here. But we may observe that other mistakes, flowing from a like misapprehension, affect his analysis of virtue. He endeavours to make an advance in this inquiry by the question, "Why am I obliged to keep my word, or to do any other moral act?" And by his answer to this question he reduces moral obligation to two elements —external constraint, and the command of a superior. This attempt at an analysis of morality is singularly futile; for, of the two supposed elements, external constraint annihilates the morality of the act, and the reference to a superior presupposes moral obligation, since a superior is one whom it is our duty to obey. If Paley had stated his question in the simpler form, "Why *ought* I to keep my word?" he would have had before him a problem more to the purpose of moral philosophy, and one to which his answer would have been palpably inapplicable.

(8.) The argument hitherto urged has been, that the impossibility of resolving the ideas of moral right and duty into other ideas, borrowed from utility, is implied in the common use of language; and virtually acknowledged by utilitarian writers themselves. Other arguments may be drawn from the nature of the feelings with which we contemplate actions, and which, it has been truly said, are quite irreconcilable with the supposition that our moral estimate of actions arises from their bearing on happiness, and that our moral estimate of men looks only to their having calculated such consequences well or ill. Our admiration of the higher virtues, our indignation and scorn of the baser vices, are entirely different from an assent to, or dissent from, the agent's estimate of consequences. We can conceive a remorse for sins committed, which is something very distinct from a regret at having mistaken the road to happiness. A bad man, in a moral sense, is not merely a man who has had a bad head for calculating consequences, as he would be if morality resided in the intellect alone. But this argument has been sufficiently insisted upon by others.

(9.) Thus, as we separate the affections from the

desires, we distinguish the moral sense, or conscience, from both. Butler, and Mackintosh with him, express the relation of conscience to the other principles of action, by ascribing to it a *supremacy*,* or a right of command. This language is metaphorical, but in that respect it does not differ from all the rest of the language which we use concerning mental operations and relations; and the material question is, whether, in this case, the language is intelligible. It is language which has been familiarly used from the time of Aristotle and Plato to our own; and I think it will be seen by any one who reads with attention the pages of good writers who employ this language, as for instance Butler, that they have a distinct meaning in their minds, and that their expressions are fitted to convey it. Butler shows that prudential self-love is a principle differing from the desires and passions in other ways than in mere strength; and thus establishes that there is a difference of kind and order, as well as of degree and power, among our active principles. He reminds us that we can conform our acts to rules, and that this differs from acting as we please, or obeying the strongest impulse; that man is intelligibly said to contain in his own mind a law of right action; that under the influence of such a principle he approves and condemns, and thus passes judgment

* The use of the term *Supremacy*, as ascribed to the conscience, is liable to convey an erroneous and dangerous doctrine, that every one's conscience is for him the supreme rule of right and wrong. The word *Authority*, which is all that Butler and Mackintosh's argument requires, avoids this inconvenience.

See the Preface to Whewell's edition of Butler's Three Sermons on Human Nature, and Whewell's *Elements of Morality*, art. 271, 2d edit. (Note added 1862.)

on acts and dispositions; that this is the proper office of such a principle; and that right and authority are implied in this office. When we have distinguished the moral sense from the other faculties of our nature, such language appears to convey, as well as language can convey, the relation of that faculty to the others. "To declare what ought and ought not to be done," it has been said, "is the essence of command, that is, of moral command or rightful authority." And thus such authority belongs to the faculty which determines that some of our actions and emotions are, and others are not, what they ought to be.

We shall have to speak further of this supremacy of conscience in treating of Mackintosh's explanation of it. But we may, in the first place, say a few words on the application of this doctrine to questions of ethics.

(10.) Mackintosh has, with great propriety, insisted upon the importance of a distinction of two parts of Moral Philosophy, which are often confounded;—the Theory of Moral Sentiments, and the Criterion of Morality (p. 246). The question of the independent existence and character of the moral faculty belongs to the former division of the subject; the construction of our system of ethics flows from the latter. There is no necessary collision between doctrines on these two points. We may hold that morality is an original quality of actions, and may still form our rules of morality by tracing the consequences of actions.

This distinction has often been neglected. Those who hold that utility constitutes morality often call upon the advocates of a moral sense to show how the assertion of such a faculty leads us to distinguish right from wrong, or how it can supersede the criterion of general utility. To this it may be replied ;—that the existence of a moral conscience in man is an important truth, but that this truth alone cannot be expected to replace all the principles and deductions by which a sound system of philosophical ethics is to be produced ; that the construction of such a system is undoubtedly a difficult problem ;—but that we shall inevitably obtain an erroneous solution of the problem, if we do not take into our account the operation of the moral faculty. The criterion of utility cannot safely be applied without acknowledging the independent value of morality, any more than the moral faculty can always decide well without the consideration of consequences. For among the most important results of actions, we must include their effect upon the moral habits and feelings of men ; and must consider these effects as claiming attention for their own sake. The promotion of human virtue must be our aim, as well as the augmentation of human happiness. We cannot by any analysis exclude the former of these ends ; happiness depends on the exercise of the virtuous affections, far more clearly than virtue depends on the pursuit of happiness. The most wise and moderate of the utilitarian moralists do, accordingly, apply their method in this manner. Thus Paley (B. III. p. III. C. III.), in estimating the guilt of corrupting a person to the commission of one offence, states it as one ground of condemnation, that such seduction is the destruction of the person's moral principle. And it appears, at present, to be generally allowed, that the utilitarian doctrine cannot be applied without considering the effect on the moral feelings of men as among the important consequences of action. "It often happens," it is said, "that an essential part of the morality or immorality of an action, or a rule of action, consists in its influence on the agent's own mind." "Many actions, moreover, produce effects on the characters of other persons besides the agent." The effects here spoken of are, in fact, effects on the moral habits of thought; and thus the existence of the moral attributes of the mind, as original and independent objects of the attention of the ethical philosopher, is presupposed in this mode of applying the utilitarian scheme.

If indeed we take *such* good and bad consequences into the account;—if among the useful effects of actions we conceive the most useful to be the improvement of man's moral character;—if we frame our rules so that they shall conduce as much as possible to virtuous feeling as well as to beneficial action,—to purity of heart as well as to rectitude of conduct;—if we aim at man's general well-being, and not merely at his gratification;—I know not what moralist would object to a criterion of morality so drawn from consequences, or would deny that the promotion of human happiness, and of human virtue, requires the same practical rules. Mackintosh would undoubtedly have assented to this; for he not only allows the universal coincidence of virtue with utility in the largest sense, but founds his recommendation of the highest forms of virtue on the advantage of virtuous habits and feelings, both to the possessor and to the community; as when he speaks of the trite example of Regulus, of the character of Andrew Fletcher, and of the virtue of courage. If we could take into due account the whole value of right principles, and the whole happiness produced by virtuous feelings, we could commit no practical error in making the advantageous consequences of actions the measure of their morality.

But this can happen only by considering moral good as a primary object, valuable for its own sake; not by supposing that virtue is aimed at, as subservient to some other purpose of more genuine utility: and no sagacity or fairness in estimating useful consequences can stand as a substitute for the love of right itself. It is true that honesty is the best policy; but he who is honest only out of policy does not come up even to the vulgar notion of a virtuous man. If a man were tempted by the opportunity of gaining a large estate through a safe but fraudulent proceeding, the utilitarian doctrine would seem to recommend him to weigh both sides well, though it would direct him in conclusion to decide in favour of probity; but the common judgment of mankind would hardly deem him honest if he hesitated at all. And in like manner, in regard to other temptations, the safety of virtue appears to consist so little in tracing all possible consequences, that it has been held that to deliberate is to be lost, and that the only secure protection is that purity of mind which will not look at the prospect of sensual pleasure when it forms one side of the account. We cannot help saying with Cicero, "Hæc nonne est turpe dubitare philosophos, quæ ne rustici quidem dubitent?"—(*Off.* III. 19.)

Indeed, it appears to be acknowledged by the advocates of the rule of utility, that it is not safe to apply the principle separately in each particular case. Mr. Bentham has urged with great beauty of expression (*Deontology*, vol. ii. ch. i.) the propriety of framing general rules, and conforming our practice invariably to these, so as to avoid the temptations of our frailty and passion in particular instances. If a reverence for general maxims of morality, and a constant reference to the common precepts of virtue, take the place, in the utilitarian's mind, of the direct application of his principle, there will remain little difference between him and the believer in original moral distinctions; for the practical rules of the two will rarely differ, and in both systems the rules will be the moral guides of thought and conduct.

(11.) But though the two schools agree so far, there still will be found a deficiency on the part of the consistent utilitarian. A persuasion that moral good is something different from, and superior to, mere pleasure, is requisite to give our preference of it that tone of enthusiasm and affection which belongs to virtuous feeling. To approve a rule as right, is different from liking it as profitable; to admire an act of virtuous self-devotion as we are capable of admiring, is a feeling so different from the apprehension of any usefulness the act may have, that the comparison of the two things is altogether incongruous. The moral faculty converts our perception of the quality of actions into an affection of the strongest kind; nor can we be satisfied with any account of our moral sentiments which excludes this feature in the process. Thus, as we hold the affections to be motives of an order superior to the desires which have reference to ourselves only, we maintain the moral faculty, the conscience, the affection towards duty, to be a principle of action of an order superior both to the desires and to the other affections. Without the acknowledgment of this subordination, the language and feelings of men when they compare the claims of personal pleasure, of social affection, and of duty, are altogether unintelligible and absurd.

(12.) Of those who have held the doctrine opposite of this—namely, that all these sentiments are composed of elements the same in kind—Paley has expressed the opinion in perhaps the most offensive form, being carried on partly by his love of clearness, and partly by his indifference to mere speculation. "In this inquiry," he says, "I will omit much declamation on the dignity and capacity of our nature, the superiority of the soul to the body, the rational to the animal part of our constitution: upon the worthiness, refinement, and delicacy of some satisfactions, and the meanness, grossness, and sensuality of others; because *I hold that pleasures differ in nothing but in continuance and in intensity.*"

If we could use such a term without an unbecoming disrespect towards a virtuous and useful writer, this opinion might properly be called brutish, since it recognises no difference between the pleasures of man and those of the lowest animals. If we are to promote human happiness in this sense, I do not see how the same obligation does not lie upon us to promote the happiness of brutes with the same care. And if the pleasures of sense differ only in intensity and duration from the pleasures of filial and parental affection, we ought to know how many days of luxurious living are equivalent to the pleasure of saving a father's life, that we may decide rightly when these claims happen to come in competition. If utilitarian moral obligation consists in being regulated by such calculations, we cannot be surprised at the disgust with which so many persons speak of the scheme which refers us to "the calculations of utility."

(13.) I shall not pretend to determine whether Mr. Bentham, and those who agree with him, have sometimes overlooked the conditions under which alone their principle can be safely applied; or whether, at any period, they were justly liable to Mackintosh's censure (p. 188) of "clinging to opinions because they are obnoxious; of wantonly wounding the most respectable feelings of mankind." In more recent times this cannot, I think, be said of them; for extreme opinions on the political questions of the day, however unfavourable may be their influence on the moral speculations with which they are combined, are not appropriately spoken of in such terms. At present I think we may discern in utilitarian writers a wish to conciliate rather than to shock the moral sympathies of their countrymen; and perhaps the opposite schools of moralists may thus be brought nearer to each other. If those who profess to make the utility of our actions the measure of their morality, include in utility the effect upon the moral habits of ourselves and others;—if they repel with indignation the charge that they lose sight of virtuous feeling, and of the beneficial influence of good actions on the frame of mind—if they claim to have their estimate of good interpreted in the same way as Plato's; and speak of "that generous and inspiring tone which gives so much of their usefulness as well as of their charm" to writings such as his—if they even become discontented with the name of utility, and wish to have their science called deontology;—the question at issue between them and their opponents ceases to be a difference of moral rule, and almost to be a discordance of moral feeling; and becomes rather a point of metaphysical analysis. They do not indeed become a deontological school, but they show how near a eudemonist school may approach to being so.

Whether such an approximation would gratify the writers to whom I refer, I have no means of knowing; and if I am told that I am mistaken in my interpretation of the indications to which I have alluded, I shall not attempt to maintain the opinion. It would be nothing new or strange if persons honestly seeking truth from different quarters should be led towards the same point; but if they bring with them an angry and hostile spirit, they may approach only to quarrel more bitterly. It is, however, possible to seek truth of all kinds in a calm and charitable temper; and it would be very strange if moral truths were held to be an exception to the desirableness of doing this. Captiousness and petulance, fierceness and menace, personal contumely and angry buffoonery, may be used in this as in other discussions; but I conceive that no writer on morals, duly feeling the dignity and obligations of his office, will, by any act of his, recognise those who have recourse to such modes of treating the subject, as moral philosophers.*

* Perhaps we have now reached a period, when I may remark,

III. I now proceed to notice a third principle which enters into Mackintosh's philosophy, and which, in the way in which he holds it, is more peculiar to him than the two hitherto stated. He assents, in a great measure, to the explanation suggested by Hume and Smith (p. 146), but more fully developed by Hartley (p. 159), of the formation of our passions and affections, and even of our sentiments of virtue and duty, by means of "the association of ideas." He further urges this theory more at length in his general remarks (p. 241).

(1.) But into this view, as usually understood, he introduces several modifications; and, in particular, he asserts that the effect of such "association" may be something very different from the mere juxtaposition of the component elements. Thus he says that the result may be so entirely a single sentiment, that "the originally separate feelings can no longer be disjoined" (p. 169); and, moreover, that "the compound may have properties not to be found in any of its component parts;" as constantly happens, he observes, in material compounds.

It is clear that this view of the effect of the "association of ideas" may give results very different from those often founded upon that doctrine. If we say that gratitude, or compassion, or patriotism, are *only* certain trains of pleasurable associations, we are generally understood to assert that we can again resolve those feelings into the constituent and associated elements; and that

without reviving any angry feelings, that these expressions were intended to refer to Criticisms of this Dissertation of Mackintosh which had been published, and especially to a *Fragment on Mackintosh*, the title of which was, I suppose, suggested by Bentham's *Fragment on Government*, the latter being a severe criticism on a portion of Blackstone's *Commentaries*. (Note added 1862.)

by so doing we may hope to reason upon them most philosophically and exactly. But Mackintosh's mode of considering these and other emotions would allow of neither of these inferences. He supposes "association" to be employed in the education rather than in the creation of our moral sentiments; in awakening affections rather than in connecting notions.

(2.) The ideas or the feelings which are concerned in this process are said to be *associated;* but this is, he declares, a very inadequate word to express the "complete combination and fusion" which occur (p. 164). This association presupposes laws and powers of the mind itself, according to which the conjunction produces its results. The celebrated comparison of the mind to a sheet of white paper is not just, except we consider that there may be in the paper itself many circumstances which affect the nature of the writing (p. 159). A recent writer, however, appears to me to have supplied us with a much more apt and beautiful comparison. Man's soul at first, says Professor Sedgwick, is one unvaried blank, till it has received the impressions of external experience. "Yet has this blank," he adds, "been already touched by a celestial hand; and, when plunged in the colours which surround it, it takes not its tinge from accident but design, and comes out covered with a glorious pattern."
—(*Discourse on the Studies of the University,* p. 54.) This modern image of the mind as a prepared blank is well adapted to occupy a permanent place in opposition to the ancient sheet of white paper.

(3.) Not only the word association, but also the word *ideas,* in the Lockian expression, appears to Mackintosh to be unsuited to its purpose; since an association takes place "of thoughts with emotions, as well as with each other" (p. 164). Our author has indeed shown great solicitude to bring into clear view that part of our nature which he here distinguishes from thought;—"that other part of it, hitherto without any adequate name, which feels, and desires, and loves, and hopes, and wills" (p. 63). After balancing the various terms which may be used to express. the aggregate of such feelings, he inclines finally to call it the *emotive* or *pathematic** part of man (p. 161).

Thus the "association of ideas," according to Mackintosh, would more properly be termed the composition of ideas and emotions. In his view of the composite, as losing all trace of apparent composition, the author was, in some measure, following Hartley (p. 153), though he justly claims the credit (p. 152) of seeing more distinctly than his predecessors the important truth, that the compound may have properties not found in any of its component parts.

(4.) Mackintosh maintains that this is by no means a modification of the selfish system (p. 173); for the "affections and the moral sentiments, though educed by association, only become what they are when they lose all trace of self-regard." "If the affections be *acquired*, they are justly called *natural;* and if their origin be personal, their nature may and does become *disinterested.*"

---

* These terms have not had much "luck" (to use Mackintosh's own phraseology in this passage). In common language, this part of our nature is often called the *heart,* as distinguished from *the head.* We may perhaps best describe it by the compound phrase used in the Dissertation itself; *the desires and affections.* Some recent writers have spoken of the *emotional* part of our nature. (1862.)

IV. But we must now consider another peculiarity of Mackintosh's system; I speak of what he names his *Theory of Conscience.*

(1.) Being persuaded, as we have seen, that the moral faculty exists and exercises a rightful supremacy over the active principles, he has attempted to explain and account for this relation of our emotions. His view is given in his remarks on Butler (p. 120), and again in his concluding remarks (p. 256). According to this theory, the moral faculty consists of a class of desires and affections which have dispositions and volitions for their sole object. This description of our moral sentiments will, he conceives, explain their peculiar character and attributes. He expresses the relation which he wishes to describe, by saying that the moral sentiments are *in contact with the will* (p. 121); or, as he further elucidates this, "they may and do stand between any other practical principle and its object, while it is absolutely impossible that any other shall intercept their connection with the will." The conscience requires virtuous acts and dispositions to action; and by such requisition it can check and control any desires of external objects; but no desire of any outward gratification can prevent the conscience from demanding a virtuous direction of the will; and this mental relation explains and justifies, Mackintosh conceives, that attribution of supremacy and command to the conscience on which moral writers have often insisted.

(2.) Thus conscience consists in, or rather results from, the composition of *all* those sentiments of which the final object is a state of the will, intimately and inseparably blended, and held in a perfect state of solution

(p. 260); and the conscience being thus represented as analogous to the desires, it implies, in the same way as other desires, a *sense* of what is grateful, and a faculty of dwelling, in thought, on the gratification so obtained.

(3.) But if, in order further to develop this theory, it be asked *what* states of the will are thus agreeable to the conscience; or, in other words, what, according to this system, is the general character of the dispositions and actions which we consider good and right; Mackintosh's answer would be, that the conscience, being educated and awakened by certain processes of association, is thus composed of various elements, and finds good under various forms;—that (p. 256) the beneficial volitions are delightful, and that, therefore, they strongly attract those affections which regard the will, and thus give rise to some of the elements of conscience;—that our anger against those who disappoint our wish for the happiness of others, when in like manner detached from persons and transferred to dispositions, becomes a sense of justice, another element of conscience;—that courage, energy, decision, when tamed by the society of the affections, and considered as dispositions only, become magnanimity, and gratify the moral sense; and that even those habits which mainly affect our own good, as temperance, prudence, when they become disposition and not calculation, are, for like reasons, added to the constituents of conscience.

(4.) Thus the view of the nature of conscience here presented explains how it is that the private desires and the social affections alike fall under the authority of the moral faculty. The explanation of this community of rule in sentiments of so widely different nature, Mackintosh considers a strong confirmation of the justice of his opinion.

Without pronouncing a judgment on the truth of this theory, I hope I have faithfully represented the author's meaning. But he draws from the theory certain inferences, of which I may say a few words.

V. Mackintosh, as we have seen, maintains that though the moral faculty is formed or educed by intercourse with the external world, it is a law of our nature; yet he allows that what this law prescribes agrees with the rule, rightly understood, of bringing forth the greatest happiness. He was, therefore, naturally called upon to account for this coincidence. If moral approval be a different sentiment from the estimation of general happiness, why does the moral sense of man invariably approve that which increases the happiness of his species? If this theory account for this phenomenon, such a circumstance will, he conceives, be a strong argument in its favour.

(1.) He replies to this inquiry (p. 263), that all the separate objects which conscience approves, the social affections, the decisions of justice, the maxims of enlightened prudence, tend to the happiness of some part of the species, and that thus the general rules of conscience must agree with the rules of the general happiness. All the acts which the moral faculty sanctions promote the welfare of some part of mankind, and all that reason has to do is to add up the items of the account. All the principles of which conscience is composed converge towards the happiness of man; and therefore this may be taken as its central point. And thus the coincidence just noticed is not accidental, but is a necessary consequence of the theory.

(2.) I will add, as a corollary to what Mackintosh has said, that a system of ethics, rightly constructed on the principle of promoting, in the greatest degree, the happiness of mankind, will coincide, in most of its rules of action, with a system founded on the supreme authority of conscience ; but that, in order to apply safely and well the *eudemonist* principle, we must recollect that happiness consists rather in habits of the mind than in outward gratifications ; and is to be sought rather by forming moral dispositions than by prescribing acts. In Paley's "Moral Philosophy" we have a work framed on the eudemonist basis, which has for some time possessed considerable authority in this country, and has probably in no small degree influenced men's reasonings on such subjects in recent times. Without examining here how far Paley has always applied his principle under due conditions, and traced his consequences with a sufficiently enlarged survey, we may observe that there prevails through the work a tone of practical sagacity, good sense, and good feeling, which neutralises most of its theoretical defects.

VI. Some other bearings of Mackintosh's theory may be noticed, and especially the view it offers of the relation of religion and morality. This agrees nearly with the doctrine of Butler, and many English divines, that conscience is one of the ways in which the commands of God are conveyed to us (p. 264). "The completeness and rigour acquired by conscience when all its dictates are revered as the commands of a perfectly good and wise being, are so obvious, that they cannot be questioned by any reasonable man, however wide his incredulity may be. It is thus that conscience can add the warmth of an affection to the inflexibility of principle and habit." Not only are we bound to accept all the precepts for the moral government of the will, disclosed either by Revelation or by reason, as undeniable rules for our feelings and actions ; but the relations between man and his Maker, which religion teaches us, tend to make this a work of love, no less than of duty ; and bestow on that improvement of our inward nature to which conscience is constantly urging us, an aspect of hope and joy, which human morality, without such aid, can hardly assume, and seldom long retain.

VII. I will only refer to one other consequence of this theory of conscience of Mackintosh ;—the view it appears to him to supply of the celebrated question of Free-will (p. 272). Since conscience contemplates those dispositions only which depend on the will, it excludes all consideration of the cause in which the will originated : hence the voluntary dispositions appear as the first link of the chain ; and, in the eye of conscience, will is the independent cause of action. Reason, on the other hand, must consider occurrences as bound together by the connection of cause and effect, and thus sees only the strength of the necessitarian system. Thus, while speculation appears to show that our actions are necessary, practice convinces us that they are free. The advocates of necessity and of free-will look at the question from different points of view;—that of the understanding and that of the conscience. But the conscientious view, being strengthened by the moral sympathy of mankind, is by far the most generally and strongly entertained.

I shall here close my remarks on the Dissertation which the following pages contain. The theoretical view of the nature, formation, and operation of our moral sentiments, which is given by the author, must be left to the consideration of those who pursue such speculations in a philosophical spirit and temper. His historical sketch of the progress of the subject has in it much to please and instruct, to interest and improve the ethical student. There will be found several instances in which the phraseology is defective in clearness and simplicity; and in this, as in any work, if we pay no attention to the writer's aim, if we insist upon confounding what he has distinguished, and upon interpreting his language by an analysis which he did not acknowledge, we shall not obtain his sense, or any sense. But the reader who candidly seeks for the author's meaning, will, I think, not fail to find it: and I am persuaded that most readers will derive pleasure from the comprehensive views, the tolerant temper, and the love of virtuous feeling and literary beauty which they will find pervading the work. His unfavourable judgments, in those cases in which he expresses such, are less severe than those of other philosophers, both in our own and in other countries, who look at the progress of moral philosophy from a like point of view; and he always appears to rejoice to give credit to any writers in whom he discovers the early gleams of those doctrines which he held to be important truths.

In the conclusion of his survey he speaks of the spirit of speculation on this subject as all but extinct in this country. I would willingly believe that this is too desponding a view of the fortunes of moral philosophy among us;—that the youth of England are far from indifferent to the questions which concern the nature and laws of man's highest faculties, and which excite a vigorous and generous love of speculation in other parts of Europe. To such a result I look forward the more gladly, because I do not doubt that the reigning philosophy of any age, even when it excites little direct attention, influences powerfully men's convictions and habits of thought; and I am persuaded that we cannot make the prevalent views of morals sounder, purer, and more philosophical, without improving the general intellectual and moral character of the educated classes of the nation.

W. W.

ETHICAL PHILOSOPHY.

INTRODUCTION.

The inadequacy of the words of ordinary language for the purposes of philosophy is an ancient and frequent complaint; of which the justness will be felt by all who consider the state to which some of the most important arts would be reduced, if the coarse tools of the common labourer were the only instruments to be employed in the most delicate operations of manual expertness. The watchmaker, the optician, and the surgeon, are provided with instruments which are fitted, by careful ingenuity, to second their skill; the philosopher alone is doomed to use the rudest tools for the most refined purposes. He must reason in words of which the looseness and vagueness are suitable, and even agreeable, in the usual intercourse of life, but which are almost as remote from the extreme exactness and precision required, not only in the conveyance, but in the search of truth, as the hammer and the axe would be unfit for the finest exertions of skilful handiwork; for it is not to be forgotten that he must himself think in these gross words as unavoidably as he uses them in speaking to others. He is, in this respect, in a worse condition than an astronomer who looked at the heavens only with the naked eye, whose limited and partial observation, however it might lead to error, might not directly, and would not necessarily, deceive. He might be more justly compared to an arithmetician compelled to employ numerals, not only cumbrous, but used so irregularly to denote different quantities, that they often deceive not only others, but himself.

The Natural Philosopher and Mathematician have in some degree the privilege of framing their own terms of art, though that liberty is daily narrowed by the happy diffusion of these great branches of knowledge, which daily mixes their language with the general vocabulary of educated men. The cultivator of Mental and Moral Philosophy can seldom do more than mend the faults of his words by definition ; a necessary but very inadequate expedient, in a great measure defeated in practice by the unavoidably more frequent recurrence of the terms in their vague than in their definite acceptation ; in consequence of which the mind, to which the definition is faintly and but occasionally present, naturally suffers, in the ordinary state of attention, the scientific meaning to disappear from remembrance, and insensibly ascribes to the word a great part, if not the whole, of that popular sense which is so very much more familiar even to the most veteran speculator. The obstacles which stood in the way of Lucretius and Cicero, when they began to translate the subtle philosophy of Greece into their narrow and barren tongue, are always felt by the philosopher when he struggles to express, with the necessary discrimination, his abstruse reasonings, in words which, though those of his own language, he must take from the mouths of those to whom his distinctions would be without meaning.

The Moral Philosopher is in this respect subject to peculiar difficulties. His statements and reasonings often call for nicer discriminations of language than those which are necessary in describing or discussing the purely intellectual part of human nature ; but his freedom in the choice of words is more circumscribed. As he treats of matters on which all men are disposed to form a judgment, he can as rarely hazard glaring innovations in diction, at least in an adult and mature language like ours, as the orator or the poet. If he deviates from common use, he must atone for his deviation by hiding it, and can only give a new sense to an old word by so skilful a position of it as to render the new meaning so quickly understood that its novelty is scarcely perceived. Add to this, that, in those most difficult inquiries for which the utmost coolness is not more than sufficient, he is often forced to use terms commonly connected with warm feeling, with high praise, with severe reproach ; which excite the passions of his readers when he most needs their calm attention and the undisturbed exercise of their impartial judgment. There is scarcely a neutral term left in Ethics ; so quickly are such expressions enlisted on the side of Praise or Blame, by the address of contending passions. A true philosopher must not even desire that men should less love virtue or hate vice, in order to fit them for a more unprejudiced judgment on his speculations.

There are perhaps not many occasions where the penury and laxity of language are more felt than in entering on the history of sciences where the first measure must be to mark out the boundary of the whole subject with some distinctness. But no exactness in these important operations can be approached without a new division of human knowledge, adapted to the present stage of its progress, and a reformation of all those barbarous, pedantic, unmeaning, and (what is worse) wrong-meaning names which continue to be applied to the greater part of its branches. Instances are needless where nearly all the appellations are faulty. The term *Metaphysics* affords a specimen of all the faults which the name of a science can combine. To those who know only their own language, it must, at their entrance on the study, convey no meaning. It points their attention to nothing. If they examine the language in which its parts are significant, they will be misled into the pernicious error of believing that it seeks something more than the interpretation of nature. It is only by examining the history of ancient Philosophy that the probable origin of, this name will be found, in the application of it as the running title of several essays of Aristotle, which were placed, in a collection of the manuscripts of that great philosopher, after his treatise on *Physics*. It has the greater fault of an unsteady and fluctuating signification; denoting one class of objects in the seventeenth century, and another in the eighteenth—even in the nineteenth not quite of the same import in the mouth of a German as in that of a French or English philosopher; to say nothing of the farther objection that it continues to be a badge of undue pretension among some of the followers of the science, while it has become a name of reproach and derision among those who altogether decry it.

The modern name of the very modern science called *Political Economy*, though deliberately bestowed on it by its most eminent teachers, is perhaps a still more notable sample of the like faults. It might lead the ignorant to confine it to retrenchment in national expenditure; and a consideration of its etymology alone would lead into the more mischievous error of believing it to teach, that national wealth is best promoted by the contrivance and interference of lawgivers, in opposition to its surest doctrine, which it most justly boasts of having discovered and enforced.

It is easy to conceive an exhaustive analysis of Human Knowledge and a consequent division of it into parts corresponding to all the classes of objects to which it relates:—a representation of that vast edifice, containing a picture of what is finished, a sketch of what is building, and even a conjectural outline of what, though required by completeness and convenience, as well as symmetry, is yet altogether untouched. A system of names might also be imagined derived from a few roots, indicating the objects of each part, and showing the relation of the parts to each other. An order and a language somewhat resembling those by which the objects of the sciences of Botany and Chemistry have, in the eighteenth century, been arranged and denoted, are doubtless capable of application to the sciences generally, when considered as parts of the system of knowledge. The attempts, however, which have hitherto been made to accomplish the analytical division of knowledge which must necessarily precede a new nomenclature of the sciences, have required so prodigious a superiority of genius in the single instance of approach to success by Bacon, as to discourage rivalship nearly as much as the frequent examples of failure in subsequent times. The nomenclature itself is attended with great difficulties, not indeed in its conception, but in its adoption and usefulness. In the Continental languages to the south of the Rhine, the practice of deriving the names of science from Greek must be continued; which would render the new names for a while unintelligible to the majority of men. Even in Germany, where a flexible and fertile language affords unbounded liberty of derivation and composition from native roots, or elements, and where the newly derived and compounded words would thus be as clear to the mind, and almost as little startling to the ear, of every man, as the oldest terms in the language, yet the whole nomenclature would be unintelligible to other nations. The intercommunity of the technical terms of science in Europe has been so far broken down by the Germans, and the influence of their literature and philosophy is so rapidly increasing in the greater part of the Continent, that though a revolution in scientific nomenclature be probably yet far distant, the foundation of it may be considered as already prepared.

But although so great an undertaking must be reserved for a second Bacon and a future generation, it is necessary for the historian of any branch of knowledge to introduce his work by some account of the limits and contents of the sciences of which he is about to trace the progress; and though it will be found impossible to trace throughout the treatise a distinct line of demarcation, yet a general and imperfect sketch of the boundaries of the whole, and of the parts of our present subject, may be a considerable help to the reader, as it has been a useful guide to the writer.

There is no distribution of the parts of knowledge more ancient than that of the *Physical* and *Moral* Sciences, which seems liable to no other objection than that it does not exhaust the subject. Even this division, however, cannot be safely employed, without warning the reader, that no science is entirely insulated, and that the principles of one are often only the conclusions and results of another. Every branch of knowledge has its root in the theory of the Understanding, from which even the mathematician must learn what can be known of his magnitude and his numbers; and Moral Science is founded on that other hitherto unnamed part of the philosophy of human nature (to be constantly and vigilantly distinguished from *Intellectual* Philosophy), which contemplates the laws of sensibility, of emotion, of desire and aversion, of pleasure and pain, of happiness and misery; and on which arise the august and sacred landmarks that stand conspicuous along the frontier between Right and Wrong.

But however multiplied the connections of the Moral and Physical Sciences are, it is not difficult to draw a general distinction between them. The purpose of the Physical Sciences, throughout all their provinces, is to answer the question *What is?* They consist only of facts arranged according to their likeness, and expressed by general names given to every class of similar facts. The purpose of the Moral Sciences is to answer the question *What ought to be?* They aim at ascertaining the rules which *ought* to govern voluntary action, and to which those habitual dispositions of

INTRODUCTION.

mind which are the source of voluntary actions *ought* to be adapted.

It is obvious that *Will, Action, Habit, Disposition,* are terms denoting facts in human nature, and that an explanation of them must be sought in Mental Philosophy; which, if knowledge be divided into Physical and Moral, must be placed among physical sciences; though it essentially differs from them all in having for its chief object those laws of thought which alone render any other sort of knowledge possible. But it is equally certain that the word *Ought* introduces the mind into a new region, to which nothing physical corresponds. However philosophers may deal with this most important of words, it is instantly understood by all who do not attempt to define it. No civilised speech, perhaps no human language, is without correspondent terms. It would be as reasonable to deny that *Space* and *Greenness* are significant words, as to affirm that *Ought, Right, Duty, Virtue,* are sounds without meaning. It would be fatal to an Ethical Theory that it did not explain them, and that it did not comprehend all the conceptions and emotions which they call up. There never yet was a theory which did not attempt such an explanation.

* *Anticipation of Moore's Principia Ethica* [handwritten annotation]

SECTION I.

PRELIMINARY OBSERVATIONS.

There is no man who, in a case where he was a calm bystander, would not look with more satisfaction on acts of kindness than on acts of cruelty. No man, after the first excitement of his mind has subsided, ever whispered to himself with self-approbation and secret joy that he had been guilty of cruelty or baseness. Every criminal is strongly impelled to hide these qualities of his actions from himself, as he would do from others, by clothing his conduct in some disguise of duty or of necessity. There is no tribe so rude as to be without a faint perception of a difference between right and wrong. There is no subject on which men of all ages and nations coincide in so many points as in the general rules of conduct, and in the qualities of the human character which deserve esteem. Even the grossest deviations from the general consent will appear, on close examination, to be not so much corruptions of moral feeling, as either ignorance of facts; or errors with respect to the consequences of action; or cases in which the dissentient party is inconsistent with other parts of his own principles, which destroys the value of his dissent; or where each dissident is condemned by all the other dissidents, which immeasurably augments the majority against him. In the first three cases he may be convinced by argument, that his moral judgment should be changed on principles which he recognises as just: and he can seldom, if ever, be condemned at the same time by the body of mankind who agree in their moral systems, and by those who on some other points dissent from that general code, without being also convicted of error by inconsistency with himself. The tribes who expose new-born infants condemn those who abandon their decrepit parents to destruction. Those who betray and murder strangers are condemned by the rules of faith and humanity which they acknowledge in their intercourse with their countrymen. Mr. Hume, in a dialogue in which he ingeniously magnifies the moral heresies of two nations so polished as the Athenians and the French, has very satisfactorily resolved his own difficulties. " In how many circumstances would an Athenian and a Frenchman of merit certainly resemble each other ? Humanity, fidelity, truth, justice, courage, temperance, constancy, dignity of mind. . . . The principles upon which men reason in morals are always the same, though their conclusions are often very different."* He might have added, that almost every deviation which he imputes to each nation is at variance with some of the virtues justly esteemed by both ; and that the reciprocal condemnation of each other's errors which appears in his statement, entitles us on these points to strike out the suffrages of both, when collecting the general judgment of mankind. If we bear in mind that the question relates to the coincidence of all men in considering the same qualities as virtues, and not to the preference of one class of virtues by some, and of a different class by others, the exceptions from the agreement of mankind, in their system of practical morality, will be reduced to absolute insignificance ; and we shall learn to view them as no more affecting the harmony of our moral faculties than the resemblance of the limbs and features is affected by monstrous conformations, or by the unfortunate effects of accident and disease in a very few individuals.†

* *Philosophical Works*, vol. iv. pp. 420, 422, Edin. 1826.
† " On convient le plus souvent de ces instincts de la conscience. La plus grande et la plus saine partie du genre humain leur rend té-

It is very remarkable, however, that though all men agree that there are acts which ought to be done, and acts which ought not to be done ; though the far greater part of mankind agree in their list of virtues and duties, of vices and crimes ; and though the whole race, as it advances in other improvements, is as evidently tending towards the moral system of the most civilised nations, as children in their growth tend to the opinions as much as to the experience and strength of adults ; yet there are no questions in the circle of inquiry to which answers more various have been given than—How have men thus come to agree in the rule of life ? Whence arises their general reverence for it ? and, What is meant by affirming that it ought to be inviolably observed? It is singular, that where we are most nearly agreed respecting rules, we should perhaps most differ as to the *causes* of our agreement, and as to the *reasons* which justify us for adhering to it. The discussion of these subjects composes what is usually called the *Theory of Morals*, in a sense not in all respects coincident with what is usually considered as Theory in other sciences. When we investigate the *causes* of our moral agreement, the term Theory retains its ordinary scientific sense ; but when we endeavour to ascertain the *reasons* of it, we rather employ the term as importing the theory of the rules of an art. In

moignage. Les Orientaux, et les Grecs, et les Romains conviennent en cela ; et il faudroit être aussi abruti que les sauvages Américains pour approuver leurs coutumes, pleines d'une cruauté qui passe même celle des bêtes. *Cependant ces même sauvages sentent bien ce que c'est que la justice en d'autres occasions ;* et quoique il n'y ait point de mauvaise pratique peut-être qui ne soit autorisée quelque part, il y en a peu pourtant qui ne soient condamnées le plus souvent, et par la plus grande partie des hommes." (Leibnitz, *Œuvres Philosophiques*, p. 49, Amst. et Leipz. 1765, 4to.)

There are some admirable observations on this subject in Hartley, especially in the development of the 49th Proposition. "*The rule of life drawn from the practice and opinions of mankind corrects and improves itself perpetually, till at last it determines entirely for virtue, and excludes all kinds and degrees of vice.*" (*Observations on Man*, i. 270.)

the first case, Theory denotes, as usual, the most general laws to which certain facts can be reduced; whereas, in the second, it points out the efficacy of the observance, in practice, of certain rules, for producing the effects intended to be produced in the art. These reasons also may be reduced under the general sense, by stating the question relating to them thus:— What are the causes why the observance of certain rules enables us to execute certain purposes? An account of the various answers attempted to be made to these inquiries properly forms the History of Ethics.

The attentive reader may already perceive that these momentous inquiries relate to at least two perfectly distinct subjects:—1. The nature of the distinction between right and wrong in human conduct; and 2. The nature of those feelings with which right and wrong are contemplated by human beings. The latter constitutes what has been called the *Theory of Moral Sentiments;* the former consists in an investigation into the *Criterion of Morality* in action. Other most important questions arise in this province. But the two problems which have been just stated, and the essential distinction between them, must be clearly apprehended by all who are desirous of understanding the controversies which have prevailed on ethical subjects. The discrimination has seldom been made by Moral Philosophers; the difference between the two problems has never been uniformly observed by any of them; and it will appear, in the sequel, that they have been not rarely altogether confounded by very eminent men, to the destruction of all just conception and of all correct reasoning in this most important, and perhaps most difficult, of sciences.

It may therefore be allowable to deviate so far from historical order, as to illustrate the nature and to prove the importance of the distinction, by an example of the effects of neglecting it, taken from the recent works of justly celebrated writers; in which they discuss questions much agitated in the present age, and therefore probably now familiar to most readers of this Dissertation.

Dr. Paley represents the principle of a moral sense as being opposed to that of utility.* Now, it is evident that this representation is founded on a confusion of the two questions which have been stated above. That we are endued with a moral sense, or, in other words, a faculty which immediately approves what is right, and condemns what is wrong, is only a statement of the feelings with which we contemplate actions. But to affirm that right actions are those which conduce to the wellbeing of mankind, is a proposition concerning the outward effects by which right actions themselves may be recognised. As these affirmations relate to different subjects, they cannot be opposed to each other, any more than the solidity of earth is inconsistent with the fluidity of water; and a very little reflection will show it to be easily conceivable that they may be both true. Man may be so constituted as instantaneously to approve certain actions without any reference to their consequences; and yet reason may nevertheless discover, that a tendency to produce general happiness is the essential characteristic of such actions. Mr. Bentham also contrasts the principle of utility with that of sympathy, of which he considers the moral sense as being one of the forms.† It is needless to repeat, that propositions which affirm or deny anything of different subjects cannot contradict each other. As these celebrated persons have thus inferred or implied the non-existence of a moral sense, from their opinion that the morality of actions depends upon their usefulness; so other philosophers of equal name have concluded that the utility of actions cannot be the criterion of their morality, because a perception of that

---

* *Principles of Moral and Political Philosophy.* Compare book i. chap. v. with book ii. chap. vi.

† *Introduction to the Principles of Morality and Legislation*, chap. ii.

utility appears to them to form a faint and inconsiderable part of our moral sentiments, if indeed it be at all discoverable in them.* These errors are the more remarkable, because the like confusion of perceptions with their objects, of emotions with their causes, or even the omission to mark the distinctions, would, in every other subject, be felt to be a most serious fault in philosophising. If, for instance, an element were discovered to be common to all bodies which our taste perceives to be sweet, and to be found in no other bodies, it is apparent that this discovery, perhaps important in other respects, would affect neither our perception of sweetness nor the pleasure which attends it. Both would continue to be what they have been since the existence of mankind. Every proposition concerning that element would relate to sweet bodies, and belong to the science of Chemistry; while every proposition respecting the perception or pleasure of sweetness would relate either to the body or mind of man, and accordingly belong either to the science of Physiology, or to that of Mental Philosophy. During the many ages which passed before the analysis of the sun's beams had proved them to be compounded of different colours, white objects were seen, and their whiteness was sometimes felt to be beautiful, in the very same manner as since that discovery. The qualities of light are the object of Optics; the nature of beauty can be ascertained only by each man's observation of his own mind; the changes in the living frame which succeed the refraction of light in the eye, and precede mental operation, will, if they are ever to be known by man, constitute a part of Physiology. But no proposition relating to one of these orders of phenomena can contradict or support a proposition concerning another order.

* Smith's *Theory of Moral Sentiments*, Part iv. Even Hume, in the third book of his *Treatise of Human Nature*, the most precise, perhaps, of his philosophical writings, uses the following as the title of one of the sections: "MORAL DISTINCTIONS *derived from a Moral Sense.*"

The analogy of this latter case will justify another preliminary observation. In the case of the pleasure derived from beauty, the question whether that pleasure be original or derived is of secondary importance. It has been often observed that the same properties which are admired as beautiful in the horse, contribute also to his safety and speed; and they who infer that the admiration of beauty was originally founded on the convenience of fleetness and firmness, if they at the same time hold that the usefulness is gradually effaced, and that the admiration of a certain shape at length rises instantaneously without reference to any purpose, may, with perfect consistency, regard a sense of beauty as an independent and universal principle of human nature. The laws of such a feeling of beauty are discoverable only by self-observation. Those of the qualities which call it forth are ascertained by examination of the outward things which are called beautiful. But it is of the utmost importance to bear in mind, that he who contemplates the beautiful proportions of a horse, as the signs and proofs of security or quickness, and has in view these convenient qualities, is properly said to prefer the horse for his usefulness, not for his beauty; though he may choose him for the same outward appearance which pleases the admirer of the beautiful animal. He alone who derives immediate pleasure from the appearance itself, without reflection on any advantages which it may promise, is truly said to feel the beauty. The distinction, however, manifestly depends not on the origin of the emotion, but on its object and nature when completely formed. Many of our most important perceptions through the eye are universally acknowledged to be acquired. But they are as general as the original perceptions of that organ; they arise as independently of our will, and human nature would be quite as imperfect without them. An adult who did not immediately see the different distances of objects from his eye, would be thought by every one to be as great a deviation from the ordinary state of man as if he were incapable of distinguishing the brightest sunshine from the darkest midnight. Acquired perceptions and sentiments may therefore be termed natural, as much as those which are more commonly so called, if they be as rarely found wanting. Ethical theories can never be satisfactorily discussed by those who do not constantly bear in mind that the question concerning the existence of a moral faculty in man, which immediately approves or disapproves, without reference to any further object, is perfectly distinct, on the one hand, from that which inquires into the qualities thus approved or disapproved; and on the other from an inquiry whether that faculty be derived from other parts of our mental frame, or be itself one of the ultimate constituent principles of human nature.

SECTION II.

RETROSPECT OF ANCIENT ETHICS.

INQUIRIES concerning the nature of mind, the first principles of knowledge, the origin and government of the world, appear to have been among the earliest objects which employed the understanding of civilised men. Fragments of such speculations are handed down from the legendary age of Greek philosophy. In the remaining monuments of that more ancient form of civilisation which sprang up in Asia, we see clearly that the Braminical philosophers, in times perhaps before the dawn of western history, had run round that dark and little circle of systems which an unquenchable thirst of knowledge has since urged both the speculators of ancient Greece and those of Christendom to retrace. The wall of adamant which bounds human inquiry has scarcely ever been discovered by any adventurer, until he was roused by the shock which drove him back. It is otherwise with the theory of morals. No controversy seems to have arisen regarding it in Greece, till the rise and conflict of the Stoical and Epicurean schools; and the ethical disputes of the modern world originated with the writings of Hobbes, about the middle of the seventeenth century. Perhaps the longer abstinence from debate on this subject may have sprung from reverence for morality. Perhaps also, where the world were unanimous in their practical opinions, little need was felt of exact theory. The teachers of morals were content with partial or secondary principles, with the combination of principles not always reconcilable, even with vague but specious phrases which in any degree explained or seemed to explain the rules of the art of life—which seemed at once too evident to need investigation, and too venerable to be approached by controversy.

Perhaps the subtile genius of Greece was in part withheld from indulging itself in ethical controversy by the influence of Socrates, who was much more a teacher of virtue than even a searcher after truth—

> Whom, well inspired, the oracle pronounced
> Wisest of men.

It was doubtless because he chose that better part that he was thus spoken of by the man whose commendation is glory, and who, from the loftiest eminence of moral genius ever reached by a mortal, was perhaps alone worthy to place a new crown on the brow of the martyr of virtue.

Aristippus indeed, a wit and a worldling, borrowed nothing from the conversations of Socrates but a few maxims for husbanding the enjoyments of sense. Antisthenes also, a hearer, but not a follower, founded a school of parade and exaggeration, which caused his master to disown him by the ingenious rebuke, "I see your vanity through your threadbare cloak."* The modest doubts of the most sober of moralists, and his indisposition to fruitless abstractions, were in process of time employed as the foundation of systematic scepticism; the most presumptuous, inapplicable, and inconsistent of all the results of human meditation. But though his lessons were thus distorted by the perverse ingenuity of some who heard him, the authority of his practical sense may be traced in the moral writings of those most celebrated philosophers who were directly or indirectly his disciples.

Plato, the most famous of his scholars, the most eloquent of Grecian writers, and the earliest moral philosopher whose writings have come down to us, employed his genius in the composition of dialogues, in which his master performed the

* Diog. Laert. vi. Ælian, ix. 35.

principal part. These beautiful conversations would have lost their charm of verisimilitude, of dramatic vivacity, of picturesque representation of character, if they had been subjected to the constraint of method. They necessarily presuppose much oral instruction. They frequently quote, and doubtless oftener allude to, the opinions of predecessors and contemporaries whose works have perished, and of whose doctrines only some fragments are preserved. In these circumstances, it must be difficult for the most learned and philosophical of his commentators to give a just representation of his doctrines, if he really framed or adopted a system. The moral part of his works is more accessible.* The vein of thought which runs through them is always visible. The object is to inspire the love of truth, of wisdom, of beauty, especially of goodness the highest beauty, and of that supreme and eternal Mind, which contains all truth and wisdom, all beauty and goodness. By the love or delightful comtemplation and pursuit of these transcendent aims for their own sake only, he represented the mind of man as raised from low and perishable objects, and prepared for those high destinies which are appointed for all those who are capable of them.

The application to moral qualities of terms which denote outward beauty, though by him perhaps carried to excess, is an illustrative metaphor, as well warranted by the poverty of language, as any other employed to signify the acts or attributes of mind.† The *beautiful* in his language denoted all

---

* Heusde, *Initia Philosoph. Plat.* 1827 ; a hitherto incomplete work of great perspicuity and elegance, in which we must excuse the partiality which belongs to a labour of love.

† The most probable etymology of καλος seems to be from κᾳω to burn. What burns commonly shines. *Schön*, in German, which means beautiful, is derived from *scheinen*, to shine. The word καλος was used for right so early as the Homeric Poems. (*Il.* xvii. 19.) In the philosophical age it became a technical term, with little other remains of the metaphorical sense than what the genius and art of a fine writer might

that of which the mere contemplation is in itself delightful, without any admixture of organic pleasure, and without being regarded as the means of attaining any further end. The feeling which belongs to it he called *love;* a word which, as comprehending complacency, benevolence, and affection, and reaching from the neighbourhood of the senses to the most sublime of human thoughts, is foreign from the colder and more exact language of our philosophy; but which perhaps then happily served to lure both the lovers of poetry and the votaries of superstition to the school of truth and goodness in the groves of the Academy. He enforced these lessons by an inexhaustible variety of just and beautiful illustrations,—sometimes striking from their familiarity, sometimes subduing by their grandeur; and his works are the store-house from which moralists have from age to age borrowed the means of rendering moral instruction easier and more delightful. Virtue he represented as the harmony of the whole soul;—as a peace between all its principles and desires, assigning to each as much space as they can occupy without encroaching on each other;—as a state of perfect health, in which every function was performed with ease, pleasure, and vigour;—as a well-ordered commonwealth, where the obedient passions executed with energy the laws and commands of reason. The vicious mind presented the odious character, sometimes of discord, of war;—sometimes of disease—always of passions warring with each other in eternal anarchy. Consistent with himself, and at peace with his fellows, the good man felt in the quiet of his conscience a foretaste of the approbation of God. "Oh, what ardent love would virtue inspire if she could be seen!" "If the heart of a tyrant could be laid bare, we should see how it

sometimes rekindle. *Honestum,* the term by which Cicero translates the καλον, being derived from outward honours, is a less happy metaphor. In our language the terms, being from foreign roots, contribute nothing to illustrate the progress of thought.

was cut and torn by its own evil passions, and by an avenging conscience."*

Perhaps in every one of these illustrations, an eye trained in the history of Ethics may discover the germ of the whole, or of a part, of some subsequent theory. But to examine it thus would not be to look at it with the eye of Plato. His aim was as practical as that of Socrates. He employed every topic, without regard to its place in a system, or even always to its force as argument, which could attract the small portion of the community then accessible to cultivation; who, it should not be forgotten, had no moral instructor but the philosopher, unaided, if not thwarted, by the reigning superstition; for religion had not then, besides her own discoveries, brought down the most awful and the most beautiful forms of moral truth to the humblest station in human society.†

Ethics retained her sober spirit in the hands of his great scholar and rival Aristotle, who, though he certainly surpassed all men in acute distinction, in subtile argument, in severe

---

* Let it not be forgotten, that for this terrible description, Socrates, to whom it is ascribed by Plato (*De Rep.* ix.), is called "*Præstantissimus sapientiæ*," by a writer of the most masculine understanding, the least subject to be transported by enthusiasm. (Tac. *Ann.* vi. 6.) "*Quæ vulnera!*" says Cicero, in alluding to the same passage. (*De Officiis*, iii. 21.)

† There can hardly be a finer example of Plato's practical morals than his observations on the treatment of slaves. Genuine humanity and real probity, says he, are brought to the test by the behaviour of a man to slaves, whom he may wrong with impunity. Διαδηλος γαρ ὁ φυσει και μη πλαστως σεβων την δικην, μισων δε οντως το αδικον εν τουτοις των ανθρωπων εν οἱς αυτῳ ῥᾳδιον αδικειν. (Plato *de Legibus*, lib. vi. edit. Bipont. VIII. 303.)

That Plato was considered as the fountain of ancient morals would be sufficiently evident from Cicero alone. "Ex hoc igitur Platonis, quasi quodam sancto augustoque fonte, nostra omnis manabit oratio." (*Tusc. Quæst.* v. 13.) Perhaps the sober Quintilian meant to mingle some censure with the highest praise: "Plato, qui eloquendi facultate divina quadam et Homerica, multum supra prosam orationem surgit." (*Inst. Orat.* x. 1.)

method, in the power of analysing what is most compounded, and of reducing to simple principles the most various and unlike appearances, yet appears to be still more raised above his fellows by the prodigious faculty of laying aside these extraordinary endowments whenever his present purpose required it; as in his *History of Animals*, in his *Treatises on Philosophical Criticism*, and in his *Practical Writings*, political as well as moral. Contrasted as his genius was to that of Plato, not only by its logical and metaphysical attributes, but by the regard to experience and observation of nature which, in him perhaps alone, accompanied them:—though they may be considered as the original representatives of the two antagonist tendencies of philosophy—that which would ennoble man, and that which seeks rather to explain nature: yet, opposite as they are in other respects, the master and the scholar combine to guard the Rule of Life against the licentious irruptions of the Sophists.

In Ethics alone their systems differed more in words than in things.* That happiness consisted in virtuous pleasure, chiefly dependent on the state of mind, but not unaffected by outward agents, was the doctrine of both. Both would with Socrates have called happiness "unrepented pleasure." Neither distinguished the two elements which they represented as constituting the supreme good from each other; partly, perhaps, from a fear of appearing to separate them. Plato more habitually considered happiness as the natural fruit of virtue; Aristotle oftener viewed virtue as the means of attaining happiness. The celebrated doctrine of the Peripatetics, which placed all virtues in a medium between opposite vices, was

---

* "Una et consentiens duobus vocabulis philosophiæ forma instituta est, Academicorum et Peripateticorum; qui rebus congruentes, nominibus differebant. (Cic. *Acad. Quæst.* i. 4.) Βουλεται (Αριστοτελης) διττον ειναι τον κατα φιλοσοφιαν λογον· τον μεν πρακτικον, τον δε θεωρητικον. και του πρακτικου, τον τε ηθικον και πολιτικον. του δε θεωρητικου, τον τε φυσικον και λογικον. (Diog. *Laert.* v. 28.)

probably suggested by the Platonic representation of its necessity to keep up harmony between the different parts of our nature. The perfection of a compound machine is attained where all its parts have the fullest scope for action. Where one is so far exerted as to repress others, there is a vice of excess. When any one has less activity than it might exert without disturbing others, there is a vice of defect. The point which all reach without collision against each other, is the mediocrity in which the Peripatetics placed virtue.

It was not till near a century after the death of Plato that Ethics became the scene of philosophical contest between the adverse schools of Epicurus and Zeno; whose errors afford an instructive example that, in the formation of theory, partial truth is equivalent to absolute falsehood. As the astronomer who left either the centripetal or the centrifugal force of the planets out of his view would err as completely as he who excluded both, so the Epicureans and Stoics, who each confined themselves to real but not exclusive principles in morals, departed as widely from the truth as if they had adopted no part of it. Every partial theory is indeed directly false, inasmuch as it ascribes to one or few causes what is produced by more. As the extreme opinions of one if not both of these schools have been often revived with variations and refinements in modern times, and are still not without influence on ethical systems, it may be allowable to make some observations on this earliest of moral controversies.

"All other virtues," said Epicurus, "grow from prudence, which teaches that we cannot live pleasurably without living justly and virtuously, nor live justly and virtuously without living pleasurably."* The illustration of this sentence formed the whole moral discipline of Epicurus. To him we owe the general concurrence of reflecting men in succeeding times in

---

* Epic. *Epist. ad Menœc.* apud Diog. Laert. lib. x. edit. Meibom. I. 653, 656.

the important truth, that men cannot be happy without a virtuous frame of mind and course of life ; a truth of inestimable value, not peculiar to the Epicureans, but placed by their exaggerations in a stronger light ;—a truth, it must be added, of less importance as a motive to right conduct than to the completeness of Moral Theory, which, however, it is very far from solely constituting. With that truth the Epicureans blended another position, which indeed is contained in the first words of the above statement ; namely, that because virtue promotes happiness, every act of virtue must be done in order to promote the happiness of the agent. They and their modern followers tacitly assume that the latter position is the consequence of the former ; as if it were an inference from the necessity of food to life, that the fear of death should be substituted for the appetite of hunger as a motive for eating. "Friendship," says Epicurus, "is to be pursued by the wise man only for its usefulness, but he will begin as he sows the field in order to reap."* It is obvious that if these words be confined to outward benefits, they may be sometimes true but never can be pertinent ; for outward acts sometimes show kindness, but never compose it. If they be applied to kind feeling they would indeed be pertinent, but they would be evidently and totally false ; for it is most certain that no man acquires an affection merely from his belief that it would be agreeable or advantageous to feel it. Kindness cannot indeed be pursued on account of the pleasure which belongs to it ; for man can no more know the pleasure till he has felt the affection, than he can form an idea of colour without the sense of sight. The moral character of Epicurus was excellent ; no man more enjoyed the pleasure or better performed the duties of friendship. The letter of his system was no more indul-

---

* Την φιλιαν δια της χρειας· (Diog. Laert. *ibid.*) "Hic est locus," Gassendi confesses, "ob quem Epicurus non parum vexatur, quando nemo non reprehendit, parari amicitiam non sui, sed utilitatis gratia."

gent to vice than that of any other moralist.* Although, therefore, he has the merit of having more strongly inculcated the connection of virtue with happiness, perhaps by the faulty excess of treating it as an exclusive principle; yet his doctrine was justly charged with indisposing the mind to those exalted and generous sentiments, without which no pure, elevated, bold, generous, or tender virtues can exist.†

As Epicurus represented the *tendency* of virtue, which is a most important truth in ethical theory, as the sole inducement to virtuous practice; so Zeno, in his disposition towards the opposite extreme, was inclined to consider the moral sentiments which are the motives of right conduct as being the sole principles of moral science. The confusion was equally great in a philosophical view; but that of Epicurus was more fatal to interests of higher importance than those of philosophy. Had the Stoics been content with affirming that virtue is the source of all that part of our happiness which depends on ourselves, they would have taken a position from which it would have been impossible to drive them: they would have laid down a principle of as great comprehension in practice as their wider pretensions; a simple and incontrovertible truth, beyond which everything is an object of mere curiosity to man. Our information, however, about the opinions of the more celebrated Stoics is very scanty. None of their own writings are preserved. We know little of them but from Cicero, the translator of Grecian philosophy, and from the Greek compilers of a later age; authorities which would be imperfect in the history of facts, but which

---

* It is due to him to observe that he treated humanity towards slaves as one of the characteristics of a wise man. Ουτε κολαζειν οικετας, ελεησειν μεν τοι, και συγγνωμην τινι εξειν των σπουδαιων. (Diog. Laert. *ibid.* 653.) It is not unworthy of remark that neither Plato nor Epicurus thought it necessary to abstain from these topics in a city full of slaves, many of whom were men not destitute of knowledge.

† "Nil generosum, nil magnificum sapit." (Cicero.)

are of far less value in the history of opinions, where a right conception often depends upon the minutest distinctions between words. We know that Zeno was more simple, and that Chrysippus, who was accounted the prop of the Stoic Porch, abounded more in subtile distinctions and systematic spirit.* His power was attested as much by the antagonists whom he called forth, as by the scholars whom he formed. "Had there been no Chrysippus, there would have been no Carneades," was the saying of the latter philosopher himself; as it might have been said in the eighteenth century, "Had there been no Hume, there would have been no Kant and no Reid." Cleanthes, when one of his followers would pay court to him by laying vices to the charge of his most formidable opponent, Arcesilaus the academic, answered with a justice and candour unhappily too rare, "Silence,—do not malign him;—though he attacks virtue by his arguments, he confirms its authority by his life." Arcesilaus, whether modestly or churlishly, replied, "I do not choose to be flattered." Cleanthes, with a superiority of repartee, as well as charity, replied, "Is it flattery to say that you speak one thing and do another?" It would be vain to expect that the fragments of the Professors who lectured in the Stoic School for five hundred years should be capable of being moulded into one consistent system; and we see that in Epictetus at least, the exaggeration of the sect was lowered to the level of reason, by confining the sufficiency of virtue to those cases only where happiness is attainable by our voluntary acts. It ought to be added, in extenuation of a noble error, that the power of habit and character to struggle against outward evils has been proved by experience to be in some instances so prodigious,

* "Chrysippus, qui fulcire putatur porticum Stoicorum." (Cicero.) Elsewhere, "Acutissimus, sed in scribendo exilis et jejunus, scripsit rhetoricam seu potius obmutescendi artem;" nearly as we should speak of a Schoolman.

that no man can presume to fix the utmost limit of its possible increase.

The attempt, however, of the Stoics to stretch the bounds of their system beyond the limits of nature produced the inevitable inconvenience of dooming them to fluctuate between a wild fanaticism on the one hand, and, on the other, concessions which left their differences from other philosophers purely verbal. Many of their doctrines appear to be modifications of their original opinions, introduced as opposition became more formidable. In this manner they were driven to the necessity of admitting that the objects of our desires and appetites are worthy of preference, though they are denied to be constituents of happiness. It was thus that they were obliged to invent a double morality; one for mankind at large, from whom was expected no more than the $\varkappa\alpha\theta\eta\varkappa o\nu$,—which seems principally to have denoted acts of duty done from inferior or mixed motives; and the other, which they appear to have hoped from their ideal wise man, is $\varkappa\alpha\tau o\rho\theta\omega\mu\alpha$, or perfect observance of rectitude,—which consisted only in moral acts done from mere reverence for morality, unaided by any feelings; all which (without the exception of pity) they classed among the enemies of reason and the disturbers of the human soul. Thus did they shrink from their proudest paradoxes into verbal evasions. It is remarkable that men so acute did not perceive and acknowledge that if pain were not an evil, cruelty would not be a vice; and that if patience were of power to render torture indifferent, virtue must expire in the moment of victory. There can be no more triumph when there is no enemy left to conquer.*

The influence of men's opinions on the conduct of their lives is checked and modified by so many causes—it so much

---

* "Patience, sovereign o'er transmuted ill." But as soon as the ill was really "transmuted" into good, it is evident that there was no longer any scope left for the exercise of patience.

depends on the strength of conviction, on its habitual combination and feelings, on the concurrence or resistance of interest, passion, example, and sympathy—that a wise man is not the most forward in attempting to determine the power of its single operation over human actions. In the case of an individual it becomes altogether uncertain. But when the experiment is made on a large scale, when it is long continued and varied in its circumstances, and especially when great bodies of men are for ages the subject of it, we cannot reasonably reject the consideration of the inferences to which it appears to lead. The Roman Patriciate, trained in the conquest and government of the civilised world, in spite of the tyrannical vices which sprang from that training, were raised by the greatness of their objects to an elevation of genius and character unmatched by any other aristocracy; at the moment when, after preserving their power by a long course of wise compromise with the people, they were betrayed by the army and the populace into the hands of a single tyrant of their own order —the most accomplished of usurpers, and, if humanity and justice could for a moment be silenced, one of the most illustrious of men. There is no scene in history so memorable as that in which Cæsar mastered a nobility of which Lucullus and Hortensius, Sulpicius and Catulus, Pompey and Cicero, Brutus and Cato, were members. This renowned body had, from the time of Scipio, sought the Greek philosophy as an amusement or an ornament. Some few, "in thought more elevate," caught the love of truth, and were ambitious of discovering a solid foundation for the Rule of Life. The influence of the Grecian systems was tried by their effect on a body of men of the utmost originality, energy, and variety of character, during the five centuries between Carneades and Constantine, in their successive positions of rulers of the world, and of slaves under the best and under the worst of uncontrolled masters. If we had found this influence perfectly uniform, we should have justly suspected our own love of system of having in part bestowed that appearance on it. Had there been no trace of such an influence discoverable in so great an experiment, we must have acquiesced in the paradox, that opinion does not at all affect conduct. The result is the more satisfactory, because it appears to illustrate general tendency without excluding very remarkable exceptions. Though Cassius was an Epicurean, the true representative of that school was the accomplished, prudent, friendly, good-natured timeserver Atticus, the pliant slave of every tyrant, who could kiss the hand of Antony, imbrued as it was in the blood of Cicero. The pure school of Plato sent forth Marcus Brutus, the signal humanity of whose life was both necessary and sufficient to prove that his daring breach of venerable rules flowed only from that dire necessity which left no other means of upholding the most sacred principles. The Roman orator, though in speculative questions he embraced that mitigated doubt which allowed most ease and freedom to his genius, yet in those moral writings where his heart was most deeply interested, followed the severest sect of philosophy, and became almost a Stoic. If any conclusion may be hazarded from this trial of systems, the greatest which history has recorded, we must not refuse our decided though not undistinguishing preference to that noble school which preserved great souls untainted at the court of dissolute and ferocious tyrants; which exalted the slave of one of Nero's courtiers to be a moral teacher of aftertimes; which for the first, and hitherto for the only time, breathed philosophy and justice into those rules of law which govern the ordinary concerns of every man; and which, above all, has contributed, by the examples of Marcus Porcius Cato, and of Marcus Aurelius Antoninus, to raise the dignity of our species, to keep alive a more ardent love of virtue, and a more awful sense of duty, throughout all generations.*

The result of this short review of the practical philosophy of Greece seems to be, that though it was rich in rules for the conduct of life, and in exhibitions of the beauty of virtue, and though it contains glimpses of just theory, and fragments of perhaps every moral truth, yet it did not leave behind any precise and coherent system; unless we except that of Epicurus, who purchased consistency, method, and perspicuity, too dearly by the sacrifice of truth, and by narrowing and lowering his views of human nature, so as to enfeeble, if not extinguish, all the vigorous motives to arduous virtue. It is remarkable, that while of the eight Professors who taught in the Porch, from Zeno to Posidonius, every one either softened or exaggerated the doctrines of his predecessor; and while the beautiful and reverend philosophy of Plato had, in his own Academy, degenerated into a scepticism which did not spare morality itself, the system of Epicurus remained without change; and his disciples continued for ages to show personal honours to his memory, in a manner which may seem unaccountable among those who were taught to measure propriety by a calculation of palpable and outward usefulness. This steady adherence is in part doubtless attributable to the portion of truth which the doctrine contains; in some degree perhaps to the amiable and unboastful character of Epicurus; not a little, it may be, to the dishonour of deserting an unpopular cause; but probably most of all to that mental indolence which disposes the mind to rest in a simple system,

---

* Of all testimonies to the character of the Stoics, perhaps the most decisive is the speech of the vile sycophant Capito, in the mock impeachment of Thrasea Pætus, before a senate of slaves : " Ut quondam C. Cæsarem et M. Catonem, ita nunc te, Nero, et Thraseam, avida discordiarum civitas loquitur. . . . Ista secta Tuberones et Favonios, veteri quoque reipublicæ ingrata nomina, genuit." (Tacit. *Ann.* xvi. 22.)

See Notes and Illustrations, Note A.

comprehended at a glance, and easily falling in, both with ordinary maxims of discretion, and with the vulgar commonplaces of satire on human nature.* When all instruction was conveyed by lectures, and when one master taught the whole circle of the sciences in one school, it was natural that the attachment of pupils to a Professor should be more devoted than when, as in our times, he can teach only a small portion of a knowledge spreading towards infinity, and even in his own little province finds a rival in every good writer who has treated the same subject. The superior attachment of the Epicureans to their master is not without some parallel among the followers of similar principles in our own age, who have also revived some part of that indifference to eloquence and poetry, which may be imputed to the habit of contemplating all things in relation to happiness, and to (what seems its uniform effect) the egregious miscalculation which leaves a multitude of mental pleasures out of the account. It may be said, indeed, that the Epicurean doctrine has continued with little change to the present day; at least it is certain that no other ancient doctrine has proved so capable of being restored in the same form among the moderns; and it may be added that Hobbes and Gassendi, as well as some of our own contemporaries, are as confident in their opinions, and as intolerant of scepticism, as the old Epicureans. The resemblance of modern to ancient opinions, concerning some of those questions upon which ethical controversy must always hinge, may be a sufficient excuse for a retrospect of the Greek morals; which, it is hoped, will simplify and shorten subsequent obser-

* The progress of commonplace satire on sexes or professions, and (he might have added) on nations, has been exquisitely touched by Gray in his remarks on Lydgate; a Fragment containing passages as finely thought and written as any in English prose. (Gray's *Works*, Matthias's edition, vol. i. p. 55.) General satire on mankind is still more absurd; for no invective can be so unreasonable as that which is founded on falling short of an ideal standard.

vation on those more recent disputes which form the proper subject of this discourse.

The genius of Greece fell with liberty. The Grecian philosophy received its mortal wound in the contests between scepticism and dogmatism which occupied the schools in the age of Cicero. The Sceptics could only perplex, and confute, and destroy. Their occupation was gone as soon as they succeeded. They had nothing to substitute for what they overthrew; and they rendered their own art of no further use. They were no more than venomous animals, who stung their victims to death, but also breathed their last into the wound. A third age of Grecian literature indeed arose at Alexandria, under the Macedonian kings of Egypt; laudably distinguished by exposition, criticism, and imitation, sometimes abused for the purposes of literary forgery, still more honoured by some learned and highly-cultivated poets, as well as by diligent cultivators of history and science; among whom some began, about the first preaching of Christianity, to turn their minds once more to that high philosophy which seeks for the fundamental principles of human knowledge. Philo, a learned and philosophical Hebrew, one of the flourishing colony of his nation established in that city, endeavoured to reconcile the Platonic Philosophy with the Mosaic Law and the Sacred Books of the Old Testament. About the end of the second century, when the Christians, Hebrews, Pagans, and various other sects of semi- or pseudo-Christian Gnostics appear to have studied in the same schools, the almost inevitable tendency of doctrines, however discordant, in such circumstances to amalgamate, produced its full effect under Ammonius Saccas; a celebrated Professor, who, by selection from the Greek systems, the Hebrew books, the oriental religions, and by some of that concession to the rising spirit of Christianity, of which the Gnostics had set the example, composed a very mixed system, commonly designated as the Eclectic Philosophy. The controversies between his contemporaries and followers, especially those of Clement and Origen, the victorious champions of Christianity, with Plotinus and Porphyry, who endeavoured to preserve Paganism by clothing it in a disguise of philosophical Theism, are, from the effects towards which they contributed, the most memorable in the history of human opinion.* But their connection with modern ethics is too faint to warrant any observation in this place, on the imperfect and partial memorials of them which have reached us. The death of Boethius in the west, and the closing of the Athenian schools by Justinian, may be considered as the last events in the history of ancient philosophy.†

* The change attempted by Julian, Porphyry, and their friends, by which Theism would have become the popular religion, may be estimated by the memorable passage of Tacitus on the Theism of the Jews. In the midst of all the obloquy and opprobrium with which he loads that people, his tone suddenly rises when he comes to contemplate them as the only nation who paid religious honours to the supreme and eternal Mind alone, and his style swells at the sight of so sublime and wonderful a scene. "Summum *illud* atque æternum, neque mutabile neque interiturum."

† The punishment of death was inflicted on Pagans by a law of Constantius. "Volumus cunctos sacrificiis abstinere. Si aliquid hujusmodi perpetraverint, gladio ultore sternantur." (Cod. I. tit. xi. *de Paganis*, A.D. 343 or 346.) From the authorities cited by Gibbon (note, chap. xi.), as well as from some research, it should seem that the edict for the suppression of the Athenian schools was not admitted into the vast collection of laws enacted or systematised by Justinian.

SECTION III.

RETROSPECT OF SCHOLASTIC ETHICS.

An interval of a thousand years elapsed between the close of ancient and the rise of modern philosophy; the most unexplored, yet not the least instructive portion of the history of European opinion. In that period the sources of the institutions, the manners, the characteristic distinctions of modern nations, have been traced by a series of philosophical inquirers from Montesquieu to Hallam; and there also, it may be added, more than among the ancients, are the well-springs of our speculative doctrines and controversies. Far from being inactive, the human mind, during that period of exaggerated darkness, produced discoveries in science, inventions in art, and contrivances in government, some of which, perhaps, were rather favoured than hindered by the disorders of society, and by the twilight in which men and things were seen. Had Boethius, the last of the ancients, foreseen that within two centuries of his death, in the province of Britain, then a prey to all the horrors of barbaric invasion, a chief of one of the fiercest tribes of barbarians should translate into the jargon of his freebooters the work on *The Consolations of Philosophy*, of which the composition had soothed the cruel imprisonment of the philosophic Roman himself, he must, even amid his sufferings, have derived some gratification from such an assurance of the recovery of mankind from ferocity and ignorance. But had he been allowed to revisit the earth in the middle of the sixteenth century, with what wonder and delight might he have contemplated the new and fairer order which was beginning to disclose its beauty, and to promise more than it revealed. He would have seen personal slavery nearly extinguished, and women, first released from oriental imprisonment by the Greeks, and raised to a higher dignity among the Romans,* at length fast approaching to due equality; two revolutions the most signal and beneficial since the dawn of civilisation. He would have seen the discovery of gunpowder, which for ever guarded civilised society against barbarians, while it transferred military strength from the few to the many; of paper and printing, which rendered a second destruction of the repositories of knowledge impossible, as well as opened a way by which it was to be finally accessible to all mankind; of the compass, by means of which navigation had ascertained the form of the planet, and laid open a new continent more extensive than his world. If he had turned to civil institutions, he might have learned that some nations had preserved an ancient, simple, and seemingly rude mode of legal proceeding, which threw into the hands of the majority of men a far larger share of judicial power than was enjoyed by them in any ancient democracy. He would have seen everywhere the remains of that principle of representation, the glory of the Teutonic race, by which popular government, anciently imprisoned in cities, became capable of being strengthened by its extension over vast countries, to which experience cannot even now assign any limits; and which, in times still distant, was to exhibit, in the newly-discovered continent, a republican confederacy, likely to surpass the

---

* The steps of this important progress, as far as relates to Athens and Rome, are well remarked by one of the finest of the Roman writers. "Quem enim Romanorum pudet uxorem ducere in convivium? aut cujus materfamilias non primum locum tenet ædium, atque in celebritate versatur? quod multo fit aliter in Græcia; nam neque in convivium adhibetur, nisi propinquorum, neque sedet nisi in interiore parte ædium, quæ *Gynæconitis* appellatur, quo nemo accedit, nisi propinqua cognatione conjunctus." (Cornel. Nepos *in Præfat.*)

Macedonian and Roman empires in extent, greatness, and duration, but gloriously founded on the equal rights, not like them on the universal subjection, of mankind. In one respect, indeed, he might have lamented that the race of man had made a really retrograde movement; that they had lost the liberty of philosophising; that the open exercise of their highest faculties was interdicted. But he might also have perceived that this giant evil had received a mortal wound from Luther, who in his warfare against Rome had struck a blow against all human authority, and unconsciously disclosed to mankind that they were entitled, or rather bound, to form and utter their own opinions, and most of all on the most deeply interesting subjects: for although this most fruitful of moral truths was not yet so released from its combination with the wars and passions of the age as to assume a distinct and visible form, its action was already discoverable in the divisions among the Reformers, and in the fears and struggles of civil and ecclesiastical oppressors. The Council of Trent, and the Courts of Paris, Madrid, and Rome, had before that time foreboded the emancipation of reason.

Though the middle age be chiefly memorable as that in which the foundations of a new order of society were laid, uniting the stability of the oriental system, without its inflexibility, to the activity of the Hellenic civilisation, without its disorder and inconstancy, yet it is not unworthy of notice, on account of the subterranean current which flows through it, from the speculations of ancient to those of modern times. That dark stream must be uncovered before the history of the European understanding can be thoroughly comprehended. It was lawful for the emancipators of reason in their first struggles to carry on mortal war against the Schoolmen. The necessity has long ceased; they are no longer dangerous; and it is now felt by philosophers that it is time to explore and estimate that vast portion of the history of philosophy from which we have scornfully turned our eyes.* A few sentences only can be allotted to the subject in this place. In the first moiety of the middle age, the darkness of Christendom was faintly broken by a few thinly-scattered lights. Even then, Moses Ben Maimon taught philosophy among the persecuted Hebrews, whose ancient schools had never perhaps been wholly interrupted; and a series of distinguished Mahometans, among whom two are known to us by the names of Avicenna and Averroes, translated the Peripatetic writings into their own language, expounded their doctrines in no servile spirit to their followers, and enabled the European Christians to make those versions of them from Arabic into Latin, which in the eleventh and twelfth centuries gave birth to the scholastic philosophy.

The Schoolmen were properly theologians, who employed philosophy only to define and support that system of Christian belief which they and their contemporaries had embraced. The founder of that theological system was Aurelius Augustinus† (called by us Augustin), bishop of Hippo, in the province of Africa; a man of great genius and ardent character, who adopted at different periods in his life the most various, but at all times the most decisive and systematic, as well as daring and extreme opinions. This extraordinary man became,

---

* Tenneman, *Geschichte der Philosophie*, viii. Band. 1811. Cousin, *Cours de l'Histoire de la Philos.* p. 29; Paris, 1828. My esteem for this admirable writer encourages me to say, that the beauty of his diction has sometimes the same effect on his thoughts that a sunny haze produces on outward objects; and to submit to his serious consideration, whether the allurements of Schelling's system have not betrayed him into a too frequent forgetfulness that principles, equally adapted to all phenomena, furnish in speculation no possible test of their truth, and lead, in practice, to total indifference and inactivity respecting human affairs. I quote with pleasure an excellent observation from this work. "Le moyen âge n'est pas autre chose que la formation pénible, lente et sanglante, de tous les élémens de la civilisation moderne; je dis la formation, et non leur développement." (P. 27.)

† Notes and Illustrations, Note B.

after some struggles, the chief Doctor, and for ages almost the sole oracle, of the Latin church. It happened by a singular accident that the Schoolmen of the twelfth century, who adopted his theology, instead of borrowing their defensive weapons from Plato, the favourite of their master, had recourse for the exposition and maintenance of their doctrines to the writings of Aristotle, the least pious of philosophical theists. The Augustinian doctrines of original sin, predestination, and grace, little known to the earlier Christian writers, who appear indeed to have adopted opposite and milder opinions, were espoused by Augustin himself in his old age; when by a violent swing from his youthful Manicheism, which divided the sovereignty of the world between two adverse beings, he did not shrink, in his pious solicitude for tracing the power of God in all events, from presenting the most mysterious parts of the moral government of the universe, in their darkest colours and their sternest shape, as articles of faith, the objects of the habitual meditation and practical assent of mankind. The principles of his rigorous system, though not with all their legitimate consequences, were taught in the schools; respectfully promulgated rather than much inculcated by the western church (for in the east these opinions seem to have been unknown); scarcely perhaps distinctly assented to by the majority of the clergy; and seldom heard of by laymen till the systematic genius and fervid eloquence of Calvin rendered them a popular creed in the most devout and moral portion of the Christian world. Anselm,* the Piedmontese archbishop of Canterbury, was the earliest reviver of the Augustinian opinions. Aquinas † was their most redoubted champion. To them, however, the latter joined others of a different spirit. Faith, according to him, was a virtue, not in the sense in which it denotes the things

* Died in 1109.
† Born in 1224; died in 1279. Notes and Illustrations, Note C.

believed, but in that in which it signifies the state of mind which leads to right belief. Goodness he regarded as the moving principle of the Divine government; justice, as a modification of goodness; and, with all his zeal to magnify the sovereignty of God, he yet taught, that though God always wills what is just, nothing is just solely because he wills it. Scotus,* the most subtile of doctors, recoils from the Augustinian rigour, though he rather intimates than avows his doubts. He was assailed for his tendency towards the Pelagian or anti-Augustinian doctrines by many opponents, of whom the most famous in his time was Thomas Bradwardine,† archbishop of Canterbury, formerly confessor of Edward III., whose defence of predestination was among the most noted works of that age. He revived the principles of the ancient philosophers, who, from Plato to Marcus Aurelius, taught that error of judgment, being involuntary, is not the proper subject of moral disapprobation; which indeed is implied in Aquinas's account of faith.‡ But he appears to have been the first whose language inclined towards that most pernicious of moral heresies, which represents morality to be founded on [divine] will.§ William of Ockham, the

---

* Born about 1265; died at Cologne (where his grave is still shown) in 1308. Whether he was a native of Dunston in Northumberland, or of Dunse in Berwickshire, or of Down in Ireland, was a question long and warmly contested; but which seems to be settled by his biographer, Luke Wadding, who quotes a passage of Scotus's Commentary on Aristotle's Metaphysics, where he illustrates his author thus: "As in the definition of St. Francis, or St. Patrick, man is necessarily presupposed." (Scoti *Opera*, 1, 3.) As Scotus was a Franciscan, the mention of St. Patrick seems to show that he was an Irishman. Notes and Illustrations, Note D.

† Born about 1290, died in 1349; the contemporary of Chaucer, and probably a fellow-student of Wickliffe and Roger Bacon. His principal work was entitled *De Causa Dei contra Pelagium, et de Virtute Causarum, Libri III.*

‡ Notes and Illustrations, Note E. § *Ibid.* Note F.

most justly celebrated of English schoolmen, went so far beyond this inclination of his master, as to affirm, that, "if God had commanded his creatures to hate himself, the hatred of God would ever be the duty of man;" a monstrous hyperbole, into which he was perhaps betrayed by his denial of the doctrine of general ideas, the pre-existence of which in the Eternal intellect was commonly regarded as the foundation of the immutable nature of morality. The doctrine of Ockham, which, by necessary implication, refuses moral attributes to the Deity, and contradicts the existence of a moral government, is practically equivalent to Atheism.* As all devotional feelings have moral qualities for their sole object; as no being can inspire love or reverence otherwise than by those qualities which are naturally amiable or venerable, this doctrine would, if men were consistent, extinguish piety, or, in other words, annihilate religion. Yet so astonishing are the contradictions of human nature, that this most impious of all opinions probably originated in a pious solicitude to magnify the sovereignty of God, and to exalt his authority even above his own goodness. Hence we may understand its adoption by John Gerson, the oracle of the Council of Constance, and the great opponent of the spiritual monarchy of the Pope; a pious mystic, who placed religion in devout feeling.† In further explanation, it may be added, that Gerson was of the sect of the Nominalists, of which Ockham was the founder; and that he was the more ready to follow his master, because they both courageously maintained the independence of the State on the church, and the authority of the church over the Pope. The general opinion of the schools was, however, that of Aquinas,

* A passage to this effect, from Ockham, with nearly the same remark, has, since the text was written, been discovered on a re-perusal of Cudworth's *Immutable Morality*. See p. 10.

† "Remitto ad quod Occam de hac materia in Lib. Sentent. dicit in qua explicatione si rudis judicetur, nescio quid appellabitur subtilitas." (Gerson *de vita Spirit.* Op. iii. 14. Hag. Com. 1728.)

who, from the native soundness of his own understanding, as well as from the excellent example of Aristotle, was averse from all rash and extreme dogmas on questions which had any relation, however distant, to the duties of life.

It is very remarkable, though hitherto unobserved, that Aquinas anticipated those controversies respecting perfect disinterestedness in the religious affections which occupied the most illustrious members of his communion* four hundred years after his death; and that he discussed the like question respecting the other affections of human nature with a fulness and clearness, an exactness of distinction, and a justness of determination, scarcely surpassed by the most acute of modern philosophers.† It ought to be added, that, according to the most natural and reasonable construction of his words, he allowed to the church a control only over spiritual concerns, and recognised the supremacy of the civil powers in all temporal affairs.‡

It has already been stated that the scholastic system was a collection of dialectical subtilties, contrived for the support of the corrupted Christianity of that age by a succession of divines, whose extraordinary powers of distinction and reasoning were morbidly enlarged in the long meditation of the cloister, by the exclusion of every other pursuit, and the consequent palsy of every other faculty; who were cut off from all the materials on which the mind can operate, and doomed for ever to toil in defence of what they must never dare to examine; to whom their age and their condition denied the

* Bossuet and Fénelon.

† See Aquinas, *Comm. in* iii. *Lib. Sentent.* distinctio xxix. quæst. i. art. 3. " Utrum Deus sit super omnia diligendus ex charitate." Art. 4. "Utrum in dilectione Dei possit haberi respectus ad aliquam mercedem." (*Opera*, ix. 322, 325.) Some illustrations of this memorable anticipation, which has escaped the research even of the industrious Tenneman, will be found in the Notes and Illustrations, Note G.

‡ Notes and Illustrations, Note H.

means of acquiring literature, of observing nature, or of studying mankind. The few in whom any portion of imagination and sensibility survived this discipline, retired from the noise of debate to the contemplation of pure and beautiful visions. They were called Mystics. The greater part, driven back on themselves, had no better employment than to weave cobwebs out of the terms of art which they had vainly, though ingeniously, multiplied. The institution of clerical celibacy, originating in an enthusiastic pursuit of purity, promoted by a mistake in moral prudence, which aimed at raising religious teachers in the esteem of their fellows, and at concentrating their whole minds on professional duties, at last encouraged by the ambitious policy of the See of Rome, desirous of detaching them from all ties but her own, had the effect of shutting up all the avenues which Providence has opened for the entrance of social affection and virtuous feeling into the human heart. Though this institution perhaps prevented knowledge from becoming once more the exclusive inheritance of a sacerdotal caste; though the rise of innumerable laymen, of the lowest condition, to the highest dignities of the church, was the grand democratical principle of the middle age, and one of the most powerful agents in impelling mankind towards a better order; yet celibacy must be considered as one of the peculiar infelicities of these secluded philosophers; not only as it abridged their happiness, nor even solely, though chiefly, as it excluded them from the school in which the heart is humanised, but also (an inferior consideration, but more pertinent to our present purpose) because the extinction of these moral feelings was as much a subtraction from the moralist's store of facts and means of knowledge, as the loss of sight or of touch could prove to those of the naturalist.

Neither let it be thought that to have been destitute of letters was to them no more than a want of ornament, and a curtailment of gratification. Every poem, every history, every oration, every picture, every statue, is an experiment on human feeling, the grand object of investigation by the moralist. Every work of genius, in every department of ingenious art and polite literature, in proportion to the extent and duration of its sway over the spirits of men, is a repository of ethical facts, of which the moral philosopher cannot be deprived by his own insensibility or by the iniquity of the times, without being robbed of the most precious instruments and invaluable materials of his science. Moreover, letters, which are closer to human feeling than science can ever be, have another influence on the sentiments with which the sciences are viewed, on the activity with which they are pursued, on the safety with which they are preserved, and even on the mode and spirit in which they are cultivated: they are the channels by which ethical science has a constant intercourse with general feeling. As the arts called useful maintain the popular honour of physical knowledge, so polite letters allure the world into the neighbourhood of the sciences of mind and of morals. Whenever the agreeable vehicles of literature do not convey their doctrines to the public, they are liable to be interrupted by the dispersion of a handful of recluse doctors, and the overthrow of their barren and unlamented seminaries. Nor is this all: these sciences themselves suffer as much when they are thus released from the curb of common sense and natural feeling, as the public loses by the want of those aids to right practice which moral knowledge in its sound state is qualified to afford. The necessity of being intelligible at least to all persons who join superior understanding to habits of reflection, who are themselves in constant communication with the far wider circle of intelligent and judicious men, which slowly but surely forms general opinion, is the only effectual check on the natural proneness of metaphysical speculations to degenerate into gaudy dreams or a mere war of words. The disputants who are set free from the wholesome check of sense and feeling, generally carry their dogmatism so far as to rouse the sceptic, who from time to time is provoked to look into the flimsiness of their cobwebs, and rushes in with his besom to sweep them and their systems into oblivion. It is true that literature, which thus draws forth moral science from the schools into the world, and recalls her from thorny distinctions to her natural alliance with the intellect and sentiments of mankind, may, in ages and nations otherwise situated, produce the contrary evil of rendering Ethics shallow, declamatory, and inconsistent. Europe at this moment affords, in different countries, specimens of these opposite and alike mischievous extremes. But we are now concerned only with the temptations and errors of the scholastic age.

We ought not so much to wonder at the mistakes of men so situated, as that they, without the restraints of the general understanding, and with the clogs of system and establishment, should in so many instances have opened questions untouched by the more unfettered ancients, and veins of speculation since mistakenly supposed to have been first explored in more modern times. Scarcely any metaphysical controversy agitated among recent philosophers was unknown to the Schoolmen, unless we except that which relates to liberty and necessity, which would be an exception of doubtful propriety; for the disposition to it is clearly discoverable in the disputes of the Thomists and Scotists respecting the Augustinian and Pelagian doctrines,* although restrained from the avowal of legitimate consequences on either side by the theological authority which both parties acknowledged. The Scotists steadily affirmed the blamelessness of erroneous opinion—a principle which is the only effectual security for conscientious inquiry, for mutual kindness, and for public quiet. The con-

* Notes and Illustrations, Note I.

troversy between the Nominalists and Realists, treated by some modern writers as an example of barbarous wrangling, was in truth an anticipation of that modern dispute which still divides metaphysicians, whether the human mind can form general ideas, and whether the words which are supposed to convey such ideas be not general terms, representing only a number of particular perceptions?—questions so far from frivolous, that they deeply concern both the nature of reasoning and the structure of language; on which Hobbes, Berkeley, Hume, Stewart, and Tooke, have followed the Nominalists; and Descartes, Locke, Reid, and Kant, have, with various modifications and some inconsistencies, adopted the doctrine of the Realists.* With the Schoolmen appears to have originated the form, though not the substance, of the celebrated maxim, which, whether true or false, is pregnant with systems, "There is nothing in the understanding which was not before in the senses."† Ockham ‡ the Nominalist first denied the Peripatetic doctrine of the existence of certain species (since the time of Descartes called *ideas*) as the direct objects of perception and thought, interposed between the mind and outward objects; the modern opposition to which by Dr. Reid has been supposed to justify the allotment of so high a station to that respectable philosopher. He taught also

---

* Locke speaks on this subject inconsistently; Reid calls himself a conceptualist; Kant uses terms so different that he ought perhaps to be considered as of neither party. Leibnitz, varying in some measure from the general spirit of his speculations, warmly panegyrises the Nominalists; "Secta Nominalium, omnium inter scholasticos profundissima, et hodiernæ reformatæ philosophandi rationi congruentissima." (Leibn. *Op.* iv. Pars i. p. 59.)

† *Nil est in intellectu quod non prius fuit in sensu.*

‡ "Maximi vir ingenii, et eruditionis pro illo ævo summæ, Wilhelmus Occam, Anglus." (Leibn. *ibid.* p. 60.) The writings of Ockham, which are very rare, I have never seen. I owe my knowledge of them to Tenneman, who, however, quotes the words of Ockham, and of his disciple Biel.

that we know nothing of mind but its acts, of which we are conscious. More inclination towards an independent philosophy is to be traced among the Schoolmen than might be expected from their circumstances. Those who follow two guides will sometimes choose for themselves, and may prefer the subordinate on some occasions. Aristotle rivalled the church; and the church herself safely allowed considerable latitude to the philosophical reasonings of those who were only heard or read in colleges or cloisters, on condition that they neither impugned her authority, nor dissented from her worship, nor departed from the language of her creeds. The Nominalists were a freethinking sect, who, notwithstanding their defence of kings against the court of Rome, were persecuted by the civil power. It should not be forgotten that Luther was a Nominalist.*

If not more remarkable it is more pertinent to our purpose, that the ethical system of the Schoolmen, or, to speak more properly, of Aquinas, as the moral master of Christendom for three centuries, was in its practical part so excellent as to leave little need of extensive change, with the inevitable exception of the connection of his religious opinions with his precepts and counsels. His rule of life is neither lax nor impracticable. His grounds of duty are solely laid in the nature of man, and in the well-being of society. Such an intruder as subtilty seldom strays into his moral instructions. With a most imperfect knowledge of the Peripatetic writings, he came near the great master, by abstaining in practical philosophy from the unsuitable exercise of that faculty of distinction, in which he would probably have shown that he was little inferior to Aristotle, if he had been equally unrestrained. His very frequent coincidence with modern moralists is

* "In Martini Lutheri scriptis prioribus amor Nominalium satis elucet, donec in omnes monachos æqualiter affectus esse cœpit." (Leibn. iv. Pars i. p. 60.)

doubtless to be ascribed chiefly to the nature of the subject, but in part also to that unbroken succession of teachers and writers, which preserved the observations contained in what had been long the text-book of the European Schools, after the books themselves had been for ages banished and forgotten. The praises bestowed on Aquinas by every one of the few great men who appear to have examined his writings since the downfall of his power, among whom may be mentioned Erasmus, Grotius, and Leibnitz, are chiefly, though not solely, referable to his ethical works.*

Though the Schoolmen had thus anticipated many modern controversies of a properly metaphysical sort, they left untouched most of those questions of ethical theory which were unknown to or neglected by the ancients. They do not appear to have discriminated between the nature of moral sentiments and the criterion of moral acts; to have considered to what faculty of our mind moral approbation is referable; or to have inquired whether our moral faculty, whatever it may be, is implanted or acquired. Those who measure only by palpable results have very consistently regarded the metaphysical and theological controversies of the schools as a mere waste of intellectual power. But the contemplation of the athletic vigour and versatile skill manifested by the European understanding at the moment when it emerged from this tedious and rugged discipline, leads, if not to approbation yet to more qualified censure. What might have been the result of a different combination of circumstances, is an inquiry which, on a large scale, is beyond human power. We may, however, venture to say, that no abstract science, unconnected with religion, was likely to be respected in a barbarous age; and we may be allowed to doubt whether any knowledge, dependent directly on experi-

---

* See especially the excellent Preface of Leibnitz to Nizolius, sect. 37.

ence, and applicable to immediate practice, would have so trained the European mind as to qualify it for that series of inventions, and discoveries, and institutions, which begins with the sixteenth century, and of which no end can now be foreseen but the extinction of the race of man.

The fifteenth century was occupied by the disputes of the Realists with the Nominalists, in which the scholastic doctrine expired. After its close no Schoolman of note appeared. The sixteenth may be considered as the age of transition from the scholastic to the modern philosophy. The former, indeed, retained possession of the Universities, and was long after distinguished by all the ensigns of authority. But the mines were already prepared. The revolution in opinion had commenced. The moral writings of the preceding times had generally been commentaries on that part of the *Summa Theologiæ* of Aquinas which relates to Ethics. Though these still continued to be published, yet the most remarkable moralists of the sixteenth century indicated the approach of other modes of thinking, by the adoption of the more independent titles of Treatises on Justice and Law. These titles were suggested, and the spirit, contents, and style of the writings themselves were materially affected, by the improved cultivation of the Roman law, by the renewed study of ancient literature, and by the revival of various systems of Greek philosophy, now studied in the original, which at once mitigated and rivalled the scholastic doctors, and, while they rendered philosophy more free, reopened its communications with society and affairs. The speculative theology which had arisen under the French governments of Paris and London in the twelfth century, which flourished in the thirteenth in Italy in the hands of Aquinas, which was advanced in the British Islands by Scotus and Ockham in the fourteenth, was in the sixteenth, with unabated acuteness, but with a clearness and elegance unknown before the restoration of letters, cultivated by Spain, in that age the most powerful and magnificent of the European nations.

Many of these writers treated the law of war and the practice of hostilities in a juridical form.* Francis Victoria, who began to teach at Valladolid in 1525, is said to have first expounded the doctrines of the schools in the language of the age of Leo the Tenth. Dominic Soto,† a Dominican, the confessor of Charles V., and the oracle of the Council of Trent, to whom that assembly were indebted for much of the precision and even elegance for which their doctrinal decrees are not unjustly commended, dedicated his treatise on *Justice and Law* to Don Carlos, in terms of praise which, used by a writer who is said to have declined the high dignities of the church, lead us to hope that he was unacquainted with the brutish vices of that wretched prince. It is a concise and not inelegant compound of the scholastic Ethics, which continued to be of considerable authority for more than a century.‡ Both he and his master Victoria deserve to be had in everlasting remembrance for the part which they took, on behalf of the natives of America and of Africa, against the

* Many of the separate dissertations, on points of this nature, are contained in the immense collection entitled *Tractatus Tractatuum*, published at Venice, in 1584, under the patronage of the Roman See. There are three *de Bello;* one by Lupus of Segovia when Francis I. was prisoner in Spain; another, more celebrated, by Francis Arias, who, on the 11th June 1532, discussed before the College of Cardinals the legitimacy of a war by the Emperor against the Pope. There are two *de Pace;* and others *de Potestate Regia, de Pœna Mortis*, etc. The most ancient and scholastic is that of J. de Lignano of Milan *de Bello*. The above writers are mentioned in the Prolegomena to Grotius *de Jure Belli*. Pietro Belloni (Councillor of the Duke of Savoy), *de Re Militari*, treats his subject with the minuteness of a Judge-Advocate, and has more modern examples, chiefly Italian, than Grotius.

† Born in 1494; died in 1560. (Antonii *Bibliotheca Hispana Nova*.) The opinion of Soto's knowledge entertained by his contemporaries is expressed in a jingle, *Qui scit Sotum scit totum*.

‡ Notes and Illustrations, Note K.

rapacity and cruelty of the Spaniards. Victoria pronounced war against the Americans for their vices or for their paganism to be unjust.* Soto was the authority chiefly consulted by Charles V., on occasion of the conference held before him at Valladolid in 1542, between Sepulveda, an advocate of the Spanish colonists, and Las Casas, the champion of the unhappy Americans; of which the result was a very imperfect edict of reformation in 1543, which, though it contained little more than a recognition of the principle of justice, almost excited a rebellion in Mexico. Sepulveda, a scholar and a reasoner, advanced many maxims which were specious, and in themselves reasonable, but which practically tended to defeat even the scanty and almost illusive reform which ensued. Las Casas was a passionate missionary, whose zeal, kindled by the long and near contemplation of cruelty, prompted him to exaggerations of fact and argument;† yet, with all its errors, it afforded the only hope of preserving the natives of America from extirpation. The opinion of Soto could not fail to be conformable to his excellent principle, that "there can be no difference between Christians and Pagans, for the law of nations is equal to all nations." ‡ To Soto belongs the signal honour of being the first writer who condemned the African slave-trade. "It is affirmed," says he, "that the unhappy Ethiopians are by fraud or force carried away and sold as slaves. If this is true, neither those who have taken them, nor those who purchased them, nor those who hold them in bondage, can ever have a quiet conscience till they emancipate them, even if no compensation should be obtained."§ As the work which contains this memorable

* "Indis non debere auferri imperium, ideo quia sunt peccatores, vel ideo quia non sunt Christiani," were the words of Victoria.
† Notes and Illustrations, Note L.
‡ "Neque discrepantia (ut reor) est inter Christianos et infideles, quoniam ius gentium cunctis gentibus æquale est."
§ Soto *de Justitia et Jure*, lib. iv. quæst. ii. art. 2.

condemnation of man-stealing and slavery was the substance of lectures many years delivered at Salamanca, philosophy and religion appear, by the hand of their faithful minister, to have thus smitten the monsters in their earliest infancy. It is hard for any man of the present age to conceive the praise which is due to the excellent monks who courageously asserted the rights of those whom they never saw, against the prejudices of their order, the supposed interest of their religion, the ambition of their government, the avarice and pride of their countrymen, and the prevalent opinions of their time.

Francis Suarez,* a Jesuit, whose voluminous works amount to twenty-four volumes in folio, closes the list of writers of his class. His work on *Laws, and on God the Lawgiver*, may be added to the above treatise of Soto, as exhibiting the most accessible and perspicuous abridgment of the theological philosophy in its latest form.

Grotius, who, though he was the most upright and candid of men, could not have praised a Spanish Jesuit beyond his deserts, calls Suarez the most acute of philosophers and divines.† On a practical matter, which may be naturally mentioned here, though in strict method it belongs to another subject, the merit of Suarez is conspicuous. He first saw that international law was composed not only of the simple principles of justice applied to the intercourse between states, but of those usages, long observed in that intercourse by the European race, which have since been more exactly distinguished as the consuetudinary law acknowledged by the Christian nations of Europe and America.‡ On this im-

---

* Born in 1538; died in 1617.

† "Tantæ subtilitatis philosophum et theologum, ut vix quemquam habeat parem." (Grotii *Epist.* apud Anton. *Bibl. Hisp. Nova.*)

‡ "Nunquam enim civitates sunt sibi tam sufficientes quin indigeant mutuo juvamine et societate, interdum ad majorem utilitatem, interdum ob necessitatem moralem. Hac igitur ratione indigent aliquo jure quo dirigantur et recte ordinentur in hoc genere societatis. Et

portant point his views are more clear than those of his contemporary Alberico Gentili.* It must even be owned, that the succeeding intimation of the same general doctrine by Grotius is somewhat more dark, perhaps from his excessive pursuit of concise diction.†

quamvis magna ex parte hoc fiat per rationem naturalem, non tamen sufficienter et immediate quoad omnia, *ideoque specialia jura poterant usu earundem gentium introduci.*" (Suarez *de Legibus,* lib. ii. cap. ii. 9 *et seq.*)

* Born in the March of Ancona in 1550; died at London in 1608.

† Grotius *de Jure Belli,* lib. i. cap. i. sect. 14. [Jus gentium in its wider sense: id est quod gentium omnium, aut multarum voluntate vim obligandi accepit. *Multarum* addidi, quia vix ullum jus referitur extra jus naturale quod ipsum quoque [*jus*] *gentium* dici solet omnibus gentibus commune.]

SECTION IV.

MODERN ETHICS.

GROTIUS.

Born 1583—died 1645.

THE introduction to the great work of Grotius,* composed in the first years of his exile, and published at Paris in 1625, contains the most clear and authentic statement of the general principles of morals prevalent in Christendom after the close of the schools, and before the writings of Hobbes had given rise to those ethical controversies which more peculiarly belong to modern times. That he may lay down the fundamental principles of Ethics he introduces Carneades on the stage as denying altogether the reality of moral distinctions; teaching that law and morality are contrived by powerful men for their own interest; that they vary in different countries, and change in successive ages; that there can be no natural law, since nature leads men as well as other animals to prefer their own interest to every other object; that therefore there is either no justice, or if there be, it is another name for the height of folly, inasmuch as it is a fond attempt to persuade a human being to injure himself for the unnatural purpose of benefiting his fellow-men.†

* *Prolegomena.* His letter to Vossius, of 1st August 1625, determines the exact period of the publication of this famous work. Grotii *Epist.* 74.

† The same commonplace paradoxes were retailed by the Sophists, whom Socrates is introduced as chastising in the Dialogues of Plato. They were common enough to be put by the historian into the mouth of an ambassador in a public speech. Ανδρι δε τυραννω η πολει αρχην εχουση ουδεν αλογον ὁ τι ξυμφερον. (Thucyd. vi. 85.)

To this Grotius answered, that even inferior animals, under the powerful though transient impulse of parental love, prefer their young to their own safety or life; that gleams of compassion, and, he might have added, of gratitude and indignation, appear in the human infant long before the age of moral discipline; that man at the period of maturity is a social animal, who delights in the society of his fellow-creatures for its own sake, independently of the help and accommodation which it yields; that he is a reasonable being, capable of framing and pursuing general rules of conduct, of which he discerns that the observance contributes to a regular, quiet, and happy intercourse between all the members of the community; and that, from these considerations, all the precepts of morality, and all the commands and prohibitions of just law, may be derived by impartial reason. "And these principles," says the pious philosopher, "would have their weight, even if it were to be granted (which could not be conceded without the highest impiety) that there is no God, or that he exercises no moral government over human affairs."* "Natural law is the dictate of right reason, pronouncing that there is in some actions a moral obligation, and in other actions a moral deformity, arising from their respective suitableness or repugnance to the reasonable and social nature; and that consequently such acts are either forbidden or enjoined by God, the author of nature. Actions which are the subject of this exertion of reason, are in themselves lawful or unlawful, and

* "Et hæc quidem locum aliquem haberent, etiamsi daretur (quod sine summo scelere dari nequit) non esse Deum, aut non curari ab eo negotia humana." (*Proleg.* 11.) And in another place, "Jus naturale est dictatum rectæ rationis, indicans actui alicui, ex ejus convenientia aut disconvenientia cum ipsa natura rationali et Sociali, inesse moralem turpitudinem aut necessitatem moralem, ac consequenter ab auctore naturæ Deo talem actum aut vetari aut præcipi. Actus de quibus tale extat dictatum, debiti sunt aut illiciti per se, atque ideo a Deo necessario præcepti aut vetiti intelliguntur." (Lib. i. cap. i. sect. 10.)

are therefore as such necessarily commanded or prohibited by God."

Such was the state of opinion respecting the first principles of the moral sciences, when, after an imprisonment of a thousand years in the cloister, they began once more to hold intercourse with the general understanding of mankind. It will be seen in the laxity and confusion, as well as in the prudence and purity of this exposition, that some part of the method and precision of the schools was lost with their endless subtilties and their barbarous language. It is manifest that the latter paragraph is a proposition, not what it affects to be, a definition; that as a proposition, it contains too many terms very necessary to be defined; that the purpose of the excellent writer is not so much to lay down a first principle of morals, as to exert his unmatched power of saying much in few words, in order to assemble within the smallest compass the most weighty inducements, and the most effectual persuasions, to well-doing.

This was the condition in which ethical theory was found by Hobbes, with whom the present Dissertation should have commenced, if it had been possible to state modern controversies in a satisfactory manner, without a retrospect of the revolutions in opinion from which they in some measure flowed.

HOBBES.

Born 1588—died 1679.

THOMAS HOBBES of Malmesbury may be numbered among those eminent persons born in the latter half of the sixteenth century, who gave a new character to European philosophy in the succeeding age.* He was one of the late writers and late learners. It was not till he was nearly thirty that he supplied

---

* Bacon, Descartes, Hobbes, and Grotius. The writings of the first are still as delightful and wonderful as they ever were, and his

the defects of his early education by classical studies, so successfully prosecuted, that he wrote well in the Latin then used by his scientific contemporaries; and made such proficiency in Greek as, in his earliest work, the Translation of Thucydides, published when he was forty, to afford a specimen of a version still valued for its remarkable fidelity; though written with a stiffness and constraint very opposite to the masterly facility of his original compositions. It was after forty that he learned the first rudiments of geometry (so miserably defective was his education); but yielding to the paradoxical disposition apt to infect those who begin to learn after the natural age of commencement, he exposed himself by absurd controversies with the masters of a science which looks down with scorn on the Sophist. A considerable portion of his mature age was passed on the Continent, where he travelled as tutor to two successive Earls of Devonshire; a family with whom he seems to have passed near half-a-century of his long life. In France his reputation, founded at that time solely on personal intercourse, became so great, that his observations on the *Meditations* of Descartes were published in the works of that philosopher, together with those of Gassendi and Arnauld.* It was about his sixtieth year that he began to publish those philosophical writings which contain his peculiar opinions;—which set the understanding of Europe into general motion, and stirred up controversies among metaphysicians and moralists not even yet

authority will have no end. Descartes forms an era in the history of Metaphysics, of Physics, of Mathematics. The controversies excited by Grotius have long ceased, but the powerful influence of his works will be doubted by those only who are unacquainted with the disputes of the seventeenth century.

* The prevalence of freethinking under Louis XIII., to a far greater degree than was avowed, appears not only from the complaints of Mersenne and of Grotius, but from the disclosures of Guy Patin, who, in his *Letters*, describes his own conversations with Gassendi and Naudé, so as to leave no doubt of their opinions.

determined. At the age of eighty-seven he had the boldness to publish metrical versions of the Iliad and Odyssey, which the greatness of his name, and the singularity of the undertaking, still render objects of curiosity, if not of criticism. He owed his influence to various causes; at the head of which may be placed that genius for system, which though it cramps the growth of knowledge,* perhaps finally atones for that mischief, by the zeal and activity which it rouses among followers and opponents, who discover truth by accident, when in pursuit of weapons for their warfare. A system which attempts a task so hard as that of subjecting vast provinces of human knowledge to one or two principles, if it presents some striking instances of conformity to superficial appearances, is sure to delight the framer; and, for a time, to subdue and captivate the student too entirely for sober reflection and rigorous examination. The evil does not indeed very frequently recur. Perhaps Aristotle, Hobbes, and Kant, are the only persons who united in the highest degree the great faculties of comprehension and discrimination which compose the *Genius of System*. Of the three, Aristotle alone could throw it off where it was glaringly unsuitable; and it is deserving of observation, that the reign of system seems, from these examples, progressively to shorten in proportion as reason is cultivated and knowledge advances. But, in the first instance, consistency passes for truth. When principles in some instances have proved sufficient to give an unexpected explanation of facts, the delighted reader is content to accept as true all other deductions from the principles. Specious premises being assumed to be true, nothing more can be

---

* "Another error," says the Master of Wisdom, "is the over-early and peremptory reduction of knowledge into arts and methods, from which time commonly receives small augmentation." (Bacon's *Advancement of Learning*, book i.) "Method," says he, "carrying a show of total and perfect knowledge, has a tendency to generate acquiescence." What pregnant words!

required than logical inference. Mathematical forms pass current as the equivalent of mathematical certainty. The unwary admirer is satisfied with the completeness and symmetry of the plan of his house—unmindful of the need of examining the firmness of the foundation and the soundness of the materials. The system-maker, like the conqueror, long dazzles and overawes the world; but when their sway is past, the vulgar herd, unable to measure their astonishing faculties, take revenge by trampling on fallen greatness.

The dogmatism of Hobbes, was, however unjustly, one of the sources of his fame. The founders of systems deliver their novelties with the undoubting spirit of discoverers; and their followers are apt to be dogmatical, because they can see nothing beyond their own ground. It might seem incredible, if it were not established by the experience of all ages, that those who differ most from the opinions of their fellow-men are most confident of the truth of their own. But it commonly requires an overweening conceit of the superiority of a man's own judgment, to make him espouse very singular notions; and when he has once embraced them, they are endeared to him by the hostility of those whom he contemns as the prejudiced vulgar. The temper of Hobbes must have been originally haughty. The advanced age at which he published his obnoxious opinions rendered him more impatient of the acrimonious opposition which they necessarily provoked; until at length a strong sense of the injustice of the punishment impending over his head, for the publication of what he believed to be truth, co-operated with the peevishness and timidity of his years, to render him the most imperious and morose of dogmatists. His dogmatism has indeed one quality more offensive than that of most others. Propositions the most adverse to the opinions of mankind, and the most abhorrent from their feelings, are introduced into the course of his argument with mathematical coldness. He presents them as demonstrated conclusions, without deigning to explain to his fellow-creatures how they all happened to believe the opposite absurdities; without even the compliment of once observing how widely his discoveries were at variance with the most ancient and universal judgments of the human understanding. The same quality in Spinoza indicates a recluse's ignorance of the world. In Hobbes it is the arrogance of a man who knows mankind and despises them.

A permanent foundation of his fame consists in his admirable style, which seems to be the very perfection of didactic language. Short, clear, precise, pithy, his language never has more than one meaning, which never requires a second thought to find. By the help of his exact method it takes so firm a hold on the mind, that it will not allow attention to slacken. His little tract on *Human Nature* has scarcely an ambiguous or a needless word. He has so great a power of always choosing the most significant term, that he never is reduced to the poor expedient of using many in its stead. He had so thoroughly studied the genius of the language, and knew so well to steer between pedantry and vulgarity, that two centuries have not superannuated probably more than a dozen of his words. His expressions are so luminous, that he is clear without the help of illustration. Perhaps no writer of any age or nation, on subjects so abstruse, has manifested an equal power of engraving his thoughts on the mind of his readers. He seems never to have taken a word for ornament or pleasure; and he deals with eloquence and poetry as the natural philosopher who explains the mechanism of children's toys, or deigns to contrive them. Yet his style so stimulates attention that it never tires; and, to those who are acquainted with the subject, appears to have as much spirit as can be safely blended with reason. He compresses his thoughts so unaffectedly, and yet so tersely, as to produce occasionally maxims which excite the same agreeable surprise with wit, and have become a sort of philosophical proverbs; the success of which he partly owed to the suitableness of such forms of expression to his dictatorial nature. His words have such an appearance of springing from his thoughts, as to impress on the reader a strong opinion of his originality, and indeed to prove that he was not conscious of borrowing; though conversation with Gassendi must have influenced his mind; and it is hard to believe that his coincidence with Ockham should have been purely accidental, on points so important as the denial of general ideas, the reference of moral distinctions to superior power, and the absolute thraldom of religion under the civil power, which he seems to have thought necessary, to maintain that independence of the state on the Church with which Ockham had been contented.

His philosophical writings might be read without reminding any one that the author was more than an intellectual machine. They never betray a feeling except that insupportable arrogance which looks down on men as a lower species of beings; whose almost unanimous hostility is so far from shaking the firmness of his conviction, or even ruffling the calmness of his contempt, that it appears too petty a circumstance to require explanation, or even to merit notice. Let it not be forgotten that part of his renown depends on the application of his admirable powers to expound truth when he meets it. This great merit is conspicuous in that part of his treatise of *Human Nature* which relates to the percipient and reasoning faculties. It is also very remarkable in many of his *secondary principles* on the subject of government and law, which, while the first principles are false and dangerous, are as admirable for truth as for his accustomed and unrivalled propriety of expression.* In many of these observations he

---

* See *De Corpore Politico*, Part i. chap. ii. iii. iv., and *Leviathan*, Part i. chap. xiv. xv., for remarks of this sort, full of sagacity.

even shows a disposition to soften his paradoxes, and to conform to the common sense of mankind.*

It was with perfect truth observed by my excellent friend Mr. Stewart, that "the ethical principles of Hobbes are completely interwoven with his political system."† He might have said that the whole of Hobbes's system, moral, religious, and in part philosophical, depended on his political scheme; not indeed logically, as conclusions depend on premises, but (if the word may be excused) *psychologically*, as the formation of one opinion may be influenced by a disposition to adapt it to previously cherished opinions. The Translation of Thucydides, as he himself boasts, was published to show the evils of popular government.‡ Men he represented as being originally equal, and having an equal right to all things, but as being taught by reason to sacrifice this right for the advantages of peace, and to submit to a common authority, which can preserve quiet only by being the sole depositary of force, and must therefore be absolute and unlimited. The supreme authority cannot be sufficient for its purpose, unless it be wielded by a single hand; nor even then, unless his absolute power extends over religion, which may prompt men to discord by the fear

---

* "The laws of nature are *immutable and eternal;* for injustice, ingratitude, arrogance, pride, iniquity, acception of persons, and the rest, can never be made lawful. For it can never be that war shall preserve life, and peace destroy it." (*Leviathan*, Part i. chap. xv. See also Part ii. chap. xxvi. xxviii., on Laws and on Punishments.)

† See Dissertation First, p. 42. The political state of England is indeed said by himself to have occasioned his first philosophical publication.

        Nascitur interea scelus execrabile belli.
        . . . . Horreo spectans,
        Meque ad dilectam confero Lutetiam,
        Postque duos annos edo De Cive Libellum.   (*Vita* Hobbesii.)

‡ The speech of Euphemus in the sixth book of that historian, and the conference between the ministers from Athens and the Melian chiefs, in the fifth book, exhibit an undisguised *Hobbism*, which was very dramatically put into the mouth of Athenian statesmen at a time when, as we learn from Plato and Aristophanes, it was preached by the Sophists.

of an evil greater than death. The perfect state of a community, according to him, is where law prescribes the religion and morality of the people, and where the will of an absolute sovereign is the sole fountain of law. Hooker had inculcated the simple truth, that "to live by one man's will is the cause of many men's misery." Hobbes embraced the daring paradox, that to live by one man's will is the only means of all men's happiness. Having thus rendered religion the slave of every human tyrant, it was an unavoidable consequence that he should be disposed to lower her character, and lessen her power over men; that he should regard atheism as the most effectual instrument of preventing rebellion; at least that species of rebellion which prevailed in his time, and had excited his alarm. The formidable alliance of religion with liberty haunted his mind, and urged him to the bold attempt of rooting out both these mighty principles; which, when combined with interests and passions, when debased by impure support, and provoked by unjust resistance, have indeed the power of fearfully agitating society; but which are, nevertheless, in their own nature, and as far as they are unmixed and undisturbed, the fountains of justice, of order, of peace, as well as of those moral hopes, and of those glorious aspirations after higher excellence, which encourage and exalt the soul in its passage through misery and depravity. A Hobbist is the only consistent persecutor; for he alone considers himself as bound, by whatever conscience he has remaining, to conform to the religion of the sovereign. He claims from others no more than he is himself ready to yield to any master ;* while the religionist who persecutes a member

---

* Spinoza adopted precisely the same first principles with Hobbes, that all men have a natural right to all things. (*Tractatus Politicus,* cap. ii. sect. 3.) He even avows the absurd and detestable maxim, that States are not bound to observe their treaties longer than the interest or danger which first formed the treaties continues. But on the internal constitution of States he embraces opposite opinions. *Servitutis enim*

of another communion exacts the sacrifice of conscience and sincerity, though professing that rather than make it himself he is prepared to die.

Remarks.—The fundamental errors on which the ethical system of Hobbes is built are not peculiar to him; though he has stated them with a bolder precision, and placed them in a more conspicuous station in the van of his main force, than any other of those who have either frankly avowed or tacitly assumed them, from the beginning of speculation to the present moment. They may be shortly stated as follows:—

1. The first and most inveterate of these errors is, that he does not distinguish *thought* from *feeling*, or rather that he in express words confounds them. The mere *perception* of an object, according to him, differs from the *pleasure* or *pain* which that perception may occasion, no otherwise than as they affect different organs of the bodily frame. The action of the mind in perceiving or conceiving an object is precisely the same with that of feeling the agreeable or disagreeable.* The

---

non pacis interest omnem potestatem ad unum transferre. (*Ibid.* cap. vi. sect. 4.) Limited monarchy he considers as the only tolerable example of that species of government. An Aristocracy nearly approaching to the Dutch system during the suspension of the Stadtholdership, he seems to prefer. He speaks favourably of Democracy, but the chapter on that subject is left unfinished. "Nulla plane templa urbium sumptibus ædificanda, nec jura de opinionibus statuenda." He was the first republican atheist of modern times, and probably the earliest irreligious opponent of an ecclesiastical establishment.

* This doctrine is explained in his tract on *Human Nature*, c. vii.-x. "*Conception is a motion* in some internal substance of the head, which proceeding to the heart, when it helpeth the motion there, it is called *pleasure;* when it weakeneth or hindereth the motion it is called *pain.*" The same matter is handled more cursorily, agreeably to the practical purpose of the work, in *Leviathan*, Part i. chap. vi. These passages are here referred to as proofs of the statement in the text. With the materialism of it we have here no concern. If the multiplied suppositions were granted, we should not advance one step towards understanding what they profess to explain. The first four words are

necessary result of this original confusion is to extend the laws of the intellectual part of our nature over that other part of it, hitherto without any adequate name, which feels, and desires, and loves, and hopes, and wills. In consequence of this long confusion, or want of distinction, it has happened that, whilst the simplest act of the merely intellectual part has many names (such as sensation, perception, impression, etc.), the correspondent act of the other not less important portion of man is not denoted by a technical term in philosophical systems; nor by a convenient word in common language. *Sensation* has another more common sense. *Emotion* is too warm for a generic term. *Feeling* has some degree of the same fault, besides its liability to confusion with the sense of touch. *Pleasure* and *pain* represent only two properties of this act, which render its repetition the object of desire or aversion; which last states of mind presuppose the act. Of these words *emotion* seems to be the least objectionable,* since it has no absolute double meaning, and does not require so much vigilance in the choice of the accompanying words as would be necessary if we were to prefer *feeling;* which, however, being a more familiar word, may, with due caution, be also sometimes employed. Every man who attends to the state of his own mind will acknowledge, that these words, *emotion* and *feeling,* thus used, are perfectly simple, and as incapable of further explanation by words as sight or hearing; which may indeed be rendered into synonymous words, but never can be defined by any more simple or more clear.

---

as unmeaning as if one were to say that greenness is very loud. It is obvious that many motions which promote the motion of the heart are extremely painful.

* ["The part of our nature," of which the author here speaks, has often been described by the compound phrase, "the desires and affections." The proposal to call these "the Emotions" has not been generally accepted; but the adjective "emotional" is not unfrequently used.—W. W.]

Reflection will in like manner teach that perception, reasoning, and judgment, may be conceived to exist without being followed by emotion. Some men hear music without gratification; one may distinguish a taste without being pleased or displeased by it; or at least the relish or disrelish is often so slight, without lessening the distinctness of the sapid qualities, that the distinction of it from the perception cannot be doubted.

The multiplicity of errors which have flowed into Moral Science from this original confusion is very great. They have spread over many schools of philosophy; and many of them are prevalent to this day. Hence the laws of the understanding have been applied to the affections; virtuous feelings have been considered as just reasonings; evil passions represented as mistaken judgments; and it has been laid down as a principle, that the will always follows the last decision of the practical intellect.*

2. By this great error, Hobbes was led to represent all the variety of the desires of men as being only so many instances of objects deliberately and solely pursued, because they were the means, and at the time perceived to be so, of directly or indirectly procuring organic gratification to the individual.† The human passions are described as if they reasoned accurately, deliberated coolly, and calculated exactly. It is assumed that, in performing these operations, there is and can be no act of life in which a man does not bring distinctly before his eyes the pleasure which is to accrue to himself from the act. From this single and simple principle, all human conduct may, according to him, be explained and even foretold.

The true laws of this part of our nature (so totally different from those of the percipient part) were, by this grand mistake,

---

* "Voluntas semper sequitur ultimum indicium intellectus practici."
† See the passages before quoted.

entirely withdrawn from notice. Simple as the observation is, it seems to have escaped not only Hobbes, but many, perhaps most philosophers, that our desires seek a great diversity of objects; that the attainment of these objects is indeed followed by, or rather called, Pleasure; but that it could not be so, if the objects had not been previously desired. Many besides him have really represented *self* as the ultimate object of every action; but none ever so hardily thrust forward the selfish system in its harshest and coarsest shape. The mastery which he shows over other metaphysical subjects forsakes him on this. He does not scruple, for the sake of this system, to distort facts of which all men are conscious; and to do violence to the language in which the result of their uniform experience is conveyed, "Acknowledgment of power is called Honour."* His explanations are frequently sufficient confutations of the doctrine which required them. "Pity is the imagination of future calamity to ourselves, proceeding from the sense (observation) of another man's calamity." "Laughter is occasioned by sudden glory in our eminence, or in comparison with the infirmity of others." Every man who ever wept or laughed may determine whether this be a true account of the state of his mind on either occasion. "Love is a conception of his need of the one person desired;" a definition of love, which, as it excludes kindness, might perfectly well comprehend the hunger of a cannibal, provided that it were not too ravenous to exclude choice. "Good-will, or charity, which containeth the natural affection of parents to their children, consists in a man's conception that he is able not only to accomplish his own desires, but to assist other men in theirs:" from which it follows, as the pride of power is felt in destroy-

---

* *Human Nature*, chap. viii. The ridiculous explanation of the admiration of personal beauty, "as a sign of power generative," shows the difficulties to which this extraordinary man was reduced by a false system.

ing as well as in saving men, that cruelty and kindness are the same passion.*

Such were the expedients to which a man of the highest class of understanding was driven, in order to evade the admission of the simple and evident truth, that there are in our nature perfectly disinterested passions, which seek the wellbeing of others as their object and end, without looking beyond it to self, or pleasure, or happiness. A proposition, from which such a man could attempt to escape only by such means, may be strongly presumed to be true.

3. Hobbes having thus struck the affections out of his map of human nature, and having totally misunderstood (as will appear in a succeeding part of this work) the nature even of the appetites, it is no wonder that we should find in it not a trace of the moral sentiments. Moral good† he considers merely as consisting in the signs of a power to produce pleasure; and repentance is no more than regret at having missed the way; so that, according to this system, a disinterested approbation of and reverence for virtue, are no more possible than disinterested affections towards our fellow-creatures. There is no sense of duty, no compunction for our own offences, no indignation against the crimes of others, unless they affect our own safety; no secret cheerfulness shed over the heart by the practice of well-doing. From his philosophical writings it would be impossible to conclude that there are in man a set of emotions, desires, and aversions, of which the sole and final objects are the voluntary actions and habitual dispositions of himself and of all other

---

* *Human Nature*, chap. ix. I forbear to quote the passage on Platonic love, which immediately follows. But, considering Hobbes's blameless and honourable character, that passage is perhaps the most remarkable instance of the shifts to which his selfish system reduced him.

† Which he calls the *pulchrum*, for want, as he says, of an English word to express it. (*Leviathan*, Part i. c. vi.)

voluntary agents; which are properly called *Moral Sentiments;* and which, though they vary more in degree, and depend more on cultivation, than some other parts of human nature, are as seldom as most of them found to be entirely wanting.

4. A theory of man which comprehends in its explanations neither the social affections nor the moral sentiments, must be owned to be sufficiently defective. It is a consequence, or rather a modification of it, that Hobbes should constantly represent the deliberate regard to personal advantage as the only possible motive of human action; and that he should altogether disdain to avail himself of those refinements of the selfish scheme which allow the pleasures of benevolence and of morality, themselves, to be a most important part of that interest which reasonable beings pursue.

5. Lastly, though Hobbes does in effect acknowledge the necessity of morals in society, and the general coincidence of individual with public interest—truths so palpable, that they never have been excluded from any ethical system—he betrays his utter want of moral sensibility by the coarse and odious form in which he has presented the first of these great principles; and his view of both leads him most strongly to support that common and pernicious error of moral reasoners, that a perception of the tendency of good actions to preserve the being and promote the well-being of the community, and a sense of the dependence of our own happiness upon the general security, either are essential constituents of our moral feelings, or are ordinarily mingled with the most effectual motives to right conduct.

The Court of Charles II. were equally pleased with Hobbes's poignant brevity, and his low estimate of human motives. His ethical epigrams became the current coin of profligate wits. Sheffield, Duke of Buckinghamshire, who represented the class still more perfectly in his morals than in his faculties, has expressed their opinion in verses, of which one line is good enough to be quoted:

> Fame bears no fruit till the vain planter dies.

Dryden speaks of "the philosopher and *poet* (for such is the condescending term employed) of Malmesbury," as resembling Lucretius in haughtiness. But Lucretius, though he held many of the opinions of Hobbes, had the sensibility as well as genius of a poet. His dogmatism is full of enthusiasm; and his philosophical theory of society discovers occasionally as much tenderness as can be shown without reference to individuals. He was a Hobbist in only half his nature.

The moral and political system of Hobbes was a palace of ice, transparent, exactly proportioned, majestic, admired by the unwary as a delightful dwelling; but gradually undermined by the central warmth of human feeling, before it was thawed into muddy water by the sunshine of true philosophy.

When Leibnitz, in the beginning of the eighteenth century, reviewed the moral writers of modern times, his penetrating eye saw only two who were capable of reducing morals and jurisprudence to a science. "So great an enterprise," says he, "might have been executed by the deep-searching genius of Hobbes, if he had not set out from evil principles; or by the judgment and learning of the incomparable Grotius, if his powers had not been scattered over many subjects, and his mind distracted by the cares of an agitated life."[*] Perhaps, in this estimate, admiration of the various and excellent qualities of Grotius may have overrated his purely philosophical powers, great as they unquestionably were. Certainly the failure of Hobbes was owing to no inferiority in strength of intellect. Probably his fundamental errors may be imputed,

---

[*] "Et tale aliquid potuisset vel ab incomparabilis Grotii judicio et doctrina, vel a profundo Hobbii ingenio præstari; nisi illum multa distraxissent; hic vero prava constituisset principia." (Leibnitii *Epist. ad Molanum;* iv. Pars iii. p. 276.)

in part, to the faintness of his moral sensibilities, insufficient to make him familiar with those sentiments and affections † which can be known only by being felt :—a faintness perfectly compatible with his irreproachable life, but which obstructed, and at last obliterated, the only channel through which the most important materials of ethical science enter into the mind.

Against Hobbes, says Warburton, the whole church-militant took up arms. The answers to the *Leviathan* would form a library. But the far greater part have followed the fate of all controversial pamphlets. Sir Robert Filmer was jealous of any rival theory of servitude. Harrington defended liberty, and Clarendon the church, against a common enemy. His philosophical antagonists were, Cumberland, Cudworth, Shaftesbury, Clarke, Butler, and Hutcheson. Though the last four writers cannot be considered as properly polemics, their labours were excited, and their doctrines modified by, the stroke from a vigorous arm which seemed to shake Ethics to its foundation. They lead us far into the eighteenth century; and their works, occasioned by the doctrines of Hobbes, sowed the seed of the ethical writings of Hume, Smith, Price, Kant, and Stewart; in a less degree, also, of those of Tucker and Paley : not to mention Mandeville, the buffoon and sophister of the ale-house ; or Helvetius, an ingenious but flimsy writer, the low and loose moralist of the vain, the selfish, and the sensual.

SECTION V.

CONTROVERSIES CONCERNING THE MORAL FACULTIES AND THE SOCIAL AFFECTIONS.

Cumberland—Cudworth—Clarke—Shaftesbury—Bossuet—Fénélon—Leibnitz—Malebranche—Edwards—Buffier.

DR. RICHARD CUMBERLAND.
Born 1632—died 1718.

RAISED to the see of Peterborough after the Revolution of 1688, Cumberland was the only professed answerer of Hobbes.* His work on *The Law of Nature* still retains a place on the shelf, though not often on the desk. The philosophical epigrams of Hobbes form a contrast to the verbose, prolix, and languid diction of his answerer. The forms of scholastic argument serve more to encumber his style than to insure his exactness. But he has substantial merits. He justly observes that all men can only be said to have had originally a right to all things in a sense in which right has the same meaning with power. He shows that Hobbes is at variance with himself; inasmuch as the dictates of right reason, which, by his own statement, teach men for their own safety to forego the exercise of that right, and which he calls *Laws of Nature*, are coeval with it; and that mankind perceive the moral limits of their power as clearly and as soon as they are conscious of its existence. He enlarges the intimations of Grotius on the social feelings, which prompt men to the pleasures of pacific intercourse, as certainly as the

---

* [Answers to Hobbes were published also by Clarendon, Tenison, Bramhall, Sharrock, as I have noticed in my *Lectures on the History of Moral Philosophy in England*. Lectures II. and III.—W. W.]

apprehension of danger and destruction urges them to avoid hostility. The fundamental principle of his Ethics is, that "the greatest benevolence of every rational agent to all others is the happiest state of each individual, as well as of the whole."* The happiness accruing to each man from the observance and cultivation of benevolence, he considers as appended to it by the Supreme Ruler; through which he sanctions it as his law, and reveals it to the mind of every reasonable creature. From this principle he deduces the rules of morality, which he calls the *Laws of Nature*. The surest, or rather only mark that they are the commandments of God, is, that their observance promotes the happiness of man: for that reason alone could they be imposed by that Being whose essence is love. As our moral faculties must to us be the measure of all moral excellence, he infers that the moral attributes of the Divinity must in their nature be only a transcendent degree of those qualities which we most approve, love, and revere, in those moral agents with whom we are familiar.† He had a momentary glimpse of the possibility that some human actions might be performed with a view to the happiness of others, without any consideration of the pleasure reflected back on ourselves.‡ But it is too faint and transient to be worthy of observation, otherwise than as a new proof how often great truths must flit before the understanding, before they can be firmly and finally held in its grasp. His only attempt to explain the nature of the moral faculty, is the substitution of practical reason (a phrase of the schoolmen, since become celebrated from its renewal by Kant) for right reason;§ and his definition of the first, as that

* Cumberland, *De Legibus Naturæ*, cap. i. sect. 12, first published in London, 1672, and then so popular as to be reprinted at Lubeck in 1683. † *Ibid.* cap. v. sect. 19.
‡ *Ibid.* cap. ii. sect. 20.
§ "Whoever determines his judgment and his will by right reason must agree with all others who judge according to right reason in the

which points out the ends and means of action. Throughout his whole reasoning, he adheres to the accustomed confusion of the quality which renders actions virtuous, with the sentiments excited in us by the contemplation of them. His language on the identity of general and individual interest is extremely vague; though it be, as he says, the foundation-stone of the Temple of Concord among men.

It is little wonder that Cumberland should not have disembroiled this ancient and established confusion, since Leibnitz himself, in a passage where he reviews the theories of morals which had gone before him, has done his utmost to perpetuate it. "It is a question," says he, "whether the preservation of human society be the first principle of the law of nature. This our author denies, in opposition to Grotius, who laid down sociability to be so; to Hobbes, who ascribed that character to mutual fear; and to Cumberland, who held that it was mutual benevolence; which are all three only different names for the safety and welfare of society."* Here the great philosopher considered benevolence or fear, two feelings of the human mind, to be the first principles of the law of nature; in the same sense in which the tendency of certain actions to the well-being of the community may be so regarded. The confusion, however, was then common to him with many, as it even now is with most. The comprehensive view was his own. He perceives the close resemblance of

same matter." (Cumberland, *De Legibus Naturæ*, cap. ii. sect. 8.) This is in one sense only a particular instance of the identical proposition, that two things which agree with a third thing must agree with each other in that in which they agree with the third. But the difficulty entirely consists in the particular third thing here introduced, namely, "right reason," the nature of which not one step is made to explain. The position is curious, as coinciding with "the universal categorical imperative," adopted as a first principle by Kant.

* Leibn. iv. Pars iii. p. 271. The unnamed work, which occasioned these remarks (perhaps one of Thomasius), appeared in 1699. How long after this Leibnitz's Dissertation was written does not appear.

these various and even conflicting opinions, in that important point of view in which they relate to the effects of moral and immoral actions on the general interest. The tendency of virtue to preserve amicable intercourse was enforced by Grotius; its tendency to prevent injury was dwelt on by Hobbes; its tendency to promote an interchange of benefits was inculcated by Cumberland.

CUDWORTH.

Born 1617—died 1688.

CUDWORTH, one of the eminent men educated or promoted in the English Universities during the Puritan rule, was one of the most distinguished of the Latitudinarian or Arminian party who came forth at the Restoration, with a love of liberty imbibed from their Calvinistic masters, as well as from the writings of antiquity, yet tempered by the experience of their own agitated age; and with a spirit of religious toleration more impartial and mature, though less systematic and professedly comprehensive, than that of the Independents, the first sect who preached that doctrine. Taught by the errors of their time, they considered religion as consisting not in vain efforts to explain unsearchable mysteries, but in purity of heart, exalted by pious feelings, and manifested by virtuous conduct.* The government of the church was placed in their

* See the beautiful account of them by Burnet (*Hist.* i. 321, Oxford edit. 1823), who was himself one of the most distinguished of this excellent body; with whom may be classed, notwithstanding some shades of doctrinal difference, his early master, Leighton, Bishop of Dunblane, a beautiful writer, and one of the best of men. The earliest account of them is in a curious contemporary pamphlet, entitled, *An Account of the new Sect of Latitude-men at Cambridge*, republished in the collection of tracts entitled *Phœnix Britannicus*. Jeremy Taylor deserves the highest and perhaps the earliest place among them. But Cudworth's excellent sermon before the House of Commons (31st March

hands by the Revolution, and their influence was long felt among its rulers and luminaries. The first generation of their scholars turned their attention too much from the cultivation of the heart to the mere government of outward action; and in succeeding times the tolerant spirit, not natural to an establishment, was with difficulty kept up by a government whose existence depended on discouraging intolerant pretensions. No sooner had the first sketch of the Hobbian philosophy* been privately circulated at Paris, than Cudworth seized the earliest opportunity of sounding the alarm against the most justly odious of the modes of thinking which it cultivates, or forms of expression which it would introduce;† the prelude to a war which occupied the remaining forty years of his life. The *Intellectual System*, his great production, is directed against the atheistical opinions of Hobbes; it touches ethical questions but occasionally and incidentally. It is a work of stupendous erudition, of much more acuteness than at first appears, of frequent mastery over diction and illustration on subjects where it is most rare; and it is distinguished, perhaps beyond any other volume of controversy, by that best proof of the deepest conviction of the truth of a man's principles, a fearless statement of the most formidable objections to them; a fairness rarely practised but by him who is conscious of his power to answer them. In all his writings, it must be owned that his learning obscures his reasonings, and seems even to oppress his powerful intellect. It is an unfortunate effect of the redundant fulness of his mind, that

---

1647) in the year of the publication of Taylor's *Liberty of Prophesying*, may be compared even to Taylor in charity, piety, and the most liberal toleration.

* *De Cive*, 1642.

† *Dantur boni et mali rationes æternæ et indispensabiles.* Thesis for the degree of B.D. at Cambridge in 1644. (Birch's *Life of Cudworth*, prefixed to his edition of the *Intellectual System*, p. vii. Lond. 1743, 2 vols. 4to.)

it overflows in endless digressions, which break the chain of argument, and turn aside the thoughts of the reader from the main object. He was educated before usage had limited the naturalisation of new words from the learned languages; before the failure of those great men, from Bacon to Milton, who laboured to follow a Latin order in their sentences,— and the success of those men of inferior powers, from Cowley to Addison, who were content with the order, as well as the words, of pure and elegant conversation,—had, as it were, by a double series of experiments, ascertained that the involutions and inversions of the ancient languages are seldom reconcilable with the genius of ours ; and, unless' skilfully as well as sparingly introduced, are at variance with the natural beauties of our prose composition. His mind was more that of an ancient than of a modern philosopher. He often indulged in that sort of amalgamation of fancy with speculation, the delight of the Alexandrian doctors, with whom he was most familiarly conversant; and the *Intellectual System*, both in thought and expression, has an old and foreign air, not unlike a translation from the work of a later Platonist. Large ethical works of this eminent writer are extant in manuscript in the British Museum.* One posthumous volume on morals was published by Dr. Chandler, Bishop of Durham, entitled, *A Treatise concerning Eternal and Immutable Morality.*† But there is the more reason to regret (as far as relates to the history of opinion) that the larger treatises are still unpublished, because the above volume is not so much an ethical treatise as an introduction to one. Protagoras of old, and Hobbes then alive, having concluded that right and wrong were unreal, because they were not perceived by the senses, and because all human knowledge consists only in such perception, Cudworth

---

* A curious account of the history of these MSS., by Dr. Kippis, is to be found in the *Biographia Britannica*, iv. 549.

† London, 1731, 8vo.

endeavours to refute them, by disproving that part of their premises which forms the last-stated proposition. The mind has many conceptions (νοήματα) which are not cognisable by the senses; and though they are *occasioned* by sensible objects, yet could not be formed but by a faculty superior to sense. The conceptions of justice and duty he places among them. The distinction of right from wrong is discerned by reason; and as soon as these words are defined, it becomes evident that it would be a contradiction in terms to affirm that any power, human or divine, could change their nature; or, in other words, make the same act to be just and unjust at the same time. They had existed eternally in the only mode in which truths can be said to be eternal, in the eternal Mind; and they were indestructible and unchangeable like that Supreme Intelligence.*

Whatever judgment may be formed of this reasoning, it is manifest that it relates merely to the philosophy of the *understanding*, and does not attempt any explanation of what constitutes the very essence of morality, its relation to the *will*. That we perceive a distinction between right and wrong as much as between a triangle and a square, is indeed true; and may possibly lead to an explanation of the reason why men should adhere to the one and avoid the other. But it is not that reason. A command or a precept is not a proposition. It cannot be said that either is true or false. Cud-

* "There are many objects of our mind which we can neither see, hear, feel, smell, nor taste, and which did never enter into it by any sense; and therefore we can have no sensible pictures or ideas of them, drawn by the pencil of that inward limner or painter which borrows all his colours from sense, which we call Fancy: and if we reflect on our own cogitations of these things, we shall sensibly perceive that they are not *phantastical* but *noematical*: as, for example, justice, equity, duty and obligation, cogitation, opinion, intellection, volition, memory, verity, falsity, cause, effect, genus, species, nullity, contingency, possibility, impossibility, and innumerable others." (*Eternal and Immutable Morality*, p. 140.) We have here an anticipation of Kant.

worth, as well as many who succeeded him, confounded the mere apprehension by the understanding that right is different from wrong, with the practical authority of these important conceptions, exercised over voluntary actions, in a totally distinct province of the human soul.

Though his life was devoted to the assertion of divine Providence, and though his philosophy was imbued with the religious spirit of Platonism,* yet he had placed Christianity too purely in the love of God and man to be considered as having much regard for. those controversies about rites and opinions with which zealots disturb the world. They represented him as having fallen into the same heresy with Milton and with Clarke ;† and some of them even charged him with atheism, for no other reason than that he was not afraid to state the atheistic difficulties in their fullest force. As blind anger heaps inconsistent accusations on each other, they called him at least an " Arian, a Socinian, or a Deist." ‡ The courtiers of Charles II., who were delighted with every part of Hobbes but his integrity, did their utmost to decry his antagonist. They turned the railing of the bigots into a sarcasm against religion ; as we learn from him who represented them with unfortunate fidelity. "He has raised," says Dryden, "such strong objections against the being of God, that many think he has not answered them ;"—"the common fate," as Lord Shaftesbury tells us, " of those who dare to appear fair authors."§ He had, indeed, earned the

* Ευσεβει, ω τεκνον, ὁ γαρ ευσεβων ακρως χριστιανιζει. Be pious, my son, for piety is the sum of Christianity. (Motto affixed to the sermon above mentioned.)

† The following doctrine is ascribed to Cudworth by Nelson, a man of good understanding and great worth : " Dr. Cudworth maintained that the Father, absolutely speaking, is the only supreme God ; the Son and Spirit being God only by his concurrence with them, and their subordination and subjection to him." (Nelson's *Life of Bull*, p. 339.)

‡ Turner's *Discourse on the Messiah*, p. 335.

§ *Moralists*, Part ii. sect. iii.

hatred of some theologians, better than they could know from the writings published during his life; for in his posthumous work he classes with the ancient atheists those of his contemporaries, whom he forbears to name, who held "that God may command what is contrary to moral rules; that he has no inclination to the good of his creatures; that he may justly doom an innocent being to eternal torments; and that whatever God does will, for that reason is just, because he wills it."* It is an interesting incident in the life of a philosopher, that Cudworth's daughter, Lady Masham, had the honour to nurse the infirmities and to watch the last breath of Mr. Locke, who was opposed to her father in speculative philosophy, but who heartily agreed with him in the love of truth, liberty, and virtue.

CLARKE.

Born 1675—died 1729.

CONNECTED with Cudworth by principle, though separated by some interval of time, was Dr. Samuel Clarke, a man eminent at once as a divine, a mathematician, a metaphysical philosopher, and a philologer; who, as the interpreter of Homer and Cæsar, the scholar of Newton, and the antagonist of Leibnitz, approved himself not unworthy of correspondence with the

* *Eternal and Immutable Morality*, p. 11. He names only one book published at Franeker. He quotes Ockham as having formerly maintained the same monstrous positions. To many, if not to most, of these opinions or expressions, ancient and modern, reservations are adjoined, which render them *literally* reconcilable with practical morals. But the dangerous abuse to which the incautious language of ethical theories is liable, is well illustrated by an anecdote related in Plutarch's Life of Alexander. A sycophant named Anaxarchas consoled that monarch for the murder of Clitus, by assuring him that every act of a ruler must be just. Παν το πραχθεν υπο του κρατουντος δικαιον. (Plut. *Oper.* i. 639, Franc. 1599.)

highest order of human spirits. Roused by the prevalence of the doctrines of Spinoza and Hobbes, he endeavoured to demonstrate the being and attributes of God from a few axioms and definitions, in the manner of Geometry; an attempt in which, with all his powers of argument, it must be owned that he is compelled sometimes tacitly to assume what the laws of reasoning required him to prove; and that, on the whole, his failure may be regarded as a proof that such a mode of argument is beyond the faculties of man.* Justly considering the moral attributes of the Deity as what alone renders him the object of religion, and to us constitutes the difference between theism and atheism, he laboured with the utmost zeal to place the distinctions of right and wrong on a more solid foundation; and to explain the conformity of morality to reason, in a manner calculated to give a precise and scientific signification to that phraseology which all philosophers had, for so many ages, been content to employ, without thinking themselves obliged to define.

It is one of the most rarely successful efforts of the human mind, to place the understanding at a point from which a philosopher takes the views that compose his system; to recollect constantly his purposes; to adopt for a moment his previous opinions and prepossessions; to think in his words and to see with his eyes; especially when the writer widely dissents from the system which he attempts to describe, and after a general change in the modes of thinking and in the use of terms. Every part of the present work requires

* This admirable person had so much candour as in effect to own his failure, and to recur to those other arguments in support of this great truth, which have in all ages satisfied the most elevated minds. In proposition viii. (*Being and Attributes of God*, p. 47) which affirms that the first cause *must* be "intelligent" (where, as he truly states, "lies the main question between us and the atheists"), he owns that the proposition cannot be demonstrated strictly and properly *a priori.* See Notes and Illustrations, Note M.

such an excuse; but perhaps it may be more necessary in a case like that of Clarke, where the alterations in both respects have been so insensible, and in some respects appear so limited, that they may escape attention, than after those total revolutions in doctrine, where the necessity of not measuring other times by our own standard must be apparent to the most undistinguishing.

The sum of his moral doctrine may be stated as follows. Man can conceive nothing without at the same time conceiving its relations to other things. He must ascribe the same law of perception to every being to whom he ascribes thought. He cannot therefore doubt that all the relations of all things to all must have always been present to the Eternal Mind. The relations in this sense are eternal, however recent the things may be between which they subsist. The whole of these relations constitute truth. The knowledge of them is omniscience. These eternal *different* relations of things involve a consequent eternal *fitness* or *unfitness* in the application of things one to another; with a regard to which the will of God always chooses, and which ought likewise to determine the wills of all subordinate rational beings. These eternal differences make it fit and reasonable for the creatures so to act; they cause it to be their duty, or lay an *obligation* on them so to do, separate from the will of God,* and antecedent to any prospect of advantage or reward.† Nay, wilful wickedness is the same absurdity and insolence in morals, as it would be in natural things to pretend to alter the relations of numbers, or to take away the properties of mathematical figures.‡

* "Those who found all moral obligation on the will of God must recur to the same thing, only they do not explain how the nature and will of God is good and just." (*Being and Attributes of God*, Proposition xii.)

† *Evidence of Natural and Revealed Religion*, p. 4, sixth edit. Lond. 1724. ‡ *Ibid.* p. 42.

"Morality," says one of his most ingenious scholars, "is the practice of reason."*

Clarke, like Cudworth, considered such a scheme as the only security against Hobbism, and probably against the Calvinistic theology from which they were almost as averse. Not content, with Cumberland, to attack Hobbes on ground which was in part his own, they thought it necessary to build on entirely new foundations. Clarke more especially, instead of substituting social and generous feeling for the selfish appetites, endeavoured to bestow on morality the highest dignity, by thus deriving it from reason. He made it more than disinterested; for he placed its seat in a region where interest never enters, and passion never disturbs. By ranking her principles with the first truths of science, he seemed to render them pure and impartial, infallible and unchangeable. It might be excusable to regret the failure of so noble an attempt, if the indulgence of such regrets did not betray an unworthy apprehension that the same excellent ends could only be attained by such frail means; and that the dictates of the most severe reason would not finally prove reconcilable with the majesty of virtue.

Remarks.—The adoption of mathematical forms and terms was, in England, a prevalent fashion among writers on moral subjects during a large part of the eighteenth century. The ambition of mathematical certainty, on matters concerning which it is not given to man to reach it, is a frailty from which the disciple of Newton ought in reason to have been withheld, but to which he was naturally tempted by the example of his master. Nothing but the extreme difficulty of detaching assent from forms of expression to which it has been long wedded, can explain the fact that the incautious expression above cited, into which Clarke was hurried by his

* Lowman on the *Unity and Perfections of God*, p. 29. Lond. 1737.

moral sensibility, did not awaken him to a sense of the error into which he had fallen. As soon as he had said that "a wicked act was as absurd as an attempt to take away the properties of a figure," he ought to have seen that principles which led logically to such a conclusion were untrue. As it is an impossibility to make three and three cease to be six, it ought, on his principles, to be impossible to do a wicked act. To act without regard to the relations of things, as if a man were to choose fire for cooling, or ice for heating, would be the part either of a lunatic or an idiot. The murderer who poisons by arsenic, acts agreeably to his knowledge of the power of that substance to kill, which is a relation between two things; as much as the physician who employs an emetic after the poison, acts upon his belief of the tendency of that remedy to preserve life, which is another relation between two things. All men who seek a good or bad end by good or bad means, must alike conform their conduct to some relation between their actions as means and their object as an end. All the relations of inanimate things to each other are undoubtedly observed as much by the criminal as by the man of virtue.

It is therefore singular that Dr. Clarke suffered himself to be misled into the representation that virtue is a conformity with the relations of things universally, vice a universal disregard of them, by the certain, but here insufficient truth, that the former necessarily implied a regard to *certain particular relations*, which were always disregarded by those who chose the latter. The distinction between right and wrong, can, therefore, no longer depend on relations as such, but on a particular class of relations. And it seems evident that no relations are to be considered except those in which a living, intelligent, and voluntary agent is one of the beings related. His acts may relate to a law, as either observing or infringing it; they may relate to his own moral sentiments and those of his fellows, as they are the objects of approbation or disapprobation; they may relate to his own welfare, by increasing or abating it; they may relate to the well-being of other sentient beings, by contributing to promote or obstruct it; but in all these, and in all supposable cases, the inquiry of the moral philosopher must be, not whether there be a relation, but what the relation is; whether it be that of obedience of law, or agreeableness to moral feeling, or suitableness to prudence, or coincidence with benevolence. The term *relation* itself, on which Dr. Clarke's system rests, being common to right and wrong, must be struck out of the reasoning. He himself incidentally drops intimations which are at variance with his system. "The Deity," he tells us, "acts according to the eternal relations of things, in order to the welfare of the whole universe;" and subordinate moral agents ought to be governed by the same rules, "for the good of the public."* No one can fail to observe that a new element is here introduced—the well-being of communities of men, and the general happiness of the world—which supersedes the consideration of abstract relations and fitnesses.

There are other views of this system, however, of a more general nature, and of much more importance, because they extend in a considerable degree to all systems which found moral distinctions or sentiments, solely or ultimately, upon reason. A little reflection will discover an extraordinary vacuity in this system. Supposing it were allowed that it satisfactorily accounts for moral judgments, there is still an important part of our moral sentiments which it passes by without an attempt to explain them. Whence, on this scheme, the pleasure or pain with which we review our own actions, or survey those of others? What is the nature of remorse? Why do we feel shame? Whence is indignation against injustice? These are surely no exercise

* *Evidence of Natural and Revealed Religion*, p. 4.

of reason. Nor is the assent of reason to any other class of propositions followed or accompanied by emotions of this nature, by any approaching them, or indeed necessarily by any emotion at all. It is a fatal objection to a moral theory that it contains no means of explaining the most conspicuous, if not the most essential, parts of moral approbation and disapprobation.

But to rise to a more general consideration: Perception and emotion are states of mind perfectly distinct; and an emotion of pleasure or pain differs much more from a mere perception, than the perceptions of one sense do from those of another. The perceptions of all the senses have some qualities in common. But an emotion has not necessarily anything in common with a perception, but that they are both states of mind. We perceive exactly the same qualities in coffee when we may dislike it, as afterwards when we come to like it. In other words, the perception remains the same when the sensation of pain is changed into the opposite sensation of pleasure. The like change may occur in every case where pleasure or pain (in such instances called sensations) enter the mind with perceptions through the eye or the ear. The prospect or the sound which was disagreeable may become agreeable, without any alteration in our idea of the objects. We can easily imagine a percipient and thinking being without a capacity of receiving pleasure or pain. Such a being might perceive what we do; if we could conceive him to reason, he might reason justly; and if he were to judge at all, there seems no reason why he should not judge truly. But what could induce such a being to *will* or to *act?* It seems evident that his existence could only be a state of passive contemplation. Reason, as reason, can never be a motive to action. It is only when we superadd to such a being sensibility, or the capacity of emotion or sentiment (or what in corporeal cases is called sensation), of desire and aversion, that we introduce him into the world of action. We then clearly discern, that when the conclusion of a process of reasoning presents to his mind an object of desire, or the means of obtaining it, a motive of action begins to operate; and reason may then, but not till then, have a powerful though indirect influence on conduct. Let any argument to dissuade a man from immorality be employed, and the issue of it will always appear to be an appeal to a feeling. You prove that drunkenness will probably ruin health. No position founded on experience is more certain. Most persons with whom you reason must be as much convinced of it as you are. But your hope of success depends on the drunkard's fear of ill health; and he may always silence your argument by telling you that he loves wine more than he dreads sickness. You speak in vain of the infamy of an act to one who disregards the opinion of others; or of its imprudence to a man of little feeling for his own future condition. You may truly, but vainly, tell of the pleasures of friendship to one who has little affection. If you display the delights of liberality to a miser, he may always shut your mouth by answering, "The spendthrift may prefer such pleasures; I love money more." If you even appeal to a man's conscience, he may answer you, that you have clearly proved the immorality of the act, and that he himself knew it before; but that now when you had renewed and freshened his conviction, he was obliged to own, that his love of virtue, even aided by the fear of dishonour, remorse, and punishment, was not so powerful as the desire which hurried him into vice.

Nor is it otherwise, however confusion of ideas may cause it to be so deemed, with that calm regard to the welfare of the agent, to which philosophers have so grossly misapplied the hardly intelligible appellation of self-love. The general tendency of right conduct to permanent well-being is indeed one of the most evident of all truths. But the success of persuasives or dissuasives addressed to it, must always be directly proportioned not to the clearness with which the truth is discerned, but to the strength of the principle addressed, in the mind of the individual ; and to the degree in which he is accustomed to keep an eye on its dictates. A strange prejudice prevails, which ascribes to what is called *self-love* an invariable superiority over all the other motives of human action. If it were to be called by a more fit name, such as foresight, prudence, or, what seems most exactly to describe its nature, a sympathy with the future feelings of the agent, it would appear to every observer to be, very often, too languid and inactive, always of late appearance, and sometimes so faint as to be scarcely perceptible. Almost every human passion in its turn prevails over self-love.

It is thus apparent that the influence of reason on the will is indirect, and arises only from it being one of the channels by which the objects of desire or aversion are brought near to these springs of voluntary action. It is only one of these channels. There are many other modes of presenting to the mind the proper objects of the emotions which it is intended to excite, whether of a calmer or of a more active nature ; so that they may influence conduct more powerfully than when they reach the will through the channel of conviction. The distinction between conviction and persuasion would indeed be otherwise without a meaning ; to teach the mind would be the same thing as to move it ; and eloquence would be nothing but logic, although the greater part of the power of the former is displayed in the direct excitement of feeling ;—on condition, indeed (for reasons foreign to our present purpose), that the orator shall never appear to give counsel inconsistent with the duty or the lasting welfare of those whom he would persuade. In like manner it is to be observed, that though reasoning be one of the instruments of education, yet education is not a proof of reasoning, but a wise disposal of all the circumstances which influence character, and of the means of producing those habitual dispositions which insure well-doing, of which reasoning is but one. Very similar observations are applicable to the great arts of legislation and government; which are here only alluded to as forming a strong illustration of the present argument.

The abusive extension of the term *Reason* to the moral faculties, one of the predominant errors of ancient and modern times, has arisen from causes which it is not difficult to discover. Reason does in truth perform a great part in every case of moral sentiment. To reason often belong the preliminaries of the act; to reason altogether belongs the choice of the means of execution. The operations of reason, in both cases, are comparatively slow and lasting; they are capable of being distinctly recalled by memory. The emotion which intervenes between the previous and the succeeding exertions of reason is often faint, generally transient, and scarcely ever capable of being reproduced by an effort of the mind. Hence the name of reason is applied to this mixed state of mind; more especially when the feeling, being of a cold and general nature, and scarcely ruffling the surface of the soul, such as those of prudence and of ordinary kindness and propriety, almost passes unnoticed, and is irretrievably forgotten. Hence the mind is, in such conditions, said by moralists to act from *reason*, in contradistinction to its more excited and disturbed state, when it is said to act from *passion*. The calmness of reason gives to the whole compound the appearance of unmixed reason. The illusion is further promoted by a mode of expression used in most languages. A man is said to act reasonably, when his conduct is such as may be reasonably expected. Amidst the disorders of a vicious mind, it is difficult to form a reasonable conjecture concerning future conduct; but the quiet and well-ordered state of virtue renders the probable acts of her fortunate votaries the object of very rational expectation.

As far as it is not presumptuous to attempt a distinction between modes of thinking foreign to the mind which makes the attempt, and modes of expression scarcely translatable into the only technical language in which that mind is wont to think, it seems [to me] that the systems of Cudworth and Clarke, though they appear very similar, are in reality different in some important points of view. The former, a Platonist, sets out from those IDEAS (a word, in this acceptation of it, which has no corresponding term in English), the eternal models of created things, which, as the Athenian master taught, pre-existed in the everlasting intellect, and, of right, rule the will of every inferior mind. The illustrious scholar of Newton, with a manner of thinking more natural to his age and school, considered primarily the very relations of things themselves; conceived indeed by the Eternal Mind, but which, if such inadequate language may be pardoned, are the law of its will, as well as the model of its works.*

EARL OF SHAFTESBURY.
Born 1671—died 1713.

LORD SHAFTESBURY, the author of the *Characteristics*, was the grandson of Sir Anthony Ashley Cooper, created Earl of Shaftesbury, one of the master spirits of the English nation, whose vices, the bitter fruits of the insecurity of a troublous time, succeeded by the corrupting habits of an inconstant,

---

* Mr. Wollaston's system, that morality consisted in acting according to truth, seems to coincide with that of Dr. Clarke. The murder of Cicero by Popilius Lenas, was, according to him, a practical falsehood; for Cicero had been his benefactor, but Popilius acted as if that were untrue. If the truth spoken of be, that gratitude is due for benefits, the reasoning is evidently a circle. If *any truth* be meant, indifferently, it is plain that the assassin acted in perfect conformity to several certain truths: such as the malignity of Antony, the ingratitude and venality of Popilius, and the probable impunity of his crime, when law was suspended, and good men without power.

venal, and profligate court, have led an ungrateful posterity to overlook his wisdom and disinterested perseverance, in obtaining for the English nation the unspeakable benefits of the Habeas Corpus Act. The fortune of the *Characteristics* has been singular. For a time the work was admired more undistinguishingly than its literary character warrants. In the succeeding period it was justly criticised, but too severely condemned. Of late, more unjustly than in either of the former cases, it has been generally neglected. It seemed to have the power of changing the temper of its critics. It provoked the amiable Berkeley to a harshness equally unwonted and unwarranted;* while it softened the rugged Warburton so far as to dispose the fierce yet not altogether ungenerous polemic to praise an enemy in the very heat of conflict.†

* Berkeley's *Minute Philosopher*, Dialogue iii. ; but especially his *Theory of Vision Vindicated*, Lond. 1733 (not republished in the quarto edition of his works), where this most excellent man sinks for a moment to the level of a railing polemic.

[As I have said in Lecture VIII. of my *Lectures on the History of Moral Philosophy*, this expression is far too strong. What Berkeley says is, " So long as we apprehend no judgment, harbour no fears, and cherish no hopes of a future state, but laugh at all these things with the author of the *Characteristics*, and those whom he esteems the liberal and polished part of mankind, how can we be said to be religious in any sense ? or what is here that an Atheist may not find his account in as well as a Theist ? "—W. W.]

† It is remarkable that the most impure passages of Warburton's composition are those in which he lets loose his controversial zeal, and that he is a fine writer principally where he writes from generous feeling. "Of all the virtues which were so much in this noble writer's heart and in his writings, there was not one he more revered than the love of public liberty. . . . The noble author of the *Characteristics* had many excellent qualities, both as a man and a writer. He was temperate, chaste, honest, and a lover of his country. In his writings he has shown how much he has imbibed the deep sense, and how naturally he could copy the gracious manner, of Plato." (Dedication to the Freethinkers, prefixed to the *Divine Legation.*) Warburton, however, soon relaxes, but not without excuse ; for he thought himself vindicating the memory of Locke.

Leibnitz, the most celebrated of Continental philosophers, warmly applauded the *Characteristics*, and (what was a more certain proof of admiration), though at an advanced age, criticised that work minutely.* Le Clerc, who had assisted the studies of the author, contributed to spread its reputation by his *Journal*, then the most popular in Europe. Locke is said to have aided in his education, probably rather by counsel than by tuition. The author had indeed been driven from the regular studies of his country by the insults with which he was loaded at Winchester school, when he was only twelve years old, immediatetly after the death of his grandfather; a choice of time which seemed not so much to indicate anger against the faults of a great man, as triumph over the principles of liberty, which seemed at that time to have fallen for ever. He gave a genuine proof of respect for freedom of thought, by preventing the expulsion, from Holland, of Bayle (with whom he differs in every moral, political, and, it may be truly added, religious opinion), when, it must be owned, the right of asylum was, in strict justice, forfeited by the secret services which the philosopher had rendered to the enemy of Holland and of Europe. In the small part of his short life which premature infirmities allowed him to apply to public affairs, he co-operated zealously with the friends of freedom; but, as became a moral philosopher, he supported, even against them, a law to allow those who were accused of treason to make their defence by counsel, although the parties first to benefit from this act of imperfect justice were conspirators to assassinate King William, and to re-enslave their country. On that occasion, it is well known with what admirable quickness he took advantage of the embarrassment which seized him, when he rose to address the House of Commons. "If I," said he, "who rise only to give my opinion on this bill, am so confounded that I cannot say what I in-

* *Opera*, tom. iii. pp. 39-56.

tended, what must the condition of that man be, who, without assistance, is pleading for his own life!" He was the friend of Lord Somers; and the tribute paid to his personal character by Warburton, who knew many of his contemporaries and some of his friends, may be considered as evidence of its excellence.

His fine genius and generous spirit shine through his writings; but their lustre is often dimmed by peculiarities, and, it must be said, by affectations, which, originating in local, temporary, or even personal circumstances, are particularly fatal to the permanence of fame. There is often a charm in the egotism of an artless writer, or of an actor in great scenes. But other laws are imposed on the literary artist. Lord Shaftesbury, instead of hiding himself behind his work, stands forward with too frequent marks of self-complacency, as a nobleman of polished manners, with a mind adorned by the fine arts, and instructed by ancient philosophy; shrinking with a somewhat effeminate fastidiousness from the clamour and prejudices of the multitude, whom he neither deigns to conciliate nor puts forth his strength to subdue. The enmity of the majority of churchmen to the government established at the Revolution was calculated to fill his mind with angry feelings; which overflow too often, if not upon Christianity itself, yet upon representations of it, closely intertwined with those religious feelings to which, in other forms, his own philosophy ascribes surpassing worth. His small and occasional writings, of which the main fault is the want of an object or a plan, have many passages remarkable for the utmost beauty and harmony of language. Had he imbibed the simplicity, as well as copied the expression and cadence, of the greater ancients, he would have done more justice to his genius; and his works, like theirs, would have been preserved by that quality, without which but a very few writings, of whatever mental power, have long survived their writers. Grace belongs only to natural movements; and Lord Shaftesbury, notwithstanding the frequent beauty of his thoughts and language, has rarely attained it. He is unfortunately prone to pleasantry, which is obstinately averse from constraint, and which he had no interest in raising to be the test of truth. His affectation of liveliness as a man of the world, tempts him sometimes to overstep the indistinct boundaries which separate familiarity from vulgarity. Of his two more considerable writings, *The Moralists*, on which he evidently most valued himself, and which is spoken of by Leibnitz with enthusiasm, is by no means the happiest. Yet perhaps there is scarcely any composition in our language more lofty in its moral and religious sentiments, and more exquisitely elegant and musical in its diction, than the Platonic representation of the scale of beauty and love, in the speech to Palemon, near the close of the first part.* Many passages might be quoted, which in some measure justify the enthusiasm of the septuagenarian geometer. Yet it is not to be concealed that, as a whole, it is heavy and languid. It is a modern antique. The dialogues of Plato are often very lively representations of conversations which might take place daily at a great university, full, like Athens, of rival professors and eager disciples—between men of various character, and great fame as well as ability. Socrates runs through them all. His great abilities, his still more venerable virtues, his cruel fate, especially when joined to his very characteristic peculiarities,—to his grave humour, to his homely sense, to his assumed humility, to the honest slyness with which he ensnared the Sophists, and to the intrepidity with which he dragged them to justice,—gave unity and dramatic interest to these dialogues as a whole. But Lord Shaftesbury's dialogue is between fictitious personages, and in a tone at utter variance with English conversation. He had great power of thought and command over words. But

* *Characteristics*, Treatise v. *The Moralists*, Part i. sect. 3.

he had no talent for inventing character and bestowing life on it. The *Inquiry concerning Virtue** is nearly exempt from the faulty peculiarities of the author; the method is perfect, the reasoning just, the style precise and clear. The writer has no purpose but that of honestly proving his principles; he himself altogether disappears; and he is intent only on earnestly enforcing what he truly, conscientiously, and reasonably believes. Hence the charm of simplicity is revived in this production, which is unquestionably entitled to a place in the first rank of English tracts on Moral Philosophy.

The point on which it becomes especially pertinent to the subject of this volume is, that it contains more intimations of an original and important nature on the Theory of Ethics, than perhaps any preceding work of modern times.† It is true that they are often but intimations, cursory, and appearing almost to be casual; so that many of them have escaped the notice of most readers, and even writers on these subjects. That the consequences of some of them are even yet not unfolded, must be owned to be a proof that they are inadequately stated; and may be regarded as a presumption that the author did not closely examine the bearings of his own positions. Among the most important of these suggestions is, the existence of dispositions in man, by which he takes pleasure in the well-being of others, without any further view; a doctrine, however, to all the consequences of which he has not been faithful in his other writings.‡ Another is,

---

* *Characteristics*, Treatise iv.

† I am not without suspicion that I have overlooked the claims of Dr. Henry More, who, notwithstanding some uncouthness of language, seems to have given the first intimations of a distinct moral faculty, which he calls "the Boniform Faculty;" a phrase against which an outcry would now be raised as German. Happiness, according to him, consists in a constant satisfaction, εν τῳ αγαθοειδει της ψυχης. (*Enchiridion Ethicum*, lib. i. cap. ii.)

‡ "It is the height of wisdom, no doubt, to be rightly selfish." *Charac.* I. 121.) The observation seems to be taken from what

that goodness consists in the prevalence of love for the system of which we are a part, over the passions pointing to our individual welfare; a proposition which somewhat confounds the motives of right acts with their tendency, and seems to favour the melting of all particular affections into general benevolence, because the tendency of these affections is to general good. The next, and certainly the most original, as well as important, is, that there are certain affections of the mind which, being contemplated by the mind itself through what he calls *a reflex sense*, become the objects of love, or the contrary, according to their nature. So approved and loved, they constitute *virtue* or *merit*, as distinguished from mere *goodness*, of which there are traces in animals who do not appear to *reflect* on the state of their own minds, and who seem, therefore, destitute of what he elsewhere calls *a moral sense*. These statements are, it is true, far too short and vague. He nowhere inquires into the origin of the reflex sense. What is a much more material defect, he makes no attempt to ascertain in what state of mind it consists. We discover only by implication, and by the use of the term *sense*, that he searches for the fountain of moral sentiments, not in mere reason, where Cudworth and Clarke had vainly sought for it, but in the heart, whence the main branch of them assuredly flows. It should never be forgotten that we owe to these hints the reception, into ethical theory, of a moral sense, which, whatever may be thought of its origin, or in whatever words it may be described, must always retain its place in such theory as a main principle of our moral nature.

His demonstration of the utility of virtue to the individual far surpasses all attempts of the same nature; being founded, not on a calculation of outward advantages or inconveniences, alike uncertain, precarious, and degrading, but

---

Aristotle says of Φιλαυτια: Τον μεν αγαθον δει φιλαυτον ειναι. (Arist. *Ethic.* i. x.; c. viii.) The chapter is admirable, and the assertion of Aristotle is very capable of a good sense.

on the unshaken foundation of the delight, which is of the very essence of social affection and virtuous sentiment; on the dreadful agony inflicted by all malevolent passions upon every soul that harbours the hellish inmates, on the all-important truth that to love is to be happy, and to hate is to be miserable,—that affection is its own reward, and ill-will its own punishment; or, as it has been more simply and more affectingly, as well as with more sacred authority, taught, that to give is more blessed than to receive, and that to love one another is the sum of all human virtue.

The relation of religion to morality, as far as it can be discovered by human reason, was never more justly or more beautifully stated.* If he represented the mere hope of reward and dread of punishment as selfish and therefore inferior motives to virtue and piety, he distinctly owns their efficacy in reclaiming from vice, in rousing from lethargy, and in guarding a feeble penitence; in all which he coincides with illustrious and zealous Christian writers. "If by the hope of reward be understood the love and desire of virtuous enjoyment, or of the very practice and exercise of virtue in another life: an expectation or hope of this kind is so far from being derogatory from virtue, that it is an evidence of our loving it the more sincerely, and *for its own sake*."†

* *Characteristics, Inquiry concerning Virtue.*
† *Ibid.*

So Jeremy Taylor : "He that is grown in grace pursues virtue purely and simply for its own interest. When persons come to that height of Grace, and love God for himself, that is but heaven in another sense." (*Sermon on Growth in Grace.*) So before him the once celebrated Mr. John Smith of Cambridge : "The happiness which good men shall partake is not distinct from their Godlike nature. Happiness and Holiness are but two several notions of the same thing. Hell is rather a nature than a place, and Heaven cannot be so well defined by anything *without* us, as by something within us." (*Select Discourses*, 2d edit. Cambridge, 1673.)

In accordance with these old authorities is the recent language of a most ingenious as well as benevolent and pious writer. "The *holiness*

FÉNÉLON—BOSSUET.

Fénélon, born 1651—died 1715.
Bossuet, born 1627—died 1704.

As the last question, though strictly speaking theological, is yet in truth dependent on the more general question, which relates to the reality of disinterested affections in human nature, it seems not foreign from the present purpose to give a short account of a dispute on the subject in France, between two of the most eminent persons of their time; namely, the controversy between Fénélon and Bossuet, concerning the possibility of men being influenced by the pure and disinterested love of God. Never were two great men more unlike. Fénélon, in his writings, exhibits more of the qualities which predispose to religious feelings than any other equally conspicuous person; a mind so pure as steadily to contemplate supreme excellence; a heart capable of being touched and affected by the contemplation; a gentle and modest spirit, not elated by the privilege, but seeing its own want of worth as it came nearer to such brightness, and disposed to treat with compassionate forbearance those errors in others, of which it felt a humbling consciousness. Bossuet

of heaven is still more attractive to the Christian than its happiness. The desire of doing that which is right for its own sake is a part of his desire after heaven." (*Unconditional Freeness of the Gospel*, by T. Erskine, Esq., pp. 32, 33. Edin. 1828.)

See also the Appendix to Ward's *Life of Henry More*, 247-271. This account of that ingenious and amiable philosopher (Lond. 1710) contains an interesting view of his opinions, and many beautiful passages of his writings, but unfortunately very few particulars of the man. His letters on *Disinterested Piety* (see the appendix to Mr. Ward's work), his boundless charity, his zeal for the utmost toleration, and his hope of general improvement from "a pacific and perspicacious posterity," place him high in the small number of true philosophers who, in their estimate of men, value dispositions more than opinions, and, in their search for good, more often look forward than backward.

was rather a great minister in the ecclesiastical commonwealth; employing knowledge, eloquence, argument, the energy of his character, the influence, and even the authority of his station, to vanquish opponents, to extirpate revolters, and, sometimes with a patrician firmness, to withstand the dictatorial encroachment of the Roman Pontiff on the spiritual aristocracy of France. Fénélon had been appointed tutor to the Duke of Burgundy. He had all the qualities which fit a man to be the preceptor of a prince, and which most disable him to get or to keep the office. Even birth and urbanity, and accomplishment and vivacity, were an insufficient atonement for his genius and virtue. Louis XIV. distrusted so fine a spirit, and appears to have early suspected that a fancy moved by such benevolence might imagine examples for his grandson which the world would consider as a satire on his own reign. Madame de Maintenon, indeed, favoured him; but he was generally believed to have forfeited her good graces by discouraging her projects for at least a nearer approach to a seat on the throne. He offended her by obeying her commands, in laying before her an account of her faults, and some of those of her royal husband, which was probably the more painfully felt for its mildness, justice, and refined observation.* An opportunity for driving such an intruder from a court presented itself somewhat strangely, in the form of a subtile controversy on one of the most abstruse questions of metaphysical theology. Molinos, a Spanish priest, reviving and perhaps exaggerating the maxims of the ancient Mystics, had recently taught that Christian perfection consisted in the pure love of God, without hope of reward or fear of punishment. This offence he expiated by seven years' imprisonment in the dungeons of the Roman Inquisition. His opinions were embraced by Madame Guyon, a pious French lady of strong feeling and active imagination, who appears to

* Bausset, *Histoire de Fénélon*, i. 252.

have expressed them in a hyperbolical language, not infrequent in devotional exercises, especially in those of otherwise amiable persons of her sex and character. In the fervour of her zeal she disregarded the usages of the world and the decorums imposed on females. She left her family, took a part in public conferences, and assumed an independence scarcely reconcilable with the more ordinary and more pleasing virtues of women. Her pious effusions were examined with the rigour which might be exercised on theological propositions. She was falsely charged by Harlay, the dissolute archbishop of Paris, with personal licentiousness. For these crimes she was dragged from convent to convent, imprisoned for years in the Bastile, and, as an act of mercy, confined during the latter years of her life to a provincial town, as a prison at large. A piety thus pure and disinterested could not fail to please Fénélon. He published a work in justification of Madame Guyon's character, and in explanation of the degree in which he agreed with her. Bossuet, the oracle and champion of the church, took up arms against him. It would be painful to suppose that a man of so great powers was actuated by mean jealousy, and it is needless. The union of zeal for opinion with the pride of authority, is apt to give sternness to the administration of controversial bishops; to say nothing of the haughty and inflexible character of Bossuet himself. He could not brook the independence of him who was hitherto so docile a scholar and so gentle a friend. He was jealous of novelties, and dreaded a fervour of piety likely to be ungovernable, and perhaps to excite movements of which no man could foresee the issue. It must be allowed that he had reason to be displeased with the indiscretion and turbulence of the innovators, and might apprehend that, in preaching motives to virtue and religion which he thought unattainable, the coarser but surer foundations of common morality might be loosened. A controversy ensued, in which he employed the utmost violence of polemical or factious contest. Fénélon replied with brilliant success, and submitted his book to the judgment of Rome. After a long examination, the commission of ten Cardinals appointed to examine it were equally divided, and he seemed in consequence about to be acquitted. But Bossuet had in the meantime easily gained Louis XIV. Madame de Maintenon betrayed Fénélon's confidential correspondence; and he was banished to his diocese, and deprived of his pensions and official apartments in the palace. Louis XIV. regarded the slightest differences from the authorities of the French church as rebellion against himself. Though endowed with much natural good sense, he was too grossly ignorant to be made to comprehend one of the terms of the question in dispute. He did not, however, scruple to urge the Pope to the condemnation of Fénélon. Innocent XII. (Pignatelli), an aged and pacific Pontiff, was desirous of avoiding such harsh measures. He said that "the archbishop of Cambray might have erred from excess in the love of God, but the bishop of Meux had sinned by a defect of the love of his neighbour."* But he was compelled to condemn a series of propositions, of which the first was, "There is an habitual state of love to God, which is pure from every motive of personal interest, and in which neither the fear of punishment nor the hope of reward has any part." † Fénélon read the bull which condemned him in his own cathedral, and professed as humble a submission as the lowest of his flock In some of the writings of his advanced years, which have been recently published, we observe with regret that, when wearied out by his exile, ambitious to regain a place at court through the Jesuits, or prejudiced against the Calvinising doctrines of the Jansenists, the strongest anti-papal party among Catholics, or somewhat detached from a cause of

---

* Bausset, *Histoire de Fénélon*, ii. 220, note.
† *Œuvres de* Bossuet, viii. 308. Liege, 1767, 8vo.

which his great antagonist had been the victorious leader, he made concessions to the absolute monarchy of Rome which did not become a luminary of the Gallican Church.*

Bossuet, in his writings on this occasion, besides tradition and authorities, relied mainly on the supposed principle of philosophy, that man must desire his own happiness, and cannot desire anything else, otherwise than as a means towards it; which renders the controversy an incident in the history of Ethics. It is immediately connected with the preceding part of this work by the almost literal coincidence between Bossuet's foremost objection to the disinterested piety contended for by Fénélon, and the fundamental position of a very ingenious and once noted divine of the English church, in his attack on the disinterested affections, believed by Shaftesbury to be a part of human nature.†

LEIBNITZ.

Born 1646—died 1716.

There is a singular contrast between the form of Leibnitz's writings and the character of his mind. The latter was

* *De summi Pontificis Auctoritate Dissertatio*: *Œuvres de* Fénélon, tome ii. Versailles, 1820.

† "Hæc est natura voluntatis humanæ, ut et beatitudinem, et ea quorum necessaria connexio cum beatitudine clare intelligitur, *necessario* appetat. . . . Nullus est actus ad quem revera non impellimur motivo beatitudinis, explicite vel *implicite;*" meaning by the latter that it may be concealed from ourselves, as he says, *for a short time*, by a nearer object. (*Œuvres de* Bossuet, viii. 80.) "The only motive by which individuals *can* be induced to the practice of virtue, *must* be the feeling or the prospect of private happiness." (Brown's *Essays on the Characteristics*, p. 159. Lond. 1752.) It must, however, be owned, that the selfishness of the Warburtonian is more rigid; making no provision for the object of one's own happiness slipping out of view for a moment. It is due to the very ingenious author of this forgotten book to add, that it is full of praise of his adversary, which, though just, was in the answerer generous; and that it contains an assertion of the *unbounded* right of public discussion, unusual even at the tolerant period of its appearance.

systematical, even to excess. It was the vice of his prodigious intellect, on every subject of science where it was not bound by geometrical chains, to confine his view to those most general principles, so well called by Bacon "merely notional;" which render it, indeed, easy to build a system, but only because they may be alike adapted to every state of appearances, and become thereby really inapplicable to any. Though his genius was thus naturally turned to system, his writings were, generally, occasional and miscellaneous. The fragments of his doctrines are scattered in Reviews; or over a voluminous Literary Correspondence; or in the Prefaces and Introductions to those compilations to which this great philosopher was obliged by his situation to descend. This defective and disorderly mode of publication arose partly from the jars between business and study, inevitable in his course of life; but probably yet more from the nature of his system, which, while it widely deviates from the most general principles of former philosophers, is ready to embrace their particular doctrines under its own generalities, and thus to reconcile them to each other, as well as to accommodate itself to popular or established opinions, and compromise with them according to his favourite and oft-repeated maxim, *that most received doctrines are capable of a good sense;*" * by which last words our philosopher meant a sense reconcilable with his own principles. Partial and occasional exhibitions of these principles suited better that constant negotiation with opinions, establishments, and prejudices, to which extreme generalities are well adapted, than a full and methodical statement of the whole at once. It is the lot of every philosopher who attempts to make his principles extremely flexible, that they

---

* *Nouveaux Essais sur l'Entendement Humain*, liv. i. chap. ii. p. 57. These Essays, which form the greater part of the publication entitled *Œuvres Philosophiques*, edited by Raspe, Amst. et Leipz. 1765, are not included in Dutens's edition of Leibnitz's works.

become like those tools which bend so easily as to penetrate nothing. Yet his manner of publication perhaps led him to those wide intuitions, as comprehensive as those of Bacon, of which he expressed the result as briefly and pithily as Hobbes. The fragment which contains his ethical principles is the Preface to a collection of documents illustrative of international law, published at Hanover in 1693;* to which he often referred as his standard afterwards, especially when he speaks of Lord Shaftesbury, or of the controversy between the two great theologians of France. "Right," says he, "is moral power; obligation, moral necessity. By *moral*, I understand what with a good man prevails as much as if it were physical. A good man is he who loves all men as far as reason allows. Justice is the benevolence of a wise man. *To love is to be pleased with the happiness of another; or, in other words, to convert the happiness of another into a part of one's own.* Hence is explained the possibility of a disinterested love. When we are pleased with the happiness of any being, his happiness becomes one of our enjoyments. Wisdom is the science of happiness."†

Remarks.—It is apparent from the above passage, that Leibnitz had touched the truth on the subject of disinterested affection; and that he was more near clinging to it than any modern philosopher, except Lord Shaftesbury. It is evident, however, from the latter part of it, that, like Shaftesbury, he shrunk from his own just conception; under the influence of that most ancient and far-spread prejudice of the schools, which assumed that such an abstraction as *Happiness* could be the object of love, and that the desire of so faint, distant, and refined an object, was the first principle of all moral nature, of which every other desire was only a modification or

* *Codex Juris Gentium Diplomaticus.* Hanov. 1695.
† See Notes and Illustrations, Note N.

a fruit. Both he and Shaftesbury, however, when they relapsed into the selfish system, embraced it in its most refined form; considering the benevolent affections as valuable parts of our own happiness, not in consequence of any of their effects or extrinsic advantages, but of that intrinsic delightfulness which was inherent in their very essence. But Leibnitz considered this refined pleasure as the object in the view of the benevolent man; an absurdity, or rather a contradiction, which, at least in the *Inquiry concerning Virtue*, Shaftesbury avoids. It will be seen from Leibnitz's limitation, taken together with his definition of Wisdom, that he regarded the distinction of the moral sentiments from the social affections, and the just subordination of the latter, as entirely founded on the tendency of general happiness to increase that of the agent, not merely as being real, but as being present to the agent's mind when he acts. In a subsequent passage he lowers his tone not a little. "As for the sacrifice of life, or the endurance of the greatest pain for others, these things are rather generously enjoined than solidly demonstrated by philosophers. For honour, glory, and self-congratulation, to which they appeal under the name of Virtue, are indeed mental pleasures, and of a high degree, but not to all, nor outweighing every bitterness of suffering; since all cannot imagine them with equal vivacity, and that power is little possessed by those whom neither education, nor situation, nor the doctrines of religion or philosophy, have taught to value mental gratifications."* He concludes very truly, that morality is completed by a belief of moral government. But the *Inquiry concerning Virtue* had reached that conclusion by a better road. It entirely escaped his sagacity, as it has that of nearly all other moralists, that the coincidence of morality with well-understood interest in our outward actions, is very far from being the most important part of the question; for these actions flow from habitual

* See Notes and Illustrations, Note N.

dispositions, from affections and sensibilities, which determine their nature. There may be, and there are, many immoral acts, which, in the sense in which words are commonly used, are advantageous to the actor. But the whole sagacity and ingenuity of the world may be safely challenged to point out a case in which virtuous dispositions, habits, and feelings, are not conducive in the highest degree to the happiness of the individual; or to maintain that he is not the happiest, whose moral sentiments and affections are such as to prevent the possibility of the prospect of advantage through unlawful means from presenting itself to his mind. It would indeed have been impossible to prove to Regulus that it was his interest to return to a death of torture in Africa. But what if the proof had been easy? The most thorough conviction on such a point would not have enabled him to set this example, if he had not been supported by his own integrity and generosity, by love of his country, and reverence for his pledged faith. What could the conviction add to that greatness of soul, and to these glorious attributes? With such virtues he could not act otherwise than he did. Would a father, affectionately interested in a son's happiness, of very lukewarm feelings of morality, but of good sense enough to weigh gratifications and sufferings exactly, be really desirous that his son should have these virtues in a less degree than Regulus, merely because they might expose him to the fate which Regulus chose? On the coldest calculation he would surely perceive that the high and glowing feelings of such a mind during life, altogether throw into shade a few hours of agony in leaving it. And, if he himself were so unfortunate that no more generous sentiment arose in his mind to silence such calculations, would it not be a reproach to his understanding not to discover, that though, in one case out of millions, such a character might lead a Regulus to torture, yet, in the common course of nature, it is the source not only of happiness in life, but of quiet and honour in death? A case so extreme as that of Regulus will not perplex, if we bear in mind, that though we cannot prove the *act* of heroic virtue to be conducive to the interest of the hero, yet we may perceive at once that nothing is so conducive to his interest as to have a mind so formed that it could not shrink from it, but must rather embrace it with gladness and triumph. Men of vigorous health are said sometimes to suffer most in a pestilence. No man was ever so absurd as for that reason to wish that he were more infirm. The distemper might return once in a century. If he were then alive, he might escape it; and even if he fell, the balance of advantage would be, in most cases, greatly on the side of robust health. In estimating beforehand the value of a strong bodily frame, a man of sense would throw the small chance of a rare and short evil entirely out of the account. So must the coldest and most selfish moral calculator, who, if he be sagacious and exact, must pronounce that the inconveniences to which a man may be sometimes exposed by a pure and sound mind, are no reasons for regretting that we do not escape them by possessing minds more enfeebled and distempered. Other occasions will call our attention, in the sequel, to this important part of the subject. But the great name of Leibnitz seemed to require that his degrading statement should not be cited without warning the reader against its egregious fallacy.

MALEBRANCHE.

Born 1638—died 1715.

This ingenious philosopher and beautiful writer is the only celebrated Cartesian who has professedly handled the Theory of Morals.* His theory has in some points of view a conformity to the doctrine of Clarke; while in others it has

* *Traité de Morale.* Rotterdam, 1634.

given occasion to his English follower Norris[*] to say, that if the Quakers understood their own opinion of the illumination of all men, they would explain it on the principles of Malebranche. "There is," says he, "one parent virtue, the universal virtue, the virtue which renders us just and perfect, the virtue which will one day render us happy. It is the only virtue. It is the love of the universal order, as it eternally existed in the Divine reason, where every created reason contemplates it. This order is composed of practical as well as speculative truth. Reason perceives the moral superiority of one being over another, as immediately as the equality of the radii of the same circle. The relative perfection of beings is that part of the immovable order to which men must conform their minds and their conduct. The love of order is the whole of virtue, and conformity to order constitutes the morality of actions." It is not difficult to discover, that in spite of the singular skill employed in weaving this web, it answers no other purpose than that of hiding the whole difficulty. The love of universal order, says Malebranche, requires that we should value an animal more than a stone, because it is more valuable; and love God infinitely more than man, because he is infinitely better. But without *presupposing* the reality of moral distinctions, and the power of moral feelings, the two points to be proved, how can either of these propositions be evident, or even intelligible? To say that a love of the eternal order will produce the love and practice of every virtue, is an assertion untenable unless we take morality for granted, and useless if we do.

In his work on Morals, all the incidental and secondary remarks are equally well considered and well expressed. The manner in which he applied his principle to the particulars

[*] Author of the *Theory of the Ideal World*, who well copied, though he did not equal, the clearness and choice of expression which belonged to his master.

of human duty is excellent. He is perhaps the first philosopher who has precisely laid down and rigidly adhered to the great principle *that virtue consists in pure intentions and dispositions of mind,* without which, actions, however conformable to rules, are not truly moral ; a truth of the highest importance, which, in the theological form, may be said to have been the main principle of the first Protestant Reformers. The ground of piety, according to him, is the conformity of the attributes of God to those moral qualities which we irresistibly love and revere.* "Sovereign princes," says he, "have no right to use their authority without reason. Even God has no such miserable right." † His distinction between a religious society and an established church, and his assertion of the right of the temporal power alone to employ coercion, are worthy of notice, as instances in which a Catholic, at once philosophical and orthodox, could thus speak, not only of the nature of God, but of the rights of the church.

JONATHAN EDWARDS.
Born 1703, at Windsor, Connecticut—died 1758, at Princetown, New Jersey.

THIS remarkable man, the metaphysician of America, was formed among the Calvinists of New England, when their stern doctrine retained its rigorous authority.‡ His power of subtile argument, perhaps unmatched, certainly unsurpassed among men, was joined, as in some of the ancient Mystics, with a character which raised his piety to fervour. He embraced their doctrine, probably without knowing it to be

* "Il faut aimer l'Etre infiniment parfait, et non pas un fantôme épouvantable, un Dieu injuste, absolu, puissant, mais sans bonté et sans sagesse. S'il y avoit un tel Dieu, le vrai Dieu nous défendroit de l'adorer et de l'aimer. Il y a peut-être plus de danger d'offenser Dieu lorsqu'on lui donne une forme si horrible, que de mépriser ce fantôme." (*Traité de Morale*, chap. viii.) † *Ibid.* chap. xxii.
‡ Notes and Illustrations, Note O.

theirs. "True religion," says he, "in a great measure consists in holy affections. A love of divine things, for the beauty and sweetness of their moral excellency, is the spring of all holy affections."* Had he suffered this noble principle to take the right road to all its fair consequences, he would have entirely concurred with Plato, with Shaftesbury, and Malebranche, in devotion to "the first good, first perfect, and first fair." But he thought it necessary afterwards to limit his doctrine to his own persuasion, by denying that such moral excellence could be discovered in divine things by those Christians who did not take the same view with him of their religion. All others, and some who hold his doctrines with a more enlarged spirit, may adopt his principle without any limitation. His ethical theory is contained in his *Dissertation on the Nature of True Virtue;* and in another, *On God's Chief End in the Creation,* published in London thirty years after his death. True virtue, according to him, consists in benevolence, or love to being "in general," which he afterwards limits to "intelligent being," though *sentient* would have involved a more reasonable limitation. This good-will is felt towards a particular being, first *in proportion to his degree of existence* (for, says he, "that which is great has more existence, and is farther from nothing, than that which is little"); and secondly, *in proportion to the degree in which that particular being feels benevolence to others.* Thus God, having infinitely more existence and benevolence than man, ought to be infinitely more loved; and for the same reason, God must love himself infinitely more than he does all other beings.† He can act only from regard to himself, and his

---

* Edwards on *Religious Affections,* pp. 4, 187. Lond. 1796.

† The coincidence of Malebranche with this part of Edwards is remarkable. Speaking of the Supreme Being, he says, "*Il s'aime invinciblement.*" He adds another more startling expression, "Certainement Dieu ne peut agir que pour lui-même : il n'a point d'autre motif que son amour propre." (*Traité de Morale,* chap. xvii.)

end in creation can only be to manifest his whole nature, which is called acting for his own glory.

As far as Edwards confines himself to created beings, and while his theory is perfectly intelligible, it coincides with that of universal benevolence, hereafter to be considered. The term *being* is a mere encumbrance, which serves indeed to give it a mysterious outside, but brings with it from the schools nothing except their obscurity. He was betrayed into it by the cloak which it threw over his really unmeaning assertion or assumption, that there are *degrees of existence;* without which that part of his system which relates to the Deity would have appeared to be as baseless as it really is. When we try such a phrase by applying it to matters within the sphere of our experience, we see that it means nothing but *degrees* of certain faculties and powers. But the very application of the term *being* to all things, shows that the least perfect has as much *being* as the most perfect; or rather that there can be no difference, so far as that word is concerned, between two things to which is it alike applicable. The justness of the compound proportion on which human virtue is made to depend, is capable of being tried by an easy test. If we suppose the greatest of evil spirits to have a hundred times the bad passions of Marcus Aurelius, and at the same time a hundred times his faculties, or, in Edwards's language, a hundred times his quantity of being, it follows, from this moral theory, that we ought to esteem and love the devil exactly in the same degree as we esteem and love Marcus Aurelius.

The chief circumstance which justifies so much being said on the last two writers, is their concurrence in a point towards which Ethical Philosophy had been slowly approaching from the time of the controversies raised up by Hobbes. They both indicate the increase of this tendency, by introducing an element into their theory, foreign from those cold systems of ethical abstraction, with which they continued in other respects to have much in common. Malebranche makes virtue consist in the love of *order*, Edwards in the love of *being*. In this language we perceive a step beyond the representation of Clarke, which made it a conformity to the relations of things; but a step which cannot be made without passing into a new province;—without confessing by the use of the word *love*, that not only perception and reason, but emotion and sentiment, are among the fundamental principles of morals. They still, however, were so wedded to scholastic prejudice, as to choose two of the most aerial abstractions which can be introduced into argument—*being* and *order*—to be the objects of those strong active feelings which were to govern the human mind.

BUFFIER.

Born 1661—died 1737.

The same strange disposition to fix on abstractions as the objects of our primitive feelings, and the end sought by our warmest desires, manifests itself in the ingenious writer with whom this part of the present work closes, under a form of less dignity than that which it assumes in the hands of Malebranche and Clarke. Buffier, the only Jesuit whose name has a place in the history of Abstract Philosophy, has no peculiar opinions which would have required any mention of him as a moralist, were it not for the just reputation of his treatise on *First Truths*, with which Dr. Reid so remarkably, though unaware of its existence, coincides, even in the misapplication of so practical a term as *common sense* to denote the faculty which recognises the truth of First Principles. His philosophical writings* are remarkable for that perfect clearness of expression, which, since the great examples of

* *Cours de Sciences.* Paris, 1732, folio.

Descartes and Pascal, has been so generally diffused as to have become one of the enviable peculiarities of French philosophical style, and almost of the French language. His ethical doctrine is that most commonly received among philosophers, from Aristotle to Paley and Bentham : "I desire to be happy; but, as I live with other men, I cannot be happy without consulting their happiness:" a proposition perfectly true indeed, but far too narrow, as inferring that in the most benevolent acts a man must pursue only his own interest, from the fact that the practice of benevolence does increase his happiness; and that because a virtuous mind is likely to be the happiest, our observation of that property of virtue is the cause of our love and reverence for it.

SECTION VI.

FOUNDATIONS OF A MORE JUST THEORY OF ETHICS.

Butler—Hutcheson—Berkeley—Hume—Smith—Price—Hartley—
Tucker—Paley—Bentham—Stewart—Brown.

FROM the beginning of ethical controversy to the eighteenth century, it thus appears that the care of the individual for himself, and his regard for the things which preserve self, were thought to form the first, and in the opinion of most, the earliest of all the principles which prompt men and other animals to activity; that nearly all philosophers regarded the appetites and desires, which look only to self-gratification, as modifications of this primary principle of self-love; and that a very numerous body considered even the social affections themselves as nothing more than the produce of a more latent and subtile operation of the desire of interest, and of the pursuit of pleasure. It is true, they often spoke otherwise; but it was rather from the looseness and fluctuation of their language, than from distrust in their doctrine. It is true, also, that perhaps all represented the gratifications of virtue as more unmingled, more secure, more frequent, and more lasting, than other pleasures; without which they could neither have retained a hold on the assent of mankind, nor reconciled the principles of their systems with the testimony of their hearts. We have seen how some began to be roused from a lazy acquiescence in this ancient hypothesis by the monstrous consequences which Hobbes had legitimately deduced from it. A few, of pure minds and great intellect, laboured to render morality disinterested, by tracing it to reason as its source; without considering that reason, elevated indeed far above interest, is also separated by an impassable gulf from feeling, affection, and passion. At length it was perceived by more than one, that through whatever length of reasoning the mind may pass in its advances towards action, there is placed at the end of any avenue through which it can advance, some principle wholly unlike mere reason—some *emotion* or *sentiment* which must be touched, before the springs of will and action can be set in motion. Had Lord Shaftesbury steadily adhered to his own principles—had Leibnitz not recoiled from his statement—the truth might have been regarded as promulged, though not unfolded. The writings of both prove, at least to us, enlightened as we are by what followed, that they were skilful in sounding, and that their lead had touched the bottom. But it was reserved for another moral philosopher to determine this hitherto unfathomed depth.*

BUTLER.

Born 1692—died 1752.

BUTLER, who was the son of a Presbyterian trader, early gave such promise, as to induce his father to fit him, by a proper

* The doctrine of the Stoics is thus put by Cicero into the mouth of Cato : "Placet his, inquit, quorum ratio mihi probatur, simul atque natum sit animal (hinc enim est ordiendum) ipsum sibi conciliari et commendari ad se conservandum, et ad suum statum, et ad ea quæ conservantia sunt ejus status diligenda ; alienari autem ab interitu, iisque rebus quæ interitum videantur afferre. Id ita esse sic probant, quod, antequam voluptas aut dolor attigerit, salutaria appetant parvi, aspernenturque contraria. Quod non fieret, nisi statum suum diligerent, interitum timerent. *Fieri autem non posset ut appeterent aliquid, nisi sensum haberent sui, eoque se, et sua diligerent.* EX QUO INTELLIGI DEBET, PRINCIPIUM DUCTUM ESSE A SE DILIGENDI." (*De Finibus*, lib. iii. cap. v.) We are told that *diligendo* is the reading of an ancient MS. Perhaps the omission of "a" would be the easiest and most reasonable emendation.

The above passage is perhaps the fullest and plainest statement of the doctrines prevalent till the time of Butler.

education, for being a minister of that persuasion. He was educated at one of their seminaries, under Mr. Jones of Gloucester, where Secker, afterwards Archbishop of Canterbury, was his fellow-student. Though many of the dissenters had then begun to relinquish Calvinism, the uniform effect of that doctrine, in disposing its adherents to metaphysical speculation, long survived the opinions which caused it, and cannot be doubted to have influenced the mind of Butler. When a student at the academy of Gloucester, he wrote private letters to Dr. Clarke on his celebrated *Demonstration*, suggesting objections which were really insuperable, and which are marked by an acuteness which neither himself nor any other ever surpassed. Clarke, whose heart was as well schooled as his head, published the letters, with his own answers, in the next edition of his work ; and, by his good offices with his friend and follower, Sir Joseph Jekyll, obtained for the young philosopher an early opportunity of making his abilities and opinions known, by the appointment of preacher at the Chapel of the Master of the Rolls. He was afterwards raised to one of the highest seats on the Episcopal bench, through the philosophical taste of Queen Caroline, and her influence over the mind of her husband, which continued long after her death. "He was wafted," says Horace Walpole, "to the see of Durham, on a cloud of Metaphysics."* Even in the fourteenth year of his widowhood, George II. was desirous of inserting the name of the Queen's metaphysical favourite in the Regency Bill of 1751.

His great work on the *Analogy of Religion to the Course of Nature*, though only a commentary on the singularly original and pregnant passage of Origen, which is so honestly prefixed to it as a motto, is, notwithstanding, the most original and profound work extant in any language on the Philosophy of Religion. It is entirely beyond our present scope. His

---

* Walpole's *Memoirs*.

ethical discussions are contained in those deep and sometimes dark dissertations which he preached at the Chapel of the Rolls, and afterwards published under the name of *Sermons*, while he was yet fresh from the schools, and full of that courage with which youth often delights to exercise its strength in abstract reasoning, and to push its faculties into the recesses of abstruse speculation. But his youth was that of a sober and mature mind, early taught by nature to discern the boundaries of knowledge, and to abstain from fruitless efforts to reach inaccessible ground. In these sermons,* he has taught truths more capable of being exactly distinguished from the doctrines of his predecessors, more satisfactorily established by him, more comprehensively applied to particulars, more rationally connected with each other, and therefore more worthy of the name of *discovery*, than any with which we are acquainted; if we ought not, with some hesitation, to except the first steps of the Grecian philosophers towards a Theory of Morals. It is a peculiar hardship that the extreme ambiguity of language, an obstacle which it is one of the chief merits of an ethical philosopher to vanquish, is one of the circumstances which prevent men from seeing the justice of applying to him so ambitious a term as *discovery*. Butler owed more to Lord Shaftesbury than to all other writers besides. He is just and generous towards that philosopher; yet, whoever carefully compares their writings, will without difficulty distinguish the two builders, and the larger as well as more regular and laboured part of the edifice, which is due to Butler.

Mankind have various principles of action; some leading directly to the private good, some immediately to the good of the community. But the private desires are not self-love, or

---

* See Sermons i. ii. and iii. on Human Nature; v. on Compassion; viii. on Resentment; ix. on Forgiveness; xi. and xii. on the Love of our Neighbour; and xiii. on the Love of God; together with the excellent Preface.

any form of it; for self-love is the desire of a man's own happiness, whereas the object of an appetite or passion is some outward thing. Self-love seeks things as means of happiness; the private appetites seek things, not as means, but as ends. A man eats from hunger, and drinks from thirst; and though he knows that these acts are necessary to life, that knowledge is not the motive of his conduct. No gratification can indeed be imagined without a previous desire. If all the particular desires did not exist independently, self-love would have no object to employ itself about; for there would be no happiness, which, by the very supposition of the opponents, is made up of the gratifications of various desires. No pursuit could be selfish or interested, if there were not satisfactions first gained by appetites which seek their own outward objects without regard to self; which satisfactions compose the mass which is called a man's interest.

In contending, therefore, that the benevolent affections are disinterested, no more is claimed for them than must be granted to mere animal appetites and to malevolent passions. Each of these principles alike seeks its own object, for the sake simply of obtaining it. Pleasure is the result of the attainment, but no separate part of the aim of the agent. The desire that another person may be gratified, seeks that outward object alone, according to the general course of human desire. Resentment is as disinterested as gratitude or pity, but not more so. Hunger or thirst may be, as much as the purest benevolence, at variance with self-love. A regard to our own general happiness is not a vice; but in itself an excellent quality. It were well if it prevailed more generally over craving and short-sighted appetites. The weakness of the social affections, and the strength of the private desires, properly constitute selfishness; a vice utterly at variance with the happiness of him who harbours it, and, as such, condemned by self-love. There are as few who attain the greatest satisfaction to themselves, as who do the greatest good to others. It is absurd to say, with some, that the pleasure of benevolence is selfish, because it is felt by self. Understanding and reasoning are acts of self, for no man can think by proxy; but no one ever called them *selfish*. Why? Evidently because they do not *regard* self. Precisely the same reason applies to benevolence. Such an argument is a gross confusion of self, as it is a *subject* of feeling or thought, with self considered as the *object* of either. It is no more just to refer the private appetites to self-love because they commonly promote happiness, than it would be to refer them to self-hatred in those frequent cases where their gratification obstructs it.

But besides the private or public desires, and besides the calm regard to our own general welfare, there is a principle in man, in its nature supreme over all others. This natural supremacy belongs to the faculty which surveys, approves, or disapproves, the several affections of our minds and actions of our lives. As self-love is superior to the private passions, so conscience is superior to the whole of man. Passion implies nothing but an inclination to follow it; and in that respect passions differ only in force. But no notion can be formed of the principle of reflection, or conscience, which does not comprehend judgment, direction, superintendency. Authority over all other principles of action is a constituent part of the idea of conscience, and cannot be separated from it. Had it strength as it has right, it would govern the world. The passions would have their power but according to their nature, which is to be subject to conscience. Hence we may understand the purpose at which the ancients, perhaps confusedly, aimed when they laid it down that virtue consisted in following nature. It is neither easy, nor, for the main object to the moralist, important, to render the doctrines of the ancients by modern language. If Butler returns to this phrase too often, it was rather from the remains of undistinguishing reverence for antiquity than because he could deem its employment important to his own opinions.

The tie which holds together Religion and Morality is, in the system of Butler, somewhat different from the common representations, but not less close. Conscience, or the faculty of approving or disapproving, necessarily constitutes the bond of union. Setting out from the belief of Theism, and combining it, as he had entitled himself to do, with the reality of conscience, he could not avoid discovering that the being who possessed the highest moral qualities is the object of the highest moral affections. He contemplates the Deity through the moral nature of man. In the case of a being who is to be perfectly loved, "goodness must be the simple actuating principle within him; this being the moral quality which is the immediate object of love." "The highest, the adequate object of this affection, is perfect goodness; which therefore we are to love with all our heart, with all our soul, and with all our strength." "We should refer ourselves implicitly to him, and cast ourselves entirely upon him. The whole attention of life should be to obey his commands."* Moral distinctions are thus presupposed before a step can be made towards religion: virtue leads to piety; God is to be loved, because goodness is the object of love; and it is only after the mind rises through human morality to divine perfection, that all the virtues and duties are seen to hang from the throne of God.

Remarks.—There do not appear to be any *errors* in the ethical principles of Butler. The following remarks are intended to point out some *defects* in his scheme; and even that attempt is made with the unfeigned humility of one who rejoices in an opportunity of doing justice to that part of the writings of a great philosopher which has not been so clearly

* Sermon xiii. On the Love of God.

understood, nor so justly estimated by the generality, as his other works.

1. It is a considerable defect, though perhaps unavoidable in a sermon, that he omits all inquiry into the nature and origin of the private appetites, which first appear in human nature. It is implied, but it is not expressed in his reasonings, that there is a time before the child can be called selfish, any more than social, when those appetites seem as it were separately to pursue their distinct objects, long antecedent to the state of mind in which all their gratifications are regarded as forming the mass called happiness. It is hence that they are likened to instincts, in contradiction to their subsequent distinction, which requires reason and experience.*

2. Butler shows admirably well, that unless there were principles of action independent of self, there could be no pleasures and no happiness for self-love to watch over. A step farther would have led him to perceive that self-love is altogether a secondary formation; the result of the joint operation of reason and habit upon the primary principles. It could not have existed without presupposing original appetites and organic gratifications. Had he considered this part of the subject, he would have strengthened his case by showing that self-love is as truly a derived principle, not only as any of the social affections, but as any of the most confessedly acquired passions. It would appear clear, that as self-love is not divested of its self-regarding character by considering it as acquired, so the social affections do not lose any part of their disinterested character, if they be considered as formed from simpler elements. Nothing would more tend to root out the old prejudice which treats a regard to self as analogous to a self-evident principle, than the proof, that self-

---

* The very able work ascribed to Mr. Hazlitt, entitled *Essay on the Principles of Human Action*, Lond. 1805, contains original views on this subject.

love is itself formed from certain original elements, and that a living being long subsists before its appearance.*

3. It must be owned that those parts of Butler's discourses which relate to the social affections are more satisfactory than those which handle the question concerning the moral sentiments. It is not that the real existence of the latter is not as well made out as that of the former. In both cases he occupies the unassailable ground of an appeal to consciousness. All men (even the worst) feel that they have a conscience and disinterested affections. But he betrays a sense of the greater vagueness of his notions on this subject. He falters as he approaches it. He makes no attempt to determine in what state of mind the action of conscience consists. He does not venture steadily to denote it by name. He fluctuates between different appellations, and multiplies the metaphors of authority and command, without a simple exposition of that mental operation which these metaphors should only have illustrated. It commands other principles. But the question recurs, why or how?

Some of his own hints, and some fainter intimations of Shaftesbury, might have led him to what appears to be the true solution; which, perhaps from its extreme simplicity, has escaped him and his successors. The truth seems to be that the moral sentiments, in their mature state, are *a class of feelings which have no other object but the mental dispositions leading to voluntary action, and the voluntary actions which flow from these dispositions.* We are pleased with some dispositions and actions, and displeased with others, in ourselves and our fellows. We desire to cultivate the dispositions, and to perform the actions, which we contemplate with satisfaction. These objects, like all those of human appetite

---

* Compare this statement with the Stoical doctrine explained by Cicero in the book *de Finibus*, quoted above, of which it is the direct opposite.

or desire, are sought for their own sake. The peculiarity of these desires is, that their gratification *requires the use of no means*. Nothing (unless it be a volition) is interposed between the desire and the voluntary act. It is impossible, therefore, that these passions should undergo any change by transfer from the end to the means, as is the case with other practical principles. On the other hand, as soon as they are fixed on these ends, they cannot regard any further object. When another passion prevails over them, the end of the moral faculty is converted into a means of gratification. But volitions and actions are not themselves the end, or last object in view, of any other desire or aversion. Nothing stands between the moral sentiments and their object. They are, as it were, in contact with the will. It is this sort of mental position, if the expression may be pardoned, that explains, or seems to explain, those characteristic properties which true philosophers ascribe to them, and which all reflecting men feel to belong to them. Being the only desires, aversions, sentiments, or emotions, which regard dispositions and actions, they *necessarily extend to the whole character and conduct*. Among motives to action, they alone are justly considered as *universal*. They may and do stand between any other practical principle and its object; while it is absolutely impossible that another shall intercept their connection with the will. Be it observed, that though many passions prevail over them, no other can act beyond its own appointed and limited sphere; and that the prevalence itself, leaving the natural order undisturbed in any other part of the mind, is perceived to be a disorder, when seen in another man, and felt to be so by the mind disordered, when the disorder subsides. Conscience may forbid the will to contribute to the gratification of a desire. No desire ever forbids will to obey conscience.

This result of the peculiar relation of conscience to the will justifies those metaphorical expressions which ascribe to it *authority* and the right of *universal command*. It is *immutable;* for by the law which regulates all feelings, it must rest on *action*, which is its object, and beyond which it cannot look; and as it employs no *means*, it never can be transferred to nearer objects, in the way in which he who first desires an object, as a means of gratification, may come to seek it as his end. Another remarkable peculiarity is bestowed on the moral feelings by the nature of their object. As the objects of all other desires are outward, the satisfaction of them may be frustrated by outward causes. The moral sentiments may always be gratified, because voluntary actions and moral dispositions spring from within. No external circumstance affects them. Hence their *independence*. As the moral sentiment needs *no means*, and the desire is instantaneously followed by the volition, it seems to be either that which first suggests the relation between *command* and *obedience*, or at least that which affords the simplest instance of it. It is therefore with the most rigorous precision that authority and universality are ascribed to them. Their only unfortunate property is their too frequent weakness; but it is apparent that it is from that circumstance alone that their failure arises. Thus considered, the language of Butler concerning conscience, that, "had it strength as it has right, it would govern the world," which may seem to be only an effusion of generous feeling, proves to be a just statement of the nature and action of the highest of human faculties. The union of universality, immutability, and independence, with direct action on the will, which distinguishes the moral sense from every other part of our practical nature, renders it scarcely metaphorical language to ascribe to it unbounded sovereignty and awful authority over the whole of the world within;— shows that attributes, well denoted by terms significant of command and control, are in fact inseparable from it, or rather constitute its very essence; justifies those ancient moralists who represent it as alone securing, if not forming, the moral liberty of man; and finally, when religion rises from its roots in virtuous feeling, it clothes conscience with the sublime character of representing the divine purity and majesty in the human soul. Its title is not impaired by any number of defeats; for every defeat necessarily disposes the disinterested and dispassionate bystander to wish that its force were strengthened: and though it may be doubted whether, consistently with the present constitution of human nature, it could be so invigorated as to be the only motive to action, yet every such bystander rejoices at all accessions to its force; and would own, that man becomes happier, more excellent, more estimable, more venerable, in proportion as conscience acquires a power of banishing malevolent passions, of strongly curbing all the private appetites, of influencing and guiding the benevolent affections themselves.

Let it be carefully considered whether the same observations could be made with truth, or with plausibility, on any other part or element of the nature of man. They are entirely independent of the question, whether conscience be an inherent or an acquired principle. If it be inherent, that circumstance is, according to the common modes of thinking, a sufficient proof of its title to veneration. But if provision be made in the constitution and circumstances of all men, for uniformly producing it, by processes similar to those which produce other acquired sentiments, may not our reverence be augmented by admiration of that supreme wisdom which, in such mental contrivances, yet more brightly than in the lower world of matter, accomplishes mighty purposes by instruments so simple? Should these speculations be thought to have any solidity by those who are accustomed to such subjects, it would be easy to unfold and apply them so fully, that they may be thoroughly apprehended by every intelligent person.

4. The most palpable defect of Butler's scheme is, that it

affords no answer to the question, "What is the distinguishing quality common to all right actions?" If it were answered, "Their criterion is, that they are approved and commanded by conscience," the answerer would find that he was involved in a vicious circle; for conscience itself could be no otherwise defined than as the faculty which approves and commands right actions.

There are few circumstances more remarkable than the small number of Butler's followers in Ethics; and it is perhaps still more observable, that his opinions were not so much rejected as overlooked. It is an instance of the importance of style. No thinker so great was ever so bad a writer. Indeed, the ingenious apologies which have been lately attempted for this defect amount to no more than that his power of thought was too much for his skill in language. How general must the reception have been of truths so certain and momentous as those contained in Butler's Discourses,—with how much more clearness must they have appeared to his own great understanding, if he had possessed the strength and distinctness with which Hobbes enforces odious falsehood, or the unspeakable charm of that transparent diction which clothed the unfruitful paradoxes of Berkeley!

HUTCHESON.

Born in Ireland, 1694—died at Glasgow, 1747.

This ingenious writer began to try his own strength by private letters, written in his early youth to Dr. Clarke, the metaphysical patriarch of his time; on whom young philosophers seem to have considered themselves as possessing a claim, which he had too much goodness to reject. His correspondence with Hutcheson is lost; but we may judge of its spirit by his answers to Butler, and by one to Mr. Henry

Home,* afterwards Lord Kames, then a young adventurer in the prevalent speculations. Nearly at the same period with Butler's first publication,† the writings of Hutcheson began to show coincidences with him, indicative of the tendency of moral theory to a new form, to which an impulse had been given by Shaftesbury, and which was roused to activity by the adverse system of Clarke. Lord Molesworth, the friend of Shaftesbury, patronised Hutcheson, and even criticised his manuscript. Though a Presbyterian, he was befriended by King, archbishop of Dublin, himself a metaphysician; and he was aided by Mr. Synge, afterwards a bishop, to whom speculations somewhat similar to his own had occurred.

Butler and Hutcheson coincided in the two important positions, that disinterested affections, and a distinct moral faculty, are essential parts of human nature. Hutcheson is a chaste and simple writer, who imbibed the opinions without the literary faults of his master, Shaftesbury. He has a clearness of expression, and fulness of illustration, which are wanting in Butler. But he is inferior to both these writers in the appearance at least of originality, and to Butler especially in that philosophical courage which, when it discovers the fountains of truth and falsehood, leaves others to follow the streams. He states as strongly as Butler, that "the same cause which determines us to pursue happiness for ourselves determines us both to esteem and benevolence on their proper occasions—even the very frame of our nature." ‡ It is vain, as he justly observes, for the patrons of a refined selfish-

* Woodhouselee's *Life of Lord Kames*, vol. i. Append. No. 3.

† The first edition of Butler's Sermons was published in 1726, in which year also appeared the *second* edition of Hutcheson's *Inquiry into Beauty and Virtue*. The Sermons had been preached some years before, though there is no likelihood that the contents could have reached a young teacher at Dublin. The place of Hutcheson's birth is not mentioned in any account known to me. Ireland may be truly said to be "*incuriosa suorum.*"

‡ *Inquiry*, p. 152.

ness to pretend that we pursue the happiness of others for the sake of the pleasure which we derive from it; since it is apparent that there could be no such pleasure if there had been no previous affection. "Had we no affection distinct from self-love, nothing could raise a desire of the happiness of others but when viewed as a mean of our own."* He seems to have been the first who entertained just notions of the formation of the secondary desires, which had been overlooked by Butler. "There must arise, in consequence of our original desires, *secondary* desires of everything useful to gratify the primary desire. Thus, as soon as we apprehend the use of wealth or power to gratify our original desires, we also *desire* them. From their universality as means arises the general prevalence of these desires of wealth and power." † Proceeding farther in his zeal against the selfish system than Lord Shaftesbury, who seems ultimately to rest the reasonableness of benevolence on its subserviency to the happiness of the individual, he represents the moral faculty to be, as well as self-love and benevolence, a calm general impulse, which may and does impel a good man to sacrifice not only happiness, but even life itself, to virtue.

As Mr. Locke had spoken of an internal sensation,—Lord Shaftesbury once or twice of a reflex sense, and once of a moral sense,—Hutcheson, who had a steadier, if not a clearer view of the nature of conscience than Butler, calls it a *Moral Sense;* a name which quickly became popular, and continues to be a part of philosophical language. By *sense* he understood a capacity of receiving ideas, together with pleasures and pains, from a class of objects. The term *moral* was used to describe the particular class in question. It implied only that conscience was a separate element in our nature, and that it was not a state or act of the understanding. According to him it also implied that it was an original and implanted

* *Essay on the Passions*, p. 17. † *Ibid.* p. 8.

principle; but every other part of his theory might be embraced by those who hold it to be derivative.

The object of moral approbation, according to him, is general benevolence; and he carries this generous error so far as to deny that prudence, as long as it regards ourselves, can be morally approved;—an assertion contradicted by every man's feelings, and to which we owe the Dissertation on the Nature of Virtue, which Butler annexed to his *Analogy*. By proving that all virtuous actions produce general good, he fancied that he had proved the necessity of regarding the general good in every act of virtue;—an instance of that confusion of the theory of moral sentiments with the criterion of moral actions, against which the reader was warned at the opening of this work, as fatal to Ethical Philosophy. He is chargeable, like Butler, with a vicious circle, in describing virtuous acts as those which are approved by the moral sense, while he at the same time describes the moral sense as the faculty which perceives and feels the morality of actions.

He was the father of speculative philosophy in Scotland, at least in modern times; for though in the beginning of the sixteenth century the Scotch are said to have been known throughout Europe by their unmeasured passion for dialectical subtilties,* and though this metaphysical taste was

* The character given of the Scotch by the famous and unfortunate Servetus, in his edition of Ptolemy (1533), is in many respects curious. "Gallis amicissimi, Anglorumque regi maxime infesti. Subita ingenia, et in ultionem prona, ferociaque. In bello fortes, inediæ, vigiliæ, algoris patientissimi, decenti forma sed cultu negligentiori; invidi naturâ et cæterorum mortalium contemptores; ostentant *plus nimio nobilitatem suam et in summa etiam egestate suum genus ad regiam stirpem referunt*, NEC NON DIALECTICIS ARGUTIIS SIBI BLANDIUNTUR."— *Subita ingenia* is an expression equivalent to the "Præfervidum Scotorum ingenium" of Buchanan. Churchill almost agrees in words with Servetus:—

Whose lineage springs
From great and glorious though forgotten kings.

And the strong antipathy of the late King George III. to what he called

nourished by the controversies which followed the Reformation, yet it languished with every other intellectual taste and talent, from the Restoration, first silenced by civil disorders, and afterwards repressed by an exemplary but unlettered clergy, till the philosophy of Shaftesbury was brought by Hutcheson from Ireland. We are told by the writer of his Life (a fine piece of philosophical biography) that "he had a remarkable degree of rational enthusiasm for learning, liberty, religion, virtue, and human happiness;* that he taught in public with persuasive eloquence; that his instructive conversation was at once lively and modest; that he united pure manners with a kind disposition. What wonder that such a man should have spread the love of knowledge and virtue around him, and should have rekindled in his adopted country a relish for the sciences which he cultivated! To him may also be ascribed that proneness to multiply ultimate and original principles in human nature, which characterised the Scottish School till the second extinction of a passion for metaphysical speculation in Scotland. A careful perusal of the writings of this now little studied philosopher will satisfy the well-qualified reader that Dr. Adam Smith's ethical speculations are not so unsuggested as they are beautiful.

BERKELEY.

Born near Thomastown in Ireland, 1684—died at Oxford, 1753.

This great metaphysician was so little a moralist, that it requires the attraction of his name to excuse its introduction here. His *Theory of Vision* contains a great discovery in mental philosophy. His immaterialism is chiefly valuable as a touchstone of metaphysical sagacity; showing those to be "Scotch Metaphysics," proves the permanency of the last part of the national character.

* Life by Dr. Leechman, prefixed to Hutcheson's *System of Moral Philosophy*, 1755.

altogether without it, who, like Johnson and Beattie, believed that his speculations were sceptical, that they implied any distrust in the senses, or that they had the smallest tendency to disturb reasoning or alter conduct. Ancient learning, exact science, polished society, modern literature, and the fine arts, contributed to adorn and enrich the mind of this accomplished man. All his contemporaries agreed with the satirist in ascribing

> To Berkeley every virtue under Heaven.

Adverse factions and hostile wits concurred only in loving, admiring, and contributing to advance him. The severe sense of Swift endured his visions; the modest Addison endeavoured to reconcile Clarke to his ambitious speculations. His character converted the satire of Pope into fervid praise. Even the discerning, fastidious, and turbulent Atterbury said, after an interview with him, "So much understanding, so much knowledge, so much innocence, and such humility, I did not think had been the portion of any but angels, till I saw this gentleman."* "Lord Bathurst told me that the Members of the Scriblerus Club being met at his house at dinner, they agreed to rally Berkeley, who was also his guest, on his scheme at Bermudas. Berkeley, having listened to the many lively things they had to say, begged to be heard in his turn, and displayed his plan with such an astonishing and animating force of eloquence and enthusiasm, that they were struck dumb, and after some pause, rose all up together, with earnestness exclaiming, 'Let us set out with him immediately.'"† It was when thus beloved and celebrated that he conceived, at the age of forty-five, the design of devoting his life to reclaim and convert the natives of North America; and he employed as much influence and solicitation as common men do for their most prized objects, in obtaining leave to resign his dignities and revenues, to quit his accomplished and

* Duncombe's *Letters*, 106, 107. † Warton *on Pope*.

affectionate friends, and to bury himself in what must have seemed an intellectual desert. After four years' residence at Newport in Rhode Island, he was compelled, by the refusal of Government to furnish him with funds for his college, to forego his work of heroic, or rather godlike benevolence; though not without some consoling forethought of the fortune of the country where he had sojourned.

> Westward the course of empire takes its way,
> The first four acts already past,
> A fifth shall close the drama with the day,
> TIME'S NOBLEST OFFSPRING IS ITS LAST.

Thus disappointed in his ambition of keeping a School for savage children, at a salary of a hundred pounds by the year, he was received, on his return, with open arms by the philosophical queen, at whose metaphysical parties he made one, with Sherlock, who, as well as Smalridge, was his supporter, and with Hoadley, who, following Clarke, was his antagonist. By her influence he was made bishop of Cloyne. It is one of his highest boasts, that though of English extraction, he was a true Irishman, and the first eminent Protestant, after the unhappy contest at the Revolution, who avowed his love for all his countrymen. He asked, "Whether their habitations and furniture were not more sordid than those of the savage Americans?" * "*Whether a scheme for the welfare of this nation should not take in the whole inhabitants?*" and, "*Whether it was a vain attempt to project the flourishing of our Protestant gentry, exclusive of the bulk of the natives?*" † He proceeds to promote the reformation suggested in this pregnant question by a series of Queries, intimating, with the utmost skill and address, every reason that proves the necessity and the safety, and the wisest mode of adopting his suggestion. He contributed, by a truly Christian address to the Roman Catholics of his diocese, to their perfect quiet during the re-

* See his *Querist*, 358; published in 1735. † *Ibid*. 255.

bellion of 1745; and soon after published a letter to the clergy of that persuasion, beseeching them to inculcate industry among their flocks, for which he received their thanks. He tells them that it was a saying among the negro slaves, "*If negro were not negro, Irishman would be negro.*" It is difficult to read these proofs of benevolence and foresight without emotion, at the moment when,* after a lapse of near a century, his suggestions have been at length, at the close of a struggle of twenty-five years, adopted, by the admission of the whole Irish nation to the privileges of the British Constitution. The patriotism of Berkeley was not, like that of Swift, tainted by disappointed ambition; nor was it, like Swift's, confined to a colony of English Protestants. Perhaps the *Querist* contains more hints, then original, still unapplied in legislation and political economy, than are to be found in any equal space. From the writings of his advanced years, when he chose a medical tract† to be the vehicle of his philosophical reflections, though it cannot be said that he relinquished his early opinions, it is at least apparent that his mind had received a new bent, and was habitually turned from reasoning towards contemplation. His immaterialism, indeed, modestly appears, but only to purify and elevate our thoughts, and to fix them on Mind, the paramount and primeval principle of all things. "Perhaps," says he, "the truth about innate ideas may be, that there are properly no ideas or passive objects in the mind but what are derived from sense, but that there are also, besides these, her own acts and operations—such are notions;" a statement which seems once more to admit *general conceptions*, and which might have served, as well as the parallel passage of Leibnitz, as the basis of the modern philosophy of Germany. From these compositions of his old age, he appears then to have recurred with fondness to Plato and the later Platonists; writers from whose mere reasonings an intellect

* April 1829. † *Siris,* or *Reflections on Tar Water.*

so acute could hardly hope for an argumentative satisfaction of all its difficulties, and whom he probably rather studied as a means of inuring his mind to objects beyond the visible diurnal sphere, and of attaching it, through frequent meditation, to that perfect and transcendent goodness, to which his moral feelings always pointed, and which they incessantly strove to grasp. His mind, enlarging as it rose, at length receives every theist, however imperfect his belief, to a communion in its philosophic piety. "Truth," he beautifully concludes, "is the cry of all, but the game of a few. Certainly, where it is the chief passion, it does not give way to vulgar cares, nor is it contented with a little ardour in the early time of life; active perhaps to pursue, but not so fit to weigh and revise. He that would make a real progress in knowledge, must dedicate his age as well as youth, the latter growth as well as first fruits, at the altar of Truth." So did Berkeley, and such were almost his latest words.

His general principles of Ethics may be shortly stated in his own words:—"As God is a being of infinite goodness, his end is the good of his creatures. The general well-being of all men of all nations, of all ages of the world, is that which he designs should be procured by the concurring actions of each individual." Having stated that this end can be pursued only in one of two ways—either by computing the consequences of each action, or by obeying the rules which generally tend to happiness—and having shown the first to be impossible, he rightly infers, "that the end to which God requires the concurrence of human actions must be carried on by the observation of certain determinate and universal rules or moral precepts, which in their own nature have a necessary tendency to promote the well-being of mankind, taking in all nations and ages, from the beginning to the end of the world."* A romance, of which a journey to

* *Sermon in Trinity College Chapel, on Passive Obedience,* 1712.

an Utopia, in the centre of Africa, forms the chief part, called *The Adventures of Signor Gaudentio di Lucca*, has been commonly ascribed to him; probably on no other ground than its union of pleasing invention with benevolence and elegance.* Of the exquisite grace and beauty of his diction, no man accustomed to English composition can need to be informed. His works are, beyond dispute, the finest models of philosophical style since Cicero. Perhaps they surpass those of the orator, in the wonderful art by which the fullest light is thrown on the most minute and evanescent parts of the most subtile of human conceptions. Perhaps he also surpassed Cicero in the charm of simplicity, a quality eminently found in Irish writers before the end of the eighteenth century; conspicuous in the masculine severity of Swift, in the Platonic fancy of Berkeley, in the native tenderness and elegance of Goldsmith, and not withholding its attractions from Hutcheson and Leland, writers of classical taste, though of inferior power. The two Irish philosophers of the eighteenth century may be said to have co-operated in calling forth the metaphysical genius of Scotland; for, though Hutcheson spread the taste, and furnished the principles, yet Berkeley undoubtedly produced the scepticism of Hume, which stimulated the instinctive school to activity, and was thought incapable of confutation, otherwise than by their doctrines.

DAVID HUME.

Born at Edinburgh, 1711—died there, 1776.

THE Life of Mr. Hume, written by himself, is remarkable above most, if not all, writings of that sort, for hitting the degree of interest between coldness and egotism which becomes a modest man in speaking of his private history. Few writers, whose opinions were so obnoxious, have more per-

* *Gentleman's Magazine*, January 1777.

fectly escaped every personal imputation. Very few men of so calm a character have been so warmly beloved. That he approached to the character of a perfectly good and wise man, is an affectionate exaggeration, for which his friend Dr. Smith, in the first moments of his sorrow, may well be excused.* But such a praise can never be earned without passing through either of the extremes of fortune; without standing the test of temptations, dangers, and sacrifices. It may be said with truth that the private character of Mr. Hume exhibited all the virtues which a man of reputable station, under a mild government in the quiet times of a civilised country, has often the opportunity to practise. He showed no want of the qualities which fit men for more severe trials. Though others had warmer affections, no man was a kinder relation, a more unwearied friend, or more free from meanness and malice. His character was so simple, that he did not even affect modesty; but neither his friendships nor his deportment were changed by a fame which filled all Europe. His good nature, his plain manners, and his active kindness, procured him at Paris the enviable name of *the good David*, from a society not so alive to goodness, as without reason to place it at the head of the qualities of a celebrated man.† His whole character is faithfully and touchingly represented in the story of La Roche, ‡ where Mr. Mackenzie, without concealing Mr. Hume's opinions, brings him into contact with scenes of tender piety, and yet preserves the interest inspired by genuine and unalloyed, though moderated, feelings and affections. The amiable and venerable patriarch of Scottish Literature was averse from the opinions of the philosopher on whom he has composed this best panegyric. He tells us that he read the manuscript to

---

* Dr. Smith's Letter to Mr. Strahan, annexed to the *Life of Hume*.
† See Notes and Illustrations, Note P.
‡ *Mirror*, Nos. 42, 43, 44.

Dr. Smith, "who declared he did not find a syllable to object to, but added, with his characteristic absence of mind, that he was surprised he had never heard of the anecdote before."* So lively was the delineation thus sanctioned by the most natural of all testimonies. Mr. Mackenzie indulges his own religious feelings by modestly intimating, that Dr. Smith's answer seemed to justify the last words of the tale, "that there were moments when the philosopher recalled to his mind the venerable figure of the good La Roche, and wished that he had never doubted." To those who are strangers to the seductions of paradox, to the intoxication of fame, and to the bewitchment of prohibited opinions, it must be unaccountable, that he who revered benevolence should, without apparent regret, cease to see it on the Throne of the Universe. It is a matter of wonder that his habitual esteem for every fragment and shadow of moral excellence should not lead him to envy those who contemplated its perfection in that living and paternal character which gives it a power over the human heart.

On the other hand, if we had no experience of the power of opposite opinions in producing irreconcilable animosities, we might have hoped that those who retained such high privileges would have looked with more compassion than dislike on a virtuous man who had lost them. In such cases it is too little remembered that repugnance to hypocrisy, and impatience of long concealment, are the qualities of the best formed minds; and that, if the publication of some doctrines proves often painful and mischievous, the habitual suppression of opinion is injurious to reason, and very dangerous to sincerity. Practical questions thus arise, so difficult and perplexing, that their determination generally depends on the boldness or timidity of the individual,—on his tenderness for the feelings of the good, or his greater reverence for the

* Mackenzie's *Life of John Home*, p. 21.

free exercise of reason. The time is not yet come when the noble maxim of Plato, "that every soul is *unwillingly* deprived of truth," will be practically and heartily applied by men to the honest opponents who differ from them most widely.

In his twenty-seventh year he published, at London, the *Treatise of Human Nature*, the first systematic attack on all the principles of knowledge and belief, and the most formidable, if universal scepticism could ever be more than a mere exercise of ingenuity.* This memorable work was reviewed in a Journal of that time,† in a criticism not distinguished by ability, which affects to represent the style of a very clear writer as unintelligible—sometimes from a purpose to insult, but oftener from sheer dulness; which is unaccountably silent respecting the consequences of a sceptical system;—and which concludes with a prophecy so much at variance with the general tone of the article, that it would seem to be added by a different hand. "It bears incontestable marks of a great capacity, of a soaring genius, but young, and not yet thoroughly practised. Time and use may ripen these qualities in the author, and we shall probably have reason to consider this, compared with his later productions, in the same light as we view the juvenile works of Milton, or the first manner of Raphael."

The great speculator did not, in this work, amuse himself,

* Sextus, a physician of the empirical, *i.e.* anti-theoretical school, who lived at Alexandria in the reign of Antoninus Pius, has preserved the reasonings of the ancient Sceptics as they were to be found in their most improved state, in the writings of Ænesidemus, a Cretan, who was a Professor in the same city, soon after the reduction of Egypt into a Roman province. The greater part of the grounds of doubt are very shallow and popular. There are, among them, intimations of the argument against a necessary connection of causes with effects, afterwards better presented by Glanville in his *Scepsis Scientifica*. See Notes and Illustrations, Note Q.

† *History of the Works of the Learned*, November and December 1739, pp. 353-404. This Review is attributed by some (Chalmers, *Biographical Dictionary*) to Warburton, but certainly without foundation.

like Bayle, with dialectical exercises, which only inspire a disposition towards doubt, by showing in detail the uncertainty of most opinions. He aimed at proving, not that nothing was known, but that nothing could be known;—from the structure of the understanding to demonstrate that we are doomed for ever to dwell in absolute and universal ignorance. It is true that such a system of universal scepticism never can be more than an intellectual amusement, an exercise of subtilty; of which the only use is to check dogmatism, but which perhaps oftener provokes and produces that much more common evil. As those dictates of experience which regulate conduct must be the objects of belief, all objections which attack them in common with the principles of reasoning must be utterly ineffectual. Whatever attacks every principle of belief can destroy none. As long as the foundations of knowledge are allowed to remain in the same level (be it called of certainty or uncertainty) with the maxims of life, the whole system of human conviction must continue undisturbed. When the sceptic boasts of having involved the results of experience and the elements of geometry in the same ruin with the doctrines of religion and the principles of philosophy, he may be answered, That no dogmatist ever claimed more than the same degree of certainty for these various convictions and opinions; and that his scepticism, therefore, leaves them in the relative condition in which it found them. No man knew better, or owned more frankly, than Mr. Hume, that to this answer there is no serious reply. Universal scepticism involves a contradiction in terms. *It is a belief that there can be no belief.* It is an attempt of the mind to act without its structure, and by other laws than those to which its nature has subjected its operations. To reason without assenting to the principles on which reasoning is founded, is not unlike an effort to feel without nerves, or to move without muscles. *No man can be allowed to be an opponent in reasoning, who does not set out with admitting all the principles, without the admission of which it is impossible to reason.** It is indeed a puerile, nay, in the eye of wisdom, a childish play, to attempt either to establish or to confute principles by argument, which every step of that argument must presuppose. The only difference between the two cases is, that he who tries to prove them can do so only by first taking them for granted; and that he who attempts to impugn them, falls at the very first step into a contradiction, from which he never can rise.

It must, however, be allowed, that universal scepticism has practical consequences of a very mischievous nature. This is because its *universality* is not steadily kept in view, and constantly borne in mind. If it were, the above short and plain remark would be an effectual antidote to the poison. But in practice it is an armoury from which weapons are taken to be employed against *some* opinions, while it is hidden from notice that the same weapon would equally cut down every other conviction. It is thus that Mr. Hume's theory of causation is used as an answer to arguments for the existence of the Deity, without warning the reader that it would equally lead him not to expect that the sun will rise to-morrow. It must also be added, that those who are early accustomed to dispute first principles are never likely to acquire, in a sufficient degree, that earnestness and that sincerity, that strong love of truth, and that conscientious solicitude for the formation of just

---

* This maxim, which contains a sufficient answer to all universal scepticism, or, in other words, to all scepticism properly so called, is significantly conveyed in the quaint title of an old and rare book, entitled, *Scivi, sive Scepticcs et scepticorum a Jure Disputationis Exclusio*, by Thomas White, the metaphysician of the English Catholics in modern times.—"Fortunately," says the illustrious sceptic himself, "*since Reason is incapable of dispelling these clouds, Nature herself suffices for that purpose, and cures me of this philosophical delirium*" (*Treatise of Human Nature*, i. 467); almost in the sublime and immortal words of Pascal: *La raison confond les Dogmatistes, et la Nature les Sceptiques.*

opinions, which are not the least virtues of men, but of which the cultivation is the more especial duty of all who call themselves philosophers.*

It is not an uninteresting fact, that Mr. Hume having been introduced by Lord Kames (then Mr. Henry Home) to Dr. Butler, sent a copy of his Treatise to that philosopher at the moment of his preferment to the bishopric of Durham; and that the perusal of it did not deter the philosophic prelate from "everywhere recommending Mr. Hume's *Moral and Political Essays*,"† published two years afterwards;— Essays which it would indeed have been unworthy of such a man not to have liberally commended, for they, and those which followed them, whatever may be thought of the contents of some of them, must be ever regarded as the best models in any language, of the short but full, of the clear and agreeable, though deep discussion of difficult questions.

Mr. Hume considered his *Inquiry concerning the Principles of Morals* as the best of his writings. It is very creditable to his character that he should have looked back with most complacency on a Tract the least distinguished by originality, and the least tainted with paradox, among his philosophical works; but deserving of all commendation for the elegant perspicuity of the style, and the novelty of illustration and inference with which he unfolded to general readers a doctrine too simple, too certain, and too important, to remain till his time undiscovered among philosophers. His diction has, indeed, neither the grace of Berkeley nor the strength of Hobbes; but it is without the verbosity of the former, or the rugged sternness of the latter. His manner is

* It would be an act of injustice to those readers who are not acquainted with that valuable volume entitled, *Essays on the Formation of Opinions*, not to refer them to it as enforcing that neglected part of morality. To it may be added a masterly article in the *Westminster Review*, occasioned by the *Essays*.

† Woodhouselee's *Life of Kames*, i. 86, 104.

more lively, more easy, more ingratiating, and, if the word may be so applied, more amusing than that of any other metaphysical writer.* He knew himself too well to be, as Dr. Johnson asserted, an imitator of Voltaire; who, as it were, embodied in his own person all the wit and quickness and versatile ingenuity of a people which surpasses other nations in these brilliant qualities. If he must be supposed to have had an eye on any French writer, it would be a more plausible guess that he sometimes copied, with a temperate hand, the unexpected thoughts and familiar expressions of Fontenelle. Though he carefully weeded his writings in their successive editions, yet they still contain Scotticisms and Gallicisms enough to employ the successors of such critics as those who exulted over the Patavinity of the Roman historian. His own great and modest mind would have been satisfied with the praise which cannot be withheld from him, that there is no writer in our language, who, through long works, is more agreeable; and it is no derogation from him, that, as a Scotsman, he did not reach those native and secret beauties, characteristical of a language, which are never attained in elaborate composition, but by a very small number of those who familiarly converse in it from infancy.

The *Inquiry* affords perhaps the best specimen of his style. In substance, its chief merit is the proof, from an abundant enumeration of particulars, that all the qualities and actions of the mind which are generally approved by mankind agree in the circumstance of being useful to society. In the proof (scarcely necessary) that benevolent affections and actions have

---

* These commendations are so far from being at variance with the remarks of the late most ingenious Dr. Thomas Brown, on Mr. Hume's "mode of writing" (*Inquiry into the Relation of Cause and Effect*, 3d ed. 327), that they may rather be regarded as descriptive of those excellences of which the excess produced the faults of Mr. Hume as a mere searcher and teacher; justly, though perhaps severely, animadverted on by Dr. Brown.

that tendency, he asserts the real existence of these affections with unusual warmth ; and he well abridges some of the most forcible arguments of Butler,* whom it is remarkable that he does not mention. To show the importance of his principle, he very unnecessarily distinguishes the comprehensive duty of justice, from other parts of morality, as an artificial virtue, for which our respect is solely derived from notions of utility. If all things were in such plenty that there could never be a want, or if men were so benevolent as to provide for the wants of others as much as for their own, there would, says he, in neither case be any justice, because there would be no need for it. But it is evident that the same reasoning is applicable to every good affection and right action. None of them could exist if there were no scope for their exercise. If there were no suffering, there could be no pity and no relief. If there were no offences, there could be no placability. If there were no crimes, there could be no mercy. Temperance, prudence, patience, magnanimity, are qualities of which the value depends on the evils by which they are respectively exercised.†

* *Inquiry*, sect. ii. part i., especially the concluding paragraphs ; those which precede being more his own.

† "Si nobis, cum ex hac vita migraverimus, in beatorum insulis, ut fabulæ ferunt, immortale ævum degere liceret, quid opus esset eloquentiâ, cum judicia nulla fierent ? aut ipsis etiam virtutibus ?. Nec enim fortitudine indigeremus, nullo proposito aut labore aut periculo ; *nec justitiâ, cum esset nihil quod appeteretur alieni ;* nec temperantiâ, quæ regeret eas quæ nullæ essent libidines : ne prudentiâ quidem egeremus, nullo proposito delectu bonorum et malorum. Unâ igitur essemus beati cognitione rerum et scientiâ." (Cicero, *Fragm. ap. Div.* Augustin, *Trinit.* iv. 2.) Cicero is more extensive, and therefore more consistent, than Hume ; but his enumeration errs both by excess and defect. He supposes knowledge to render beings happy in this imaginary state, without stooping to inquire how. He omits a virtue which might well exist in it, though we cannot conceive its formation in such a state—the delight in each other's well-being ; and he omits a conceivable though unknown vice, that of unmixed ill-will, which would render such a state a hell to the wretch who harboured the malevolence.

On purity of manners, it must be owned that Mr. Hume, though he controverts no rule, yet treats vice with too much indulgence. It was his general disposition to distrust virtues which are liable to exaggeration, and may be easily counterfeited. The ascetic pursuit of purity, and hypocritical pretences to patriotism, had too much withdrawn the respect of his equally calm and sincere nature from these excellent virtues ; more especially as severity in both these respects was often at apparent variance with affection, which can neither be long assumed nor ever overvalued. Yet it was singular that he who, in his Essay on *Polygamy and Divorce*,* had so well shown the connection of domestic ties with the outward order of society, should not have perceived their deeper and closer relation to all the social feelings of human nature. It cannot be enough regretted, that, in an Inquiry written with a very moral purpose, his habit of making Truth attractive by throwing over her the dress of paradox, should have given him for a moment the appearance of weighing the mere amusements of society and conversation against domestic fidelity, which is the preserver of domestic affection, the source of parental fondness and filial regard, and, indirectly, of all the kindness which exists between human beings. That families are schools where the infant heart learns to love, and that pure manners are the cement which alone holds these schools together, are truths so certain, that it is wonderful he should not have betrayed a stronger sense of their importance. No one could so well have proved that all the virtues of that class, in their various orders and degrees, minister to the benevolent affections ; and that every act which separates the senses from the affections tends, in some degree, to deprive kindness of its natural auxiliary, and to lessen its prevalence in the world. It did not require his sagacity to discover that the gentlest and tenderest feelings

* *Essays and Treatises*, vol. i.

flourish only under the stern guardianship of these severe virtues. Perhaps his philosophy was loosened, though his life was untainted, by that universal and undistinguishing profligacy which prevailed on the Continent from the regency of the Duke of Orleans to the French revolution; the most dissolute period of European history, at least since the Roman Emperors.* At Rome, indeed, the connection of licentiousness with cruelty, which though scarcely traceable in individuals, is generally very observable in large masses, bore a fearful testimony to the value of austere purity. The alliance of these remote vices seemed to be broken in the time of Mr. Hume. Pleasure, in a more improved state of society, seemed to return to her more natural union with kindness and tenderness, as well as with refinement and politeness. Had he lived fourteen years longer, however, he would have seen that the virtues which guard the natural seminaries of the affections are their only true and lasting friends. The demand of all well-informed men for the improvement of civil institutions—the demand of classes of men growing in intelligence, to be delivered from a degrading inferiority, and admitted to a share of political power proportioned to their new importance, being feebly yet violently resisted by those ruling Castes who neither knew how to yield nor how to withstand—being also attended by very erroneous principles of legislation, having suddenly broken down the barriers (imperfect as these were) of law and government, led to popular excesses, desolating wars, and a military dictatorship, which for a long time threatened to defeat the reformation, and to disappoint the hopes of mankind. This tremendous convulsion threw a fearful light on the ferocity which lies hid under the arts and pleasures of corrupted nations; as earthquakes and volcanoes disclose the layers which compose the deeper parts of our planet beneath a fer-

* See Notes and Illustrations, Note R.

tile and flowery surface. A part of this dreadful result may be ascribed, not improbably, to that relaxation of domestic ties, unhappily natural to the populace of vast capitals, and at that time countenanced and aggravated by the example of their superiors. Another part doubtless arose from the barbarising power of absolute government, or, in other words, of injustice in high places. A very large portion attests, as strongly as Roman history, though in a somewhat different manner, the humanising efficacy of the family virtues, by the consequences of the want of them in the higher classes, whose profuse and ostentatious sensuality inspired the laborious and suffering portion of mankind with contempt, disgust, envy, and hatred.

* The *Inquiry* is disfigured by another speck of more frivolous paradox. It consists in the attempt to give the name of virtue to qualities of the *understanding ;* and it would not have deserved the single remark about to be made on it, had it been the paradox of an inferior man. He has altogether omitted the circumstance on which depends the difference of our sentiments regarding moral and intellectual qualities. We *admire* intellectual excellence, but we bestow no moral *approbation* on it. Such approbation has no tendency directly to increase it, because it is not voluntary. We cultivate our natural disposition to esteem and love benevolence and justice, because these moral sentiments, and the expression of them, directly and materially dispose others, as well as ourselves, to cultivate these two virtues. We cultivate a natural anger against oppression, which guards ourselves against the practice of that vice, and because the manifestation of it deters others from its exercise. The first rude resentment of a child is against every instrument of hurt. We confine it to intentional hurt, when we are taught by experience that it prevents only that species of hurt; and at last it is still further limited to *wrong* done to ourselves or others, and in that case becomes a purely moral sentiment. We morally

approve industry, desire of knowledge, love of truth, and all the habits by which the understanding is strengthened and rectified, because their formation is subject to the will.* But we do not feel a moral anger against folly or ignorance, because they are involuntary. No one but the religious persecutor, a mischievous and overgrown child, wreaks his vengeance on involuntary, inevitable, compulsory acts or states of the understanding, which are no more affected by blame than the stone which the foolish child beats for hurting him. Reasonable men apply to every thing which they wish to move the agent which is capable of moving it;—force to outward substances, arguments to the understanding, and blame, together with all other motives, whether moral or personal, to the will alone. It is as absurd to entertain an abhorrence of intellectual inferiority or error, however extensive or mischievous, as it would be to cherish a warm indignation against earthquakes or hurricanes. It is singular that a philosopher who needed the most liberal toleration should, by representing states of the understanding as moral or immoral, have offered the most philosophical apology for persecution.

That general utility constitutes a uniform ground of moral distinctions, is a part of Mr. Hume's ethical theory which never can be impugned, until some example can be produced of a virtue generally pernicious, or of a vice generally beneficial. The religious philosopher who, with Butler, holds that benevolence must be the actuating principle of the Divine mind, will, with Berkeley, maintain that pure benevolence can prescribe no rules of human conduct but such as are beneficial to men; thus bestowing on the theory of *Moral Distinctions* the certainty of demonstration in the eyes of all who believe in God.

The other question of moral philosophy which relates to

* " In hac quæstione primas tenet Voluntas, *quâ*, ut ait Augustinus, *peccatur, et recte vivitur.*" (*Hyperaspistes, Diatribe adversus Servum Arbitrium* Martini Lutheri, *per* Desiderium Erasmum Rotterdamensem.)

the theory of *Moral Approbation*, has been by no means so distinctly and satisfactorily handled by Mr. Hume. His general doctrine is, that an interest in the well-being of others, implanted by nature, which he calls *Sympathy* in his *Treatise of Human Nature*, and much less happily *Benevolence* in his subsequent *Inquiry*,* prompts us to be pleased with all generally beneficial actions. In this respect his doctrine nearly resembles that of Hutcheson. He does not trace his principle through the variety of forms which our moral sentiments assume. There are very important parts of them, of which it affords no solution. For example, though he truly represents our approbation, in others, of qualities useful to the individual, as a proof of benevolence, he makes no attempt to explain our moral approbation of such virtues as temperance and fortitude in ourselves. . He entirely overlooks that consciousness of the *rightful supremacy of the moral faculty* over every other principle of human action, without an explanation of which ethical theory is wanting in one if its vital organs.

Notwithstanding these considerable defects, his proof from induction of the beneficial tendency of virtue, his conclusive arguments for human disinterestedness, and his decisive observations on the respective provinces of reason and sentiment in morals, concur in ranking the *Inquiry* with the ethical treatises of the highest merit in our language,— with Shaftesbury's *Inquiry concerning Virtue*, Butler's *Sermons*, and Smith's *Theory of Moral Sentiments*.

ADAM SMITH.

Born 1723—died 1790.

THE great name of Adam Smith rests upon the *Inquiry into the Nature and Causes of the Wealth of Nations;* perhaps

* *Essays and Treatises*, vol. ii.

the only book which produced an immediate, general, and irrevocable change in some of the most important parts of the legislation of all civilised States. The works of Grotius, of Locke, and of Montesquieu, which bear a resemblance to it in character, and had no inconsiderable analogy to it in the extent of their popular influence, were productive only of a general amendment, not so conspicuous in particular instances, as discoverable, after a time, in the improved condition of human affairs.* The work of Smith, as it touched those matters which may be numbered, and measured, and weighed, bore more visible and palpable fruit. In a few years it began to alter laws and treaties, and has made its way, throughout the convulsions of revolution and conquest, to a due ascendant over the minds of men, with far less than the average obstructions of prejudice and clamour, which choke the channels through which truth flows into practice. The most eminent of those who have since cultivated and improved the science will be the foremost to address their immortal master:

> Tenebris tantis *tam clarum extollere lumen*
> Qui primus potuisti, ILLUSTRANS COMMODA VITÆ.
> Te sequor! (Lucret. lib. iii.)

In a science more difficult, because both ascending to more simple general principles, and running down through more minute applications, though the success of Smith has been less complete, his genius is not less conspicuous. Perhaps there is no ethical work since Cicero's *Offices*, of which an abridgment enables the reader so inadequately to estimate the merit, as the *Theory of Moral Sentiments*. This is not chiefly owing to the beauty of diction, as in the case of Cicero; but to the variety of explanations of life and manners, which embellish the book often more than they illuminate the theory. Yet, on the other hand, it must be owned that, for purely philosophical purposes, few books more need abridgment; for the

* Notes and Illustrations, Note S.

most careful reader frequently loses sight of principles buried under illustrations. The naturally copious and flowing style of the author is generally redundant, and the repetition of certain formularies of the system is, in the later editions, so frequent as to be wearisome, and sometimes ludicrous. Perhaps Smith and Hobbes may be considered as forming the two extremes of good style in our philosophy; the first of graceful fulness falling into flaccidity; while the masterly concision of the second is oftener tainted by dictatorial dryness. Hume and Berkeley, though they are nearer the extreme of abundance,* are probably the least distant from perfection.

That mankind are so constituted as to sympathise with each other's feelings, and to feel pleasure in the accordance of these feelings, are the only facts required by Dr. Smith, and they certainly must be granted to him. To adopt the feelings of another, is to *approve* them. When the sentiments of another are such as would be excited in us by the same objects, we approve them as *morally proper*. To obtain this accord, it becomes necessary for him who enjoys or suffers to lower his expression of feeling to the point to which the bystander can raise his fellow-feelings; on which are founded all the high virtues of self-denial and self-command; and it is equally necessary for the bystander to raise his sympathy as near as he can to the level of the original feeling. In all unsocial passions, such as anger, we have a *divided sympathy* between him who feels them and those who are the objects of them. Hence the propriety of extremely moderating them. Pure malice is always to be concealed or disguised, because all *sympathy* is arrayed against it. In the private passions, where there is only a *simple sympathy*—that with the original

---

* This remark is chiefly applicable to Hume's *Essays*. His *Treatise of Human Nature* is more Hobbian in its general tenor, though it has Ciceronian passages.

passion—the expression has more liberty. The benevolent affections, where there is a *double sympathy*—with those who feel them, and those who are their objects—are the most agreeable, and may be indulged with the least apprehension of finding no echo in other breasts. Sympathy with the gratitude of those who are benefited by good actions prompts us to consider them as deserving of reward, and forms the *sense of merit;* as fellow-feeling with the resentment of those who are injured by crimes leads us to look on them as worthy of punishment, and constitutes the *sense of demerit.* These sentiments require not only beneficial actions, but benevolent motives for them; being compounded, in the case of merit, of a direct sympathy with the good disposition of the benefactor, and an indirect sympathy with the persons benefited; in the opposite case, with precisely opposite sympathies. He who does an act of wrong to another to gratify his own passions must not expect that the spectators, who have none of his undue partiality to his own interest, will enter into his feelings. In such a case he knows that they will pity the person wronged, and be full of indignation against him. When he is cooled, he adopts the sentiments of others on his own crime, feels *shame* at the *impropriety* of his former passion, pity for those who have suffered by him, and a dread of punishment from general and just resentment. Such are the constituent parts of remorse.

Our moral sentiments respecting *ourselves* arise from those which others feel concerning us. We feel a self-approbation whenever we believe that the general feeling of mankind coincides with that state of mind in which we ourselves were at a given time. "We suppose ourselves the spectators of our own behaviour, and endeavour to imagine what effect it would in this light produce in us." We must view our own conduct with the eyes of others before we can judge it. The sense of duty arises from putting ourselves in the place of others, and adopting their sentiments respecting our own conduct. In utter solitude there could have been no self-approbation. The *rules* of morality are a summary of those sentiments; and often beneficially stand in their stead when the self-delusions of passion would otherwise hide from us the nonconformity of our state of mind with that which, in the circumstances, can be entered into and approved by impartial bystanders. It is hence that we learn to raise our mind above local or temporary clamour, and to fix our eyes on the surest indications of the general and lasting sentiments of human nature. " When we approve of any character or action, our sentiments are derived from four sources : *first*, we sympathise with the motives of the agent ; *secondly*, we enter into the gratitude of those who have been benefited by his actions ; *thirdly*, we observe that his conduct has been agreeable to the general rules by which those two sympathies generally act ; and, last of all, when we consider such actions as forming part of a system of behaviour which tends to promote the happiness either of the individual or of society, they appear to derive a beauty from this utility, not unlike that which we ascribe to any well-contrived machine."*

Remarks.—That Smith is the first who has drawn the attention of philosophers to one of the most curious and important parts of human nature—who has looked closely and steadily into the workings of *Sympathy*, its sudden action and reaction, its instantaneous conflicts and its emotions, its minute play and varied illusions—is sufficient to place him high among the cultivators of mental philosophy.

He is very original in applications and explanations; though, for his principle, he is somewhat indebted to Butler, more to Hutcheson, and most of all to Hume. These writers, except Hume in his original work, had derived sympathy, or

---

* *Theory of Moral Sentiments*, ii. 304. Edinb. 1801.

great part of it, from benevolence.* Smith, with deeper insight, inverted the order. The great part performed by various sympathies in moral approbation was first unfolded by him; and besides its intrinsic importance, it strengthened the proofs against those theories which ascribe that great function to Reason. Another great merit of the theory of sympathy is, that it brings into the strongest light that most important characteristic of the moral sentiments which consists in their being the only principles leading to action, and dependent on emotion or sensibility, with respect to the objects of which it is not only possible but natural for all mankind to agree.†

The main defects of this theory seem to be the following:—

1. Though it is not to be condemned for declining inquiry into the origin of our fellow-feeling, which, being one of the most certain of all facts, might well be assumed as ultimate in speculations of this nature, it is evident that the circumstances to which some speculators ascribe the formation of sympathy at least contribute to strengthen or impair, to contract or expand it. It will appear, more conveniently, in the next article, that the theory of sympathy has suffered from the omission of these circumstances. For the present, it is enough to observe how much our compassion for various sorts of animals, and our fellow-feeling with various races of men, are proportioned to the resemblance which they bear to ourselves, to the frequency of our intercourse with them, and to other causes which, in the opinion of some, afford evidence that sympathy itself is dependent on a more general law.

* There is some confusion regarding this point in Butler's first sermon on Compassion.

† The feelings of beauty, grandeur, and whatever else is compre hended under the name of Taste, form no exception, for *they do not lead to action*, but terminate in delightful contemplation; which constitutes the essential distinction between them and the moral sentiments, to which, in some points of view, they may doubtless be likened.

2. Had Smith extended his view beyond the mere play of sympathy itself, and taken into account all its preliminaries, and accompaniments, and consequences, it seems improbable that he should have fallen into the great error of representing the sympathies in their primitive state, without undergoing any transformation, as continuing exclusively to constitute the moral sentiments. He is not content with teaching that they are the roots out of which these sentiments grow, the stocks on which they are grafted, the elements of which they are compounded;—doctrines to which nothing could be objected but their unlimited extent. He tacitly assumes, that if a sympathy in the beginning caused or formed a moral approbation, so it must ever continue to do. He proceeds like a geologist who should tell us that the layers of this planet had always been in the same state, shutting his eyes to transition states and secondary formations; or like a chemist who should inform us that no compound substance can possess new qualities entirely different from those which belong to its materials. His acquiescence in this old and still general error is the more remarkable, because Mr. Hume's beautiful *Dissertation on the Passions** had just before opened a striking view of some of the compositions and decompositions which render the mind of a formed man as different from its original state, as the organisation of a complete animal is from the condition of the first dim speck of vitality. It is from this oversight (ill supplied by moral rules, a loose stone in his building) that he has exposed himself to objections founded on experience, to which it is impossible to attempt any answer. For it is certain that in many, nay in most cases of moral approbation, the adult man approves the action or disposition merely *as right*, and with a distinct consciousness that no process of sympathy intervenes between the approval and its object. It is certain that an unbiassed person would call

* *Essays and Treatises*, vol. ii.

it *moral approbation*, only as far as it excluded the interposition of any reflection between the conscience and the mental state approved. Upon the supposition of an unchanged state of our active principles, it would follow that sympathy never had any share in the greater part of them. Had he admitted the sympathies to be only elements entering into the *formation of Conscience*, their disappearance, or their appearance only as auxiliaries, after the mind is mature, would have been no more an objection to his system than the conversion of a substance from a transitional to a permanent state is a perplexity to the geologist. It would perfectly resemble the destruction of qualities, which is the ordinary effect of chemical composition.

3. The same error has involved him in another difficulty perhaps still more fatal. The sympathies have nothing more of an *imperative* character than any other emotions. They attract or repel like other feelings, according to their intensity. If, then, the sympathies continue in mature minds to constitute the whole of conscience, it becomes utterly impossible to explain the character of command and supremacy, which is attested by the unanimous voice of mankind to belong to that faculty, and to form its essential distinction. Had he adopted the other representation, it would be possible to conceive, perhaps easy to explain, that conscience should possess a quality which belonged to none of its elements.

4. It is to this representation that Smith's theory owes that unhappy appearance of rendering the rule of our conduct dependent on the notions and passions of those who surround us, of which the utmost efforts of the most refined ingenuity have not been able to divest it. This objection or topic is often ignorantly urged; the answers are frequently solid; but to most men they must always appear to be an ingenious and intricate contrivance of cycles and epicycles, which perplex the mind too much to satisfy it, and seem devised to

evade difficulties which cannot be solved. All theories which treat conscience as built up by circumstances inevitably acting on all human minds, are, indeed, liable to somewhat of the same misconception; unless they place in the strongest light (what Smith's theory excludes) the total destruction of the scaffolding which was necessary only to the erection of the building, after the mind is adult and mature, and warn the hastiest reader that it then rests on its own foundation alone.

5. The constant reference of our own dispositions and actions to the point of view from which they are estimated by others, seems to be rather an excellent expedient for preserving our impartiality, than a fundamental principle of Ethics. But impartiality, which is no more than a removal of some hindrance to right judgment, supplies no materials for its exercise, and no rule, or even principle, for its guidance. It nearly coincides with the Christian precept of doing unto others as we would they should do unto us; an admirable practical maxim, but, as Leibnitz has said truly, intended only as a correction of self-partiality.

6. Lastly, this ingenious system renders all morality *relative*—by referring it to the pleasure of an agreement of our feelings with those of others, by confining itself entirely to the question of moral approbation, and by providing no place for the consideration of that quality which distinguishes all good from all bad actions; a defect which will appear in the sequel to be more immediately fatal to a theorist of the *sentimental*, than to one of the *intellectual* school. Smith shrinks from considering utility in that light as soon as it presents itself, or very strangely ascribes its power over our moral feelings to admiration of the mere adaptation of means to ends—which might surely be as well felt for the production of wide-spread misery, by a consistent system of wicked conduct—instead of ascribing it to benevolence, with Hutcheson and Hume, or to an extension of that very sympathy which is his own first principle.

RICHARD PRICE.

Born 1723—died 1791.

About the same time with the celebrated work of Smith, but with a popular reception very different, Dr. Richard Price, an excellent and eminent nonconformist minister, published *A Review of the principal Questions in Morals;* *—an attempt to revive the intellectual theory of moral obligation, which seemed to have fallen under the attacks of Butler, Hutcheson, and Hume, even before Smith. It attracted little observation at first; but, being afterwards countenanced by the Scottish School, may seem to deserve some notice, in connection with the kindred speculations of the German metaphysicians, which, having effected an establishment in France, became no longer unknown in England.

The understanding itself is, according to Price, an independent source of simple ideas. "The various kinds of agreement and disagreement between our ideas, spoken of by Locke, are so many new simple ideas." "This is true of our ideas of proportion, of our ideas of identity, and diversity, existence, connection, cause and effect, power, possibility, and of our ideas of right and wrong." "The first relates to quantity, the last to actions, the rest to all things." "Like all other simple ideas, they are undefinable."

It is needless to pursue this theory farther, till an answer shall be given to the observation made before, that as no perception or judgment, or other unmixed act of understanding, merely as such, and without the agency of some intermediate *emotion*, can affect the will, the account given by Dr. Price of perceptions or judgments respecting moral subjects does not advance one step towards the explanation of the authority of conscience over the will, which is the

* The third edition was published at London in 1787.

matter to be explained. Indeed, this respectable writer felt the difficulty so much as to allow, "that, in contemplating the acts of moral agents, we have both a perception of the understanding and a feeling of the heart." He even admits that it would have been highly pernicious to us if our reason had been left without such support. But he has not shown how, on such a supposition, we could have acted on a mere opinion; nor has he given any proof that what he calls *support*, is not, in truth, the whole of what directly produces the conformity of voluntary acts to morality.*

DAVID HARTLEY.

Born 1705—died 1757.

THE work of Dr. Hartley, entitled *Observations on Man*,† is distinguished by an uncommon union of originality with modesty, in unfolding a simple and fruitful principle of human nature. It is disfigured by the absurd affectation of mathematical forms then prevalent; and it is encumbered and deformed by a mass of physiological speculations, groundless, or at best uncertain, wholly foreign from its proper purpose, which repel the inquirer into mental philosophy from its perusal, and lessen the respect of the physiologist for the author's judgment. It is an unfortunate example of the disposition predominant among undistinguishing theorists to

* The following sentences will illustrate the text, and are in truth applicable to all moral theories on merely intellectual principles:— "Reason alone, did we possess it in a higher degree, would answer all the ends of the passions. Thus there would be no need of parental affection, were all parents sufficiently acquainted with the reasons for taking upon them the guidance and support of those whom nature has placed under their care, *and were they virtuous enough to be always determined by those reasons.*" (Price's *Review*, 121.) A very slight consideration will show that without the last words the preceding part would be utterly false, and with them it is utterly insignificant.

† London, 1749.

class together all the appearances which are observed at the same time, and in the immediate neighbourhood of each other. At that period chemical phenomena were referred to mechanical principles; vegetable and animal life were subjected to mechanical or chemical laws; and while some physiologists* ascribed the vital functions to the understanding, the greater part of the metaphysicians were disposed, with grosser confusion, to derive the intellectual operations from bodily causes. The error in the latter case, though less immediately perceptible, is deeper and more fundamental than in any other; since it overlooks the primordial and perpetual distinction between *the being which thinks* and *the thing which is thought of;*—not to be lost sight of, by the mind's eye, even for a twinkling, without involving all nature in darkness and confusion. Hartley and Condillac,† who, much about the same time, but seemingly without any knowledge of each other's speculations,‡ began in a very similar mode to simplify, but also to mutilate, the system of Locke, stopped short of what is called Materialism, which consummates the confusion, but touched its threshold. Thither, it must be owned, their philosophy pointed, and thither their followers proceeded.

* G. E. Stahl, born in 1660; died in 1734; a German physician and chemist of deserved eminence.

[Stahl ascribed the vital functions not to the understanding but to *the soul*. I have spoken of him as the founder of the *Psychical School*. See *Phil. of the Med. Sc.*, B. ix.—W. W.]

† Born in 1715—died in 1780.

‡ *Traité sur l'Origine des Connoissances Humaines*, 1746; *Traité des Systèmes*, 1749; *Traité des Sensations*, 1754. Foreign books were then little and slowly known in England. Hartley's reading, except on theology, seems confined to the physical and mathematical sciences; and his whole manner of thinking and writing is so different from that of Condillac, that there is not the least reason to suppose the work of the one to have been known to the other.

The work of Hartley, as we learn from the sketch of his life by his son, prefixed to the edition of 1791, was begun in 1730, and finished in 1746.

Hartley and Bonnet,* still more than Condillac, suffered themselves, like most of their contemporaries, to overlook the important truth, that all the changes in the organs which can be likened to other material phenomena, are nothing more than *antecedents and prerequisites of perception,* bearing not the faintest likeness to it ; as much *outward* in relation to the thinking principle, as if they occurred in any other part of the matter ; and of which the entire comprehension, if it were attained, would not bring us a step nearer to the nature of thought. They who would have been the first to exclaim against the mistake of a sound for a colour, fell into the more unspeakable error of confounding the perception of objects, as outward, with the consciousness of our own mental operations. Locke's doctrine, that REFLECTION was a separate source of ideas, left room for this greatest of all distinctions—though with much unhappiness of expression, and with no little variance from the course of his own speculations. Hartley, Condillac, and Bonnet, in hewing away this seeming deformity from the system of their master, unwittingly struck off the part of the building which, however unsightly, gave it the power of yielding some shelter and guard to truths, of which the exclusion rendered it utterly untenable. They became consistent Nominalists ; a controversy on which Locke expresses himself with confusion and contradiction ; but on this subject they added nothing to what had been taught by Hobbes and Berkeley. Both Hartley and Condillac † have the merit of having been unseduced by the temptations either of scepticism

---

* Born in 1720—died in 1793.

† The following note of Condillac will show how much he differed from Hartley in his mode of considering the Newtonian hypothesis of vibrations, and how far he was in that respect superior to him. "Je suppose ici et ailleurs que les perceptions de l'âme ont pour cause physique l'ébranlement des fibres du cerveau ; *non que je regard cette hypothese comme démontrée, mais parcequ' elle est la plus commode pour expliquer ma pensée.*" (*Œuvres de Condillac,* i. 60 ; Paris, 1798.)

or of useless idealism; which, even if Berkeley and Hume could have been unknown to them, must have been within sight. Both agree in referring all the intellectual operations to the *association of ideas*, and in representing that association as reducible to the single law, that ideas which enter the mind at the same time acquire a tendency to call up each other, which is in direct proportion to the frequency of their having entered together. In this important part of their doctrine they seem, whether unconsciously or otherwise, to have only repeated, and very much expanded, the opinion of Hobbes.* In its simplicity it is more agreeable than the system of Mr. Hume, who admitted five independent laws of association; and it is in comprehension far superior to the views of the same subject by Mr. Locke, whose ill-chosen name still retains its place in our nomenclature, but who only appeals to the principle as explaining some fancies and whimsies of the human mind. The capital fault of Hartley is that of a rash generalisation, which may prove imperfect, and which is at least premature. All attempts to explain instinct by this principle have hitherto been unavailing. Many of the most important processes of reasoning have not hitherto been accounted for by it.† It would appear by close examination, that even this theory, simple as it appears, *presupposes* many facts relating to the mind, of which its authors do not seem to have suspected the existence. How many ultimate facts of that nature, for example, are contained and involved in Aristotle's celebrated comparison of the mind in its first state to a sheet of unwritten paper!‡ The texture of

* *Human Nature*, chaps. iv. v. vi. For more ancient statements, see Notes and Illustrations, Note T.

† "Ce que les logiciens ont dit des raisonnements dans bien des volumes, me paroit entièrement superflu, et de nul usage" (Condillac, i. 115); an assertion of which the gross absurdity will be apparent to the readers of Dr. Whately's *Treatise on Logic*, one of the most important works of the present age.

‡ See Notes and Illustrations, Note U.

the paper, even its colour, the sort of instrument fit to act on it, its capacity to receive and to retain impressions, all its differences, from steel on the one hand to water on the other, certainly presuppose some facts, and may imply many, without a distinct statement of which the nature of writing could not be explained to a person wholly ignorant of it. How many more, as well as greater laws, may be necessary to enable mind to perceive outward objects! If the power of perception may be thus dependent, why may not what is called the association of ideas, the attraction between thoughts, the power of one to suggest another, be affected by mental laws hitherto unexplored, perhaps unobserved?

But to return from digression into the intellectual part of man: It becomes proper to say, that the difference between Hartley and Condillac, and the immeasurable superiority of the former, are chiefly to be found in the application which Hartley first made of the law of association to that other unnamed portion of our nature with which morality more immediately deals; that which feels pain and pleasure, is influenced by appetites and loathings, by desires and aversions, by affections and repugnances. Condillac's *Treatise on Sensation*, published five years after the work of Hartley, reproduces the doctrine of Hobbes with its root, namely, that love and hope are but transformed sensations,* by which he means perceptions of the senses and its wide-spread branches, consisting in desires and passions, which are only modifications of self-love. "The words *goodness* and *beauty*," says he, almost in the very words of Hobbes, "express those qualities of things by which they contribute to our pleasures."† In the whole of his philosophical works, we find no trace of any desire produced by association, of any disin-

* Condillac, iii. 21; more especially *Traité des Sensations*, part ii. chap. vi. "Its love for outward objects is only an effect of love for itself."

† *Traité des Sensations*, part iv. chap. iii.

terested principle, or indeed of any distinction between the percipient and what, perhaps, we may now venture to call the *emotive* or the *pathematic* part of human nature until some more convenient and agreeable name shall be hit on by some luckier or more skilful adventurer, in such new terms as seem to be absolutely necessary.

To the ingenious, humble, and anxiously conscientious character of Hartley, we owe the knowledge that, about the year 1730, he was informed that the Reverend Mr. Gay of Sydney College, Cambridge, then living in the west of England, asserted the possibility of deducing all our intellectual pleasures and pains from association; that this led him (Hartley) to consider the power of association; and that about that time Mr. Gay published his sentiments on this matter in a dissertation prefixed to Bishop Law's Translation of King's *Origin of Evil.** No writer deserves more the praise of abundant fairness than Hartley in this avowal. The dissertation of which he speaks is mentioned by no philosopher but himself. It suggested nothing apparently to any other reader. The general texture of it is that of home-spun selfishness. The writer had the merit to see and to own that Hutcheson had established as a fact the reality of moral sentiments and disinterested affections. He blames, perhaps justly, that most ingenious man,† for assuming that these

---

* Hartley's Preface to the *Observations on Man.* The word *intellectual* is too narrow. Even *mental* would be of very doubtful propriety. The theory in its full extent requires a word such as *inorganic* (if no better can be discovered) extending to all gratification, not distinctly referred to some specific organ, or at least to some assignable part of the bodily frame.

† It has not been mentioned in its proper place, that Hutcheson appears nowhere to greater advantage than in Letters on the *Fable of the Bees*, published when he was very young, at Dublin, in a publication called *Hibernicus.* " Private vices are public benefits," says he, " may signify any one of these five distinct propositions: 1. They are in themselves public benefits; or, 2. They naturally produce public happiness;

M

sentiments and affections are implanted, and partake of the nature of instincts. The object of his dissertation is to reconcile the mental appearances described by Hutcheson with the first principle of the selfish system, that "the true principle of all our actions is our own happiness." Moral feelings and social affections are, according to him, "resolvable into reason, pointing out our private happiness; and *whenever this end is not perceived* they are to be accounted for from the association of ideas." Even in the single passage in which he shows a glimpse of the truth, he begins with confusion, advances with hesitation, and after holding in his grasp for an instant the principle which sheds so strong a light around it, suddenly drops it from his hand. Instead of receiving the statements of Hutcheson (his silence relating to Butler is unaccountable) as enlargements of the science of man, he deals with them merely as difficulties to be reconciled with the received system of universal selfishness. In the conclusion of his fourth section, he well exemplifies the power of association in forming the love of money, of fame, of power, etc.; but he still treats these effects of association as aberrations and infirmities, the fruits of our forgetfulness and shortsightedness, and not at all as the great process employed to sow and rear the most important principles of a social and moral nature.

This precious mine may therefore be truly said to have been opened by Hartley; for he who did such superabundant justice to the hints of Gay, would assuredly not have withheld the like tribute from Hutcheson, had he observed the happy expression of "secondary passions," which ought to have led that philosopher himself farther than he ventured

or, 3. They may be made to produce it; or, 4. They may naturally flow from it; or, 5. At least they may probably flow from it in our infirm nature." (See a small volume containing *Thoughts on Laughter*, and *Observations on the Fable of the Bees*, Glasgow, 1758, in which these letters are republished.)

to advance. The extraordinary value of this part of Hartley's system has been hidden by various causes, which have also enabled writers who borrow from it to decry it. The influence of his medical habits renders many of his examples displeasing, and sometimes disgusting. He has none of that knowledge of the world, of that familiarity with literature, of that delicate perception of the beauties of nature and art, which not only supply the most agreeable illustrations of mental philosophy, but afford the most obvious and striking instances of its happy application to subjects generally interesting. His particular applications of the general law are often mistaken, and seldom more than brief notes and hasty suggestions; the germs of theories which, while some might adopt them without detection, others might discover without being aware that they were anticipated. To which it may be added, that, in spite of the imposing forms of geometry, the work is not really distinguished by good method, or even uniform adherence to that which had been chosen. His style is entitled to no praise but that of clearness, and a simplicity of diction, through which is visible a singular simplicity of mind. No book perhaps exists, which, with so few of the common allurements, comes at last so much to please by the picture it presents of the writer's character—a character which kept him pure from the pursuit, often from the consciousness, of novelty, and rendered him a discoverer in spite of his own modesty. In those singular passages in which, amidst the profound internal tranquillity of all the European nations, he foretells the approaching convulsions, to be followed by the overthrow of states and churches, his quiet and gentle spirit, elsewhere almost ready to inculcate passive obedience for the sake of peace, is supported under its awful forebodings by the hope of that general progress in virtue and happiness which he saw through the preparatory confusion. A meek piety, inclining towards mysticism, and sometimes indulging in visions, which borrow a lustre from his fervid benevolence, was beautifully, and perhaps singularly, blended in him with zeal for the most unbounded freedom of inquiry, flowing both from his own conscientious belief and his unmingled love of truth. Whoever can so far subdue his repugnance to petty or secondary faults as to bestow a careful perusal on the work, must be unfortunate if he does not see, feel, and own, that the writer was a great philosopher and a good man.

To those who thus study the work, it will be apparent that Hartley, like other philosophers, either overlooked, or failed explicitly to announce, that distinction between perception and emotion, without which no system of mental philosophy is complete. Hence arose the partial and incomplete view of truth conveyed by the use of the phrase "association of ideas." If the word *association*, which rather indicates the connection between separate things, than the perfect combination and fusion which occur in many operations of the mind, must, notwithstanding its inadequacy, still be retained, the phrase ought at least to be "association of thoughts with emotions, as well as with each other." With that enlargement an objection to the Hartleian doctrine would have been avoided, and its originality, as well as superiority over that of Condillac, would have appeared indisputable. The examples of avarice and other factitious passions are very well chosen; first, because few will be found to suppose that they are original principles of human nature;* secondly, because the process by which they are generated, being subsequent to the age of attention and recollection, may be brought home to the understanding of all men; and thirdly, because they afford the most striking instance of secondary passions, which not only

* A very ingenious man, Lord Kames, whose works had a great effect in rousing the mind of his contemporaries and countrymen, has indeed fancied that there is a "hoarding instinct" in man and other animals. But such conclusions are not so much objects of confutation as ludicrous proofs of the absurdity of the premises which lead to them.

become independent of the primary principles from which they are derived, but hostile to them, and so superior in strength as to be capable of overpowering their parents. As soon as the mind becomes familiar with the frequent case of the man who first pursued money to purchase pleasure, but at last, when he becomes a miser, loves his hoard better than all that it could purchase, and sacrifices all pleasures for its increase, we are prepared to admit that, by a like process, the affections, when they are fixed on the happiness of others as their ultimate object, without any reflection on self, may not only be perfectly detached from self-regard or private desires, but may subdue these, and every other antagonist passion which can stand in their way. As the miser loves money for its own sake, so may the benevolent man delight in the well-being of his fellows. His good-will becomes as disinterested as if it had been implanted and underived. The like process applied to what is called self-love, or the desire of permanent well-being, clearly explains the mode in which that principle is gradually formed from the separate appetites, without whose previous existence no notion of well-being could be obtained. In like manner, sympathy, perhaps itself the result of a transfer of our own personal feelings by association to other sentient beings, and of a subsequent transfer of their feelings to our own minds, engenders the various social affections, which at last generate in most minds some regard to the well-being of our country, of mankind, of all creatures capable of pleasure. Rational self-love controls and guides those far keener self-regarding passions of which it is the child, in the same manner as general benevolence balances and governs the variety of much warmer social affections from which it springs. It is an ancient and obstinate error of philosophers to represent these two calm principles as being the source of the impelling passions and affections, instead of being among the last results of them. Each of them exercises a sort of authority in its sphere, but the dominion of neither is co-existent with the whole nature of man. Though they have the power to quicken and check, they are both too feeble to impel; and if the primary principles were extinguished, they would both perish from want of nourishment. If indeed all appetites and desires were destroyed, no subject would exist on which either of these general principles could act.

The affections, desires, and emotions, having for their ultimate object the dispositions and actions of voluntary agents, which alone, from the nature of their object, are co-extensive with the whole of our active nature, are, according to the same philosophy, necessarily formed in every human mind by the transfer of feeling which is effected by the principle of association. Gratitude, pity, resentment, and shame, seem to be the simplest, the most active, and the most uniform elements in their composition.

It is easy to perceive how the complacency inspired by a benefit may be transferred to a benefactor, thence to all beneficent beings and acts. The well-chosen instance of the nurse familiarly exemplifies the manner in which the child transfers his complacency from the gratification of his senses to the cause of it, and thus learns an affection for her who is the source of his enjoyment. With this simple process concur, in the case of a tender nurse, and far more of a mother, a thousand acts of relief and endearment, of which the complacency is fixed on the person from whom they flow, and in some degree extended by association to all who resemble that person. So much of the pleasure of early life depends on others, that the like process is almost constantly repeated. Hence the origin of benevolence may be understood, and the disposition to approve all benevolent, and disapprove all malevolent acts. Hence also the same approbation and disapprobation are extended to all acts which we clearly perceive to promote or obstruct the happiness of men.

When the complacency is extended to action, benevolence may be said to be transformed into a part of conscience. The rise of sympathy may probably be explained by the process of association, which transfers the feelings of others to ourselves, and ascribes our own feelings to others;—at first and in some degree, always in proportion as the resemblance of ourselves to others is complete. The likeness in the outward signs of emotion is one of the widest channels in this commerce of hearts. Pity thereby becomes one of the grand sources of benevolence, and perhaps contributes more largely than gratitude. It is indeed one of the first motives to the conferring of those benefits which inspire grateful affection. Sympathy with the sufferer, therefore, is also transformed into a real sentiment, directly approving benevolent actions and dispositions, and more remotely all actions that promote happiness. The anger of the sufferer, first against all causes of pain, afterwards against all intentional agents who produce it, and finally against all those in whom the infliction of pain proceeds from a mischievous disposition, when it is communicated to others by sympathy, and is so far purified by gradual separation from selfish and individual interest as to be equally felt against all wrong-doers, whether the wrong be done against ourselves, our friends, or our enemies, is the root out of which springs that which is commonly and well called a *Sense of Justice*—the most indispensable, perhaps, of all the component parts of the moral faculties. It is the main guard against wrong. It relates to that portion of morality where many of the outward acts are capable of being reduced under certain rules, of which the violations, wherever the rule is sufficiently precise, and the mischief sufficiently great, may be guarded against by the terror of punishment. In the observation of the rules of justice consists *duty;* breaches of them we denominate *crimes*. An abhorrence of crimes, especially of those which indicate the absence of benevolence, as well as of regard to justice, is peculiarly strong; because well-framed penal laws, being the lasting declaration of the moral indignation of many generations of mankind, exceedingly strengthen the same feeling in every individual, as long as they remain in unison with the sentiments of the age and country for which they are destined, and indeed, wherever the laws do not so much deviate from the habitual feelings as to produce a struggle between law and sentiment, in which it is hard to say on which side success is most deplorable. A man who performs his duties may be esteemed, but is not admired; because it requires no more than ordinary virtue to act well where it is shameful and dangerous to do otherwise. The righteousness of those who act solely from such inferior motives is little better than that "of the Scribes and Pharisees." Those only are just in the eye of the moralist who act justly from a constant disposition to render to every man his own.* Acts of kindness, of generosity, of pity, of placability, of humanity, when they are long continued, can hardly fail mainly to flow from the pure fountain of an excellent nature. They are not reducible to rules; and the attempt to enforce them by punishment would destroy them. They are *virtues* of which the essence consists in a good disposition of mind. As we gradually transfer our desire from praise to praiseworthiness, this principle also is adopted into consciousness. On the other hand, when we are led by association to feel a painful contempt for those feelings and actions of our past self which we despise in others, there is developed in our hearts another element of that moral sense. It is a remarkable instance of the power of the law of association, that the contempt or abhorrence

* "Justitia est constans et perpetua voluntas suum cuique tribuendi;" an excellent definition in the mouth of the stoical moralists, from whom it is borrowed, but altogether misplaced by the Roman Jurists in a body of laws which deal only with outward acts in their relation to the order and interest of society.

which we feel for the bad actions of others may be transferred by it, in any degree of strength, to our own past actions of the like kind. And as the hatred of bad actions is transferred to the agent, the same transfer may occur in our own case in a manner perfectly similar to that of which we are conscious in our feelings towards our fellow-creatures. There are many causes which render it generally feebler : but it is perfectly evident that it requires no more than a sufficient strength of moral feeling to make it equal ; and that the most apparently hyperbolical language used by penitents, in describing their *remorse*, may be justified by the principle of association.

At this step in our progress, it is proper to observe that a most important consideration has escaped Hartley, as well as every other philosopher.* The language of all mankind implies that the moral faculty, whatever it may be, and from what origin soever it may spring, is intelligibly and properly spoken of as ONE. It is as common in mind as in matter for a compound to have properties not to be found in any of its constituent parts. The truth of this proposition is as certain in the human feelings as in any material combination. It is therefore easily understood, that originally separate feelings may be so perfectly blended by a process performed in every mind, that they can no longer be disjoined from each other, but must always co-operate, and thus reach the only union which we can conceive. The sentiment of *Moral Approbation*, formed by association out of antecedent affections, may become so perfectly independent of them, that we are no longer conscious of the means by which it was formed, and never can in practice repeat, though we may in theory perceive, the process by which it was generated. It is in that mature and sound state of our nature that our emotions at the view of *Right* and *Wrong* are ascribed to *Conscience*. But why, it may be asked, do these feelings, rather than others, run into

* See *supra*, section on Butler.

each other, and constitute Conscience? The answer seems to be what has already been intimated in the observations on Butler. The affinity between these feelings consists in this, that while all other feelings relate to outward objects, they alone contemplate exclusively the *dispositions and actions of voluntary agents*. When they are completely transferred from objects, and even persons, to dispositions and actions, they are fitted, by the perfect coincidence of their *aim*, for combining to form that one faculty which is directed only to that *aim*.

The words *Duty* and *Virtue*, and the word *Ought*, which most perfectly denotes *Duty*, but is also connected with *Virtue*, in every well-constituted mind, in this state become the fit language of the acquired, perhaps, but universally and necessarily acquired, faculty of Conscience. Some account of its peculiar nature has been attempted in the remarks on Butler;—for others a fitter occasion will occur hereafter. Some light may, however, now be thrown on the subject by a short statement of the hitherto unobserved distinction between the moral sentiments and another class of feelings with which they have some qualities in common. The pleasures (so called) of Imagination appear, at least in most cases, to originate in association. But it is not till the original cause of the gratification is obliterated from the mind that they acquire their proper character. Order and proportion may be at first chosen for their convenience: it is not until they are admired for their own sake that they become objects of taste. Though all the proportions for which a horse is valued may be indications of speed, safety, strength, and health, it is not the less true that they only can be said to admire the animal for his beauty, who leave such considerations out of the account while they admire. The pleasure of contemplation in these particulars of nature and art becomes universal and immediate, being entirely detached from all regard to individual beings. It contemplates neither use nor interest. In this important particular the pleasures of imagination agree with the moral sentiments. Hence the application of the same language to both in ancient and modern times. Hence also it arises that they may contemplate the very same qualities and objects. There is certainly much beauty in the softer virtues—much grandeur in the soul of a hero or a martyr. But the essential distinction still remains. The purest moral taste contemplates these qualities only with *quiescent* delight or reverence. It has no further view ;—it points towards no action. Conscience, on the contrary, containing in it a pleasure in the prospect of doing right, and an ardent desire to act well, having for its sole object the dispositions and acts of voluntary agents, is not, like moral taste, satisfied with passive contemplation, but constantly tends to act on the will and conduct of the man. Moral taste may aid it, may be absorbed into it, and usually contributes its part to the formation of the moral faculty ; but it is distinct from that faculty, and may be disproportioned to it. Conscience, being by its nature confined to mental dispositions and voluntary acts, is of necessity excluded from the ordinary consideration of all things antecedent to these dispositions. The circumstances from which such states of mind may arise are most important objects of consideration for the understanding ; but they are without the sphere of conscience, which never ascends beyond the heart of the man. It is thus that in the eye of conscience man becomes amenable to its authority for all his inclinations as well as deeds ; that some of them are approved, loved, and revered ; and that all the outward effects of disesteem, contempt, or moral anger, are felt to be the just lot of others.

But, to return to Hartley, from this perhaps intrusive statement of what does not properly belong to him : he represents all the social affections of gratitude, veneration, and love, inspired by the virtues of our fellow-men, as capable of being transferred by association to the transcendent and unmingled goodness of the Ruler of the world, and thus to give rise to piety, to which he gives the name of the theopathetic affection. This principle, like all the former in the mental series, is gradually detached from the trunk on which it grew: it takes separate root, and may altogether overshadow the parent-stock. As such a being cannot be conceived without the most perfect and constant reference to his goodness, so piety may become not only a part of conscience, but its governing and animating principle, which, after long lending its own energy and authority to every other, is at last described by our philosopher as swallowing up all of them in order to perform the same functions more infallibly.

In every stage of this progress we are taught by Dr. Hartley that a new product appears, which becomes perfectly distinct from the elements which formed it, which may be utterly dissimilar to them, and may attain any degree of vigour, however superior to theirs. Thus the objects of the private desires disappear when we are employed in the pursuit of our lasting welfare; that which was first sought only as a means, may come to be pursued as an end, and preferred to the original end; the good opinion of our fellows becomes more valued than the benefits for which it was at first courted; a man is ready to sacrifice his life for him who has shown generosity, even to others; and persons otherwise of common character are capable of cheerfully marching in a forlorn hope, or of almost instinctively leaping into the sea, to save the life of an entire stranger. These last acts, often of almost unconscious virtue, so familiar to the soldier and the sailor, so unaccountable on certain systems of philosophy, often occur without a thought of applause and reward; too quickly for the thought of the latter, too obscurely for the hope of the former; and they are of such a nature that no man could be impelled to them by the mere expectation of either.

The gratitude, sympathy, resentment, and shame, which are the principal constituent parts of the Moral Sense, thus lose their separate agency, and constitute an entirely new faculty, co-extensive with all the dispositions and actions of voluntary agents; though some of them are more predominant in particular cases of moral sentiment than others, and though the aid of all continues to be necessary in their original character, as subordinate but distinct motives of action. Nothing more evidently points out the distinction of the Hartleian system from all systems called selfish, not to say its superiority in respect to disinterestedness over all moral systems before Butler and Hutcheson, than that excellent part of it which relates to the Rule of Life. The various principles of human action rise in value according to the order in which they spring up after each other. We can then only be in a state of as much enjoyment as we are evidently capable of attaining, when we prefer interest to the original gratifications—honour to interest—the pleasures of imagination to those of sense—the dictates of conscience to pleasure, interest, and reputation—the well-being of fellow-creatures to our own indulgences; in a word, when we pursue moral good and social happiness chiefly and for their own sake. "With self-interest," says Hartley, somewhat inaccurately in language, "man must begin. He may end in self-annihilation. Theopathy, or piety, although the last result of the purified and exalted sentiments, may at length swallow up every other principle, and absorb the whole man." Even if this last doctrine should be an exaggeration unsuited to our present condition, it will the more strongly illustrate the compatibility, or rather the necessary connection, of this theory with the existence and power of perfectly disinterested principles of human action.

It is needless to remark on the *secondary* and *auxiliary* causes which contribute to the formation of moral sentiment; education, imitation, general opinion, laws and government. They all presuppose the moral faculty: in an improved state of society they contribute powerfully to strengthen it, and on some occasions they enfeeble, distort, and maim it; but in all cases they must themselves be tried by the test of an ethical standard.

The value of this doctrine will not be essentially affected by supposing a greater number of original principles than those assumed by Dr. Hartley. The principle of association applies as much to a greater as to a smaller number. It is a quality common to it with all theories, that the more simplicity it reaches consistently with truth, the more perfect it becomes. Causes are not to be multiplied without necessity. If, by a considerable multiplication of primary desires, the law of association were lowered nearly to the level of an auxiliary agent, the philosophy of human nature would still be under indelible obligations to the philosopher who, by his fortunate error, rendered the importance of that great principle obvious and conspicuous.

ABRAHAM TUCKER.
Born 1705—died 1774.

It has been the remarkable fortune of this writer to have been more prized by the cultivators of the same subjects, and more disregarded by the generality even of those who read books on such matters, than perhaps any other philosopher.*

---

* "I have found in this writer more original thinking and observation upon the several subjects that he has taken in hand than in any other, not to say than in all others put together. His talent also for illustration is unrivalled." (Paley, Preface to *Moral and Political Philosophy*.) See the excellent preface to an abridgment, by Mr. Hazlitt, of Tucker's work, published in London in 1807. May I venture to refer also to my own discourse on the *Law of Nature and Nations*,

He had many of the qualities which might be expected in an affluent country gentleman, living in a privacy undisturbed by political zeal, and with a leisure unbroken by the calls of a profession, at a time when England had not entirely renounced her old taste for metaphysical speculation. He was naturally endowed, not indeed with more than ordinary acuteness or sensibility, nor with a high degree of reach and range of mind, but with a singular capacity for careful observation and original reflection, and with a fancy perhaps unmatched in producing various and happy illustration. The most observable of his moral qualities appear to have been prudence and cheerfulness, good nature and easy temper. The influence of his situation and character is visible in his writings. Indulging his own tastes and fancies, like most English squires of his time, he became, like many of them, a sort of humorist. Hence much of his originality and independence ; hence the boldness with which he openly employs illustrations from homely objects. He wrote to please himself more than the public. He had too little regard for readers, either to sacrifice his sincerity to them, or to curb his own prolixity, repetition, and egotism, from the fear of fatiguing them. Hence he became as loose, as rambling, and as much an egotist as Montaigne ; but not so agreeably so, notwithstanding a considerable resemblance of genius ; because he wrote on subjects where disorder and egotism are unseasonable, and for readers whom they disturb instead of amusing. His prolixity at last increased itself, when his work became so long, that repetition in the latter parts partly arose from forgetfulness of the former ; and though his freedom from slavish deference to general opinion is very commendable, it must be owned that his want of a wholesome fear of the public renders the perusal of a work

London, 1799 ? Mr. Stewart treats Tucker and Hartley with unwonted harshness.

which is extremely interesting, and even amusing in most of its parts, on the whole a laborious task. He was by early education a believer in Christianity, if not by natural character religious. His calm good sense and accommodating temper led him rather to explain established doctrines in a manner agreeable to his philosophy, than to assail them. Hence he was represented as a time-server by free-thinkers, and as a heretic by the orthodox.* Living in a country where the secure tranquillity flowing from the Revolution was gradually drawing forth all mental activity towards practical pursuits and outward objects, he hastened from the rudiments of mental and moral philosophy, to those branches of it which touch the business of men.† Had he recast without changing his thoughts—had he detached those ethical observations for which he had so peculiar a vocation, from the disputes of his country and his day—he might have thrown many of his chapters into their proper form of essays, which might have been compared, though not likened, to those of Hume. But the country gentleman, philosophic as he was, had too much fondness for his own humours to engage in a course of drudgery and deference. It may, however, be confidently added, on the authority of all those who have fairly made the experiment, that whoever, unfettered by a previous system, undertakes the labour necessary to discover and relish the high excellences of this metaphysical Montaigne, will find his toil lightened as he proceeds, by a growing indulgence, if not partiality, for the

* This disposition to compromise and accommodation, which is discoverable in Paley, was carried to its utmost length by Mr. Hey, a man of much acuteness, Professor of Divinity at Cambridge.

† Perhaps no philosopher ever stated more justly, more naturally, or more modestly, than Tucker, the ruling maxim of his life. "My thoughts," says he, "have taken a turn from my earliest youth towards searching into the foundations and measures of right and wrong; my love for retirement has furnished me with continual leisure; and the exercise of my reason has been my daily employment."

foibles of the humorist; and at last rewarded, in a greater degree perhaps than by any other writer on mixed and applied philosophy, by being led to commanding stations and new points of view, whence the mind of a moralist can hardly fail to catch some fresh prospects of nature and duty.

It is in mixed, not in pure philosophy, that this superiority consists. In the part of his work which relates to the intellect, he has adopted much from Hartley, hiding but aggravating the offence by a change of technical terms; and he was ungrateful enough to countenance the vulgar sneer which involves the mental analysis of that philosopher in the ridicule to which his physiological hypothesis is liable.* Thus, for the Hartleian term *Association* he substitutes that of *Translation*, when he adopts the same theory of the principles which move the mind to action. In the practical and applicable part of that inquiry, he indeed far surpasses Hartley; and it is little to add, that he unspeakably exceeds that bare and naked thinker in the useful as well as admirable faculty of illustration. In the strictly theoretical part his exposition is considerably fuller; but the defect of his genius becomes conspicuous when he handles a very general principle. The very term *Translation* ought to have kept up in his mind a steady conviction that the secondary motives to action become as independent, and seek their own objects as exclusively, as the primary principles. His own examples are rich in proofs of this important truth. But there is a slippery descent in the Theory of Human Nature, by which he, like most of his forerunners, slid unawares into selfishness. He was not pre-

* *Light of Nature*, I. c. xviii., of which the conclusion may be pointed out as a specimen of perhaps unmatched fruitfulness, vivacity, and felicity of illustration. The admirable sense of the conclusion of chap. xxv. seems to have suggested Paley's good chapter *on Happiness*. The alteration of Plato's comparison of reason to a charioteer, and the passions to the horses, in chap. xxvi., is of characteristic and transcendent excellence.

N

served from this fall by seeing that all the deliberate principles which have self for their object, are themselves of *secondary formation;* and he was led to the general error by the notion that Pleasure, or, as he calls it, Satisfaction, was the original and sole object of all appetites and desires, confounding this with the true but very different proposition, that the attainment of all the objects of appetite and desire is productive of pleasure. He did not see that without presupposing Desires, the word Pleasure would have no signification; and that the representations by which he was seduced would leave only *one appetite* or *desire* in human nature. He had no adequate and constant conception, that the translation of Desire from the end to the means occasioned the formation of a new passion, which is perfectly distinct from, and altogether independent of, the original desire. Too frequently (for he was neither obstinate nor uniform in error) he considered these translations as accidental defects in human nature, not as the appointed means of supplying it with its variety of active principles. He was too apt to speak as if the selfish elements were not destroyed in the new combination, but remained still capable of being recalled, when convenient, like the links in a chain of reasoning, which we pass over from forgetfulness, or for brevity. Take him all in all, however, the neglect of his writings is the strongest proof of the disinclination of the English nation, for the last half-century, to Metaphysical Philosophy.*

* Much of Tucker's chapter *on Pleasure*, and of Paley's *on Happiness* (both of which are invaluable), is contained in the passage of *The Traveller*, of which the following couplet expresses the main object:—

"Unknown to them when sensual pleasures cloy,
To fill the languid pause with finer joy."

"An honest man," says Mr. Hume, "has the frequent satisfaction of seeing knaves betrayed by their own maxims." (*Inquiry into Morals.*)

"I used often to laugh at your honest, simple neighbour Flambo-

WILLIAM PALEY.
Born 1743—died 1805.

THIS excellent writer, who, after Clarke and Butler, ought to be ranked among the brightest ornaments of the English church in the eighteenth century, is, in the history of philosophy, naturally placed after Tucker, to whom, with praiseworthy liberality, he owns his extensive obligations. It is a mistake to suppose that he owed his system to Hume, a thinker too refined, and a writer perhaps too elegant, to have naturally attracted him. A coincidence in the principle of utility, common to both with so many other philosophers, affords no sufficient ground for the supposition. Had he been habitually influenced by Mr. Hume, who has translated so many of the dark and crabbed passages of Butler into his own transparent as well as beautiful language, it is not possible to suppose that such a mind as that of Paley should have fallen into those principles of gross selfishness of which Mr. Hume is a uniform and zealous antagonist.

The natural frame of Paley's understanding fitted it more for business and the world than for philosophy; and he accordingly enjoyed with considerable relish the few opportunities which the latter part of his life afforded, of taking a part in the affairs of his county as a magistrate. Penetration and shrewdness, firmness and coolness, a vein of pleasantry, fruitful though somewhat unrefined, with an original homeliness and significancy of expression, were perhaps more remarkable in his conversation than the restraints of authorship and profession allowed them to be in his writings. Grateful remembrance brings this assemblage of qualities with unfaded

rough, and one way or another generally cheated him once a year. Yet still the honest man went forward without suspicion, and grew rich, while I still continued tricksy and cunning, and was poor without the consolation of being honest." (*Vicar of Wakefield*, chap. xxvi.)

colours before the mind at the present moment, after the long interval of twenty-eight years. His taste for the common business and ordinary amusements of life fortunately gave a zest to the company which his neighbourhood chanced to yield, without rendering him insensible to the pleasures of intercourse with more enlightened society. The practical bent of his nature is visible in the language of his writings, which, on practical matters, is as precise as the nature of the subject requires, but, in his rare and reluctant efforts to rise to first principles, becomes indeterminate and unsatisfactory; though no man's composition was more free from the impediments which hinder a writer's meaning from being quickly and clearly seen. He seldom distinguishes more exactly than is required for palpable and direct usefulness. He possessed that chastised acuteness of discrimination, exercised on the affairs of men, and habitually looking to a purpose beyond the mere increase of knowledge, which forms the character of a lawyer's understanding, and which is apt to render a mere lawyer too subtile for the management of affairs, and yet too gross for the pursuit of general truth. His style is as near perfection in its kind as any in our language. Perhaps no words were ever more expressive and illustrative than those in which he represents the art of life to be that of rightly "setting our habits."

The most original and ingenious of his writings is the *Horæ Paulinæ*. The *Evidences of Christianity* are formed out of an admirable translation of Butler's *Analogy*, and a most skilful abridgment of Lardner's *Credibility of the Gospel History*. He may be said to have thus given value to two works, of which the first was scarcely intelligible to most of those who were most desirous of profiting by it; and the second soon wearies out the greater part of readers, though the few who are more patient have almost always been gradually won over to feel pleasure in a display of knowledge, probity, charity, and meekness, unmatched by an avowed advocate in a case deeply interesting his warmest feelings. His *Natural Theology* is the wonderful work of a man who, after sixty, had studied anatomy in order to write it; and it could only have been surpassed by a man who, to great originality of conception and clearness of exposition, added the advantage of a high place in the first class of physiologists.*

It would be unreasonable here to say much of a work which is in the hands of so many as his *Moral and Political Philosophy.* A very few remarks on one or two parts of it may be sufficient to estimate his value as a moralist, and to show his defects as a metaphysician. His general account of virtue may indeed be chosen for both purposes. The manner in which he deduces the necessary tendency of all virtuous actions to the general happiness, from the goodness of the Divine Lawgiver, though the principle be not, as has already more than once appeared, peculiar to him, but rather common to most religious philosophers, is characterised by a clearness and vigour which have never been surpassed. It is indeed nearly, if not entirely, an identical proposition, that a being of unmixed benevolence will prescribe those laws only to his creatures which contribute to their well-being. When we are convinced that a course of conduct is generally beneficial to all men, we cannot help considering it as acceptable to a benevolent Deity. The usefulness of actions is the mark set on them by the Supreme Legislator, by which reasonable beings discover it to be His will that such actions should be done. In this apparently unanswerable deduction, it is partly admitted, and universally implied, that the principles of right and wrong may be treated apart from the manifestation of them in the Scriptures. If it were otherwise, how could men of perfectly different religions deal or reason with each

* See *Animal Mechanics*, by Mr. Charles Bell, published by the Society for Useful Knowledge.

other on moral subjects? How could they regard rights and duties as subsisting between them? To what common principles could they appeal in their differences? Even the Polytheists themselves, those worshippers of

> Gods partial, changeful, passionate, unjust,
> Whose attributes are rage, revenge, or lust,

by a happy inconsistency are compelled, however irregularly and imperfectly, to ascribe some general enforcement of the moral code to their divinities. If there were no foundation for morality antecedent to revealed religion, we should want that important test of the conformity of a revelation to pure morality, by which its claim to a divine origin is to be tried. The internal evidence of religion necessarily presupposes such a standard. The Christian contrasts the precepts of the Koran with the pure and benevolent morality of the Gospel. The Mahometan claims, with justice, a superiority over the Hindoo, inasmuch as the Mussulman religion inculcates the moral perfection of one Supreme Ruler of the world. The ceremonial and exclusive character of Judaism has ever been regarded as an indication that it was intended to pave the way for a universal religion — a morality seated in the heart, and a worship of sublime simplicity. These discussions would be impossible unless morality were previously proved or granted to exist. Though the science of Ethics is thus far independent, it by no means follows that there is any equality, or that there may not be the utmost inequality, in the moral tendency of religious systems. The most ample scope is still left for the zeal and activity of those who seek to spread important truth. But it is absolutely essential to ethical science that it should contain principles, the authority of which must be recognised by men of every conceivable variety of religious opinion.

The peculiarities of Paley's mind are discoverable in the comparison, or rather contrast, between the practical chapter

on Happiness, and the philosophical portion of the chapter on Virtue. "Virtue is the doing good to mankind, in obedience to the will of God, and for the sake of everlasting happiness."*
It is not perhaps very important to observe, that these words, which he offers as "a definition," ought in propriety to have been called a proposition; but it is much more necessary to say, that they contain a false account of virtue. According to this doctrine, every action not done *for the sake* of the agent's happiness is vicious. Now, it is plain, that an act cannot be said to be done for the sake of anything which is not present to the mind of the agent at the moment of action. It is a contradiction in terms to affirm that a man acts for the sake of any object, of which, however it may be the necessary consequence of his act, he is not at the time fully aware. The *unfelt* consequences of his act can no more influence his will than its *unknown* consequences. Nay, further, a man is only with any propriety said to act for the sake of his chief object; nor can he with entire correctness be said to act for the sake of anything but his sole object. So that it is a necessary consequence of Paley's proposition, that every act which flows from generosity or benevolence is a vice. So also of every act of obedience to the will of GOD, if it arises from any motive but a desire of the reward which he will bestow. Any act of obedience influenced by gratitude and affection, and veneration towards supreme benevolence and perfection, is so far imperfect; and if it arises solely from these motives it becomes a vice. It must be owned that this excellent and most enlightened man has laid the foundations of religion and virtue in a more intense and exclusive selfishness than was avowed by the Catholic enemies of Fénélon, when they persecuted him for his doctrine of a pure and disinterested love of GOD.

In another province, of a very subordinate kind, the dis-

* PALEY, book i. chap. vii.

position of Paley to limit his principles to his own time and country, and to look at them merely as far as they are calculated to amend prevalent vices and errors, betrayed him into narrow and false views. His chapter on what he calls the *Law of Honour* is unjust, even in its own small sphere, because it supposes honour to *allow* what it does *not forbid;* though the truth be, that the vices enumerated by him are only not *forbidden* by honour, because they are not within its jurisdiction. He considers it as "a system of rules constructed by people of fashion;"—a confused and transient mode of expression, which may be understood with difficulty by our posterity, and which cannot now be exactly rendered perhaps in any other language.

The subject, however, thus narrowed and lowered, is neither unimportant in practice, nor unworthy of the consideration of the moral philosopher. Though all mankind honour virtue and despise vice, the degree of respect or contempt is often far from being proportioned to the place which virtues and vices occupy in a just system of Ethics. Wherever higher honour is bestowed on one moral quality than on others of equal or greater moral value, *what is called a point of honour may be said to exist.* It is singular that so shrewd an observer as Paley should not have observed a law of honour far more permanent than that which attracted his notice in the feelings of Europe respecting the conduct of men and women. Cowardice is not so immoral as cruelty, nor indeed so detestable, but it is more despicable and disgraceful. The female point of honour forbids indeed a great vice, but one not so great as many others by which it is not violated. It is easy enough to see, that where we are strongly prompted to a virtue by a natural impulse, we love the man who is constantly actuated by the amiable sentiment, but we do not consider that which is done without difficulty as requiring or deserving admiration and distinction. The kind affections are their own rich reward, and they are the object of affection to others. To encourage kindness by praise would be to insult it, besides its effect in producing counterfeits. It is for the conquest of fear, it would be still more for the conquest of resentment, if that were not, wherever it is real, the cessation of a state of mental agony, that the applause of mankind is reserved. Observations of a similar nature will easily occur to every reader respecting the point of honour in the other sex. The conquest of natural frailties, especially in a case of far more importance to mankind than is at first sight obvious, is well distinguished as an object of honour, and the contrary vice is punished by shame. Honour is not wasted on those who abstain from acts which are punished by the law. These acts may be avoided without a pure motive. Wherever a virtue is easily performed by good men—wherever it is its nature to be attended by delight—wherever its outward observance is so necessary to society as to be enforced by punishment —it is not the proper object of honour. Honour and shame, therefore, may be reasonably dispensed, without being strictly proportioned to the intrinsic morality of actions, if the inequality of their distribution contributes to the general equipoise of the whole moral system.

A wide disproportion, however, or indeed any disproportion not justifiable on moral grounds, would be a depravation of the moral principle. Duelling is among us a disputed case, though the improvement of manners has rendered it so much more infrequent, that it is likely in time to lose its support from opinion. Those who excuse individuals for yielding to a false point of honour, as in the suicides of the Greeks and Romans, may consistently blame the faulty principle, and rejoice in its destruction. The shame fixed on a Hindoo widow of rank who voluntarily survives her husband is regarded by all other nations with horror.

There is room for great praise and some blame in other

parts of Paley's works. His political opinions were those generally adopted by moderate Whigs in his own age. His language on the Revolution of 1688 may be very advantageously compared, both in precision and in generous boldness,* to that of Blackstone, a great master of classical and harmonious composition, but a feeble reasoner and a confused thinker, whose writings are not exempt from the taint of slavishness.

It cannot be denied that Paley was sometimes rather a lax moralist, especially on public duties. It is a sin which easily besets men of strong good sense, little enthusiasm, and much experience. They are naturally led to lower their precepts to the level of their expectations. They see that higher pretensions often produce less good, to say nothing of the hypocrisy, extravagance, and turbulence, to which they lend some colour. As those who claim more from men often gain less, it is natural for more sober and milder casuists to present a more accessible virtue to their followers. It was thus that the Jesuits began, till, strongly tempted by their perilous station as the moral guides of the powerful, some of them by degrees fell into that absolute licentiousness for which all, not without injustice, have been cruelly immortalised by Pascal. Indulgence, which is a great virtue in judgment concerning the actions of others, is too apt, when blended in the same system with the precepts of morality, to be received as a license for our own offences. Accommodation, without which society would be painful, and arduous affairs would become impracticable, is more safely imbibed

* "*Government may be too secure.* The greatest tyrants have been those whose titles were the most unquestioned. Whenever, therefore, the opinion of right becomes too predominant and superstitious *it is abated by breaking the custom.* Thus the Revolution broke the custom of succession, and thereby moderated, both in the prince and in the people, those lofty notions of hereditary right, which in the one were become a continual incentive to tyranny, and disposed the other to invite servitude, by undue compliances and dangerous concessions." (Paley, book vi. chap. ii.)

from temper and experience, than taught in early and systematic instruction. The middle region between laxity and rigour is hard to be fixed, and it is still harder steadily to remain within its boundaries. Whatever may be thought of Paley's observations on political influence and ecclesiastical subscription, as temperaments and mitigations which may preserve us from harsh judgment, they are assuredly not well qualified to form a part of that discipline which ought to breathe into the opening souls of youth, at the critical period of the formation of character, those inestimable virtues of sincerity, of integrity, of independence, which will even guide them *more safely* through life than mere prudence, while they provide an inward fountain of pure delight, immeasurably more abundant than all the outward sources of precarious and perishable pleasure.

JEREMY BENTHAM.
Born 1748.

THE general scheme of this Dissertation would be a sufficient reason for omitting the name of a living writer.* The devoted attachment and invincible repugnance which an impartial estimate of Mr. Bentham has to encounter on either side, are a strong inducement not to deviate from that scheme in his case. But the most brief sketch of ethical controversy, in England would be imperfect without it; and perhaps the utter hopelessness of any expedient for satisfying his followers, or softening his opponents, may enable a writer to look steadily and solely at what he believes to be the dictates of truth and justice. He who has spoken of former philosophers with unreserved freedom, ought perhaps to subject his courage and honesty to the severest test by an attempt to characterise such a contemporary. Should the very few who are at once

* Since dead, 1832.

enlightened and unbiassed be of opinion that his firmness and equity have stood this trial, they will be the more disposed to trust his fairness where the exercise of that quality is more easy.

The disciples of Mr. Bentham are more like the hearers of an Athenian philosopher than the pupils of a modern professor, or the cool proselytes of a modern writer. They are in general men of competent age, of superior understanding, who voluntarily embrace the laborious study of useful and noble sciences; who derive their opinions not so much from the cold perusal of his writings as from familiar converse with a master from whose lips these opinions are recommended by simplicity, disinterestedness, originality, and vivacity; aided rather than impeded by foibles not unamiable, enforced of late by the growing authority of years and of fame, and at all times strengthened by that undoubting reliance on his own judgment which mightily increases the ascendant of such a man over those who approach him. As he and they deserve the credit of braving vulgar prejudices, so they must be content to incur the imputation of falling into the neighbouring vices of seeking distinction by singularity; of clinging to opinions because they are obnoxious; of wantonly wounding the most respectable feelings of mankind; of regarding an immense display of method and nomenclature as a sure token of a corresponding increase of knowledge; and of considering themselves as a chosen few, whom an initiation into the most secret mysteries of philosophy entitles to look down with pity, if not contempt, on the profane multitude. Viewed with aversion or dread by the public, they become more bound to each other and to their master; while they are provoked into the use of language which more and more exasperates opposition to them. A hermit in the greatest of cities, seeing only his disciples, and indignant that systems of government and law which he believes to be perfect are disregarded at once by the many and the powerful, Mr. Bentham has at length been betrayed into the most unphilosophical hypothesis, that all the ruling bodies who guide the community have conspired to stifle and defeat his discoveries. He is too little acquainted with doubts to believe the honest doubts of others, and he is too angry to make allowance for their prejudices and habits. He has embraced the most extreme party in practical politics; manifesting more dislike and contempt towards those who are more moderate supporters of popular principles than towards their most inflexible opponents. To the unpopularity of his philosophical and political doctrines he has added the more general and lasting obloquy which arises from an unseemly treatment of doctrines and principles, which, if there were no other motives for reverential deference, even a regard to the feelings of the best men requires to be approached with decorum and respect.

In the year 1776 occurred the publication of Mr. Bentham's first work, *A Fragment on Government*—a considerable octavo volume, employed in the examination of a short paragraph of Blackstone—unmatched in acute hypercriticism, but conducted with a severity which leads to an unjust estimate of the writer criticised, till the like experiment be repeated on other writings. It was a waste of extraordinary power to employ it in pointing out flaws and patches in the robe occasionally stolen from the philosophical schools, which hung loosely and unbecomingly on the elegant commentator. This volume, and especially the preface, abounds in fine, original, and just observation; it contains the germs of most of his subsequent productions, and it is an early example of that disregard for the method, proportions, and occasion of a writing which, with all common readers, deeply affects its power of interesting or instructing. Two years after, he published a most excellent tract on *The Hard Labour Bill*, which, concurring with the spirit excited by Howard's inquiries, laid the foundation of just reasoning on Reformatory Punishment. The *Letters on Usury** are perhaps the best specimen of the exhaustive discussion of a moral or political question, leaving no objection, however feeble, unanswered, and no difficulty, however small, unexplained; remarkable also for the clearness and spirit of the style, for the full exposition which suits them to all intelligent readers, for the tender and skilful hand with which prejudice is touched, and for the urbanity of his admirable apology for projectors, addressed to Dr. Smith, whose temper and manner he seems for a time to have imbibed. The *Introduction to the Principles of Morals and Politics,* printed before the *Letters,* but published after them, was the first sketch of his system, and is still the only account of it by himself.

The great merit of this work, and of his other writings in relation to *Jurisprudence* properly so called, is not within

---

* They were addressed to Mr. George Wilson, who retired from the English bar to his native country, and died at Edinburgh in 1816; an early friend of Mr. Bentham, and afterwards an intimate friend of Lord Ellenborough, Sir Vicary Gibbs, and of all the most eminent of his professional contemporaries. The rectitude of judgment, purity of heart, elevation of honour, the sternness only in integrity, the scorn of baseness, and indulgence towards weakness, which were joined in him with a gravity exclusive neither of feeling nor of pleasantry, contributed still more than his abilities and attainments of various sorts to a moral authority with his friends, and in his profession, which few men more amply possessed, or more usefully exercised. The same character, somewhat softened, and the same influence, distinguished his closest friend, the late Mr. Lens. Both were inflexible and incorruptible friends of civil and religious liberty, and both knew how to reconcile the warmest zeal for that sacred cause, with a charity towards their opponents, which partisans, often more violent than steady, treated as lukewarm. The present writer hopes that the good-natured reader will excuse him for having thus, perhaps unseasonably, bestowed heartfelt commendation on those who were above the pursuit of praise, and the remembrance of whose good opinion and good-will helps to support him under a deep sense of faults and vices.

our present scope. To the Roman jurists belongs the praise of having allotted a separate portion of their digest to the signification of the words of most frequent use in law and legal discussion.* Bentham not only first perceived and taught the great value of an introductory section, composed of definitions of general terms, as subservient to brevity and precision in every part of a code, but he also discovered the unspeakable importance of natural arrangement in jurisprudence, by rendering the mere place of a proposed law in such an arrangement a short and easy test of the fitness of the proposal.† But here he does not distinguish between the value of arrangement as scaffolding, and the inferior convenience of its being the very framework of the structure. Mr. Bentham, indeed, is much more remarkable for laying down desirable rules for the determination of rights, and the punishment of wrongs, in general, than for weighing the various circumstances which require them to be modified in different countries and times, in order to render them either more useful, more easily introduced, more generally respected, or more certainly executed. The art of legislation consists in thus applying the principles of jurisprudence to the situation,

---

* Digest, lib. 1. tit. 16. *De Verborum Significatione.*

† See a beautiful article on Codification, in the *Edinburgh Review*, vol. xxix. p. 217. It needs no longer be concealed that it was contributed by Sir Samuel Romilly. The steadiness with which he held the balance in weighing the merits of his friend against his unfortunate defects, is an example of his union of the most commanding moral principle with a sensibility so warm, that, if it had been released from that stern authority, it would not so long have endured the coarseness and roughness of human concerns. From the tenderness of his feelings, and from an anger never roused but by cruelty and baseness, as much as from his genius and his pure taste, sprung that original and characteristic eloquence, which was the hope of the afflicted as well as the terror of the oppressor. If his oratory had not flowed so largely from this moral source, which years do not dry up, he would not perhaps have been the only example of an orator who, after the age of sixty, daily increased in polish, in vigour, and in splendour.

wants, interests, feelings, opinions, and habits of each distinct community at any given time. It bears the same relation to jurisprudence which the mechanical arts bear to pure mathematics. Many of these considerations serve to show that the sudden establishment of new codes can seldom be practicable or effectual for their purpose; and that reformations, though founded on the principles of jurisprudence, ought to be not only adapted to the peculiar interests of a people, but engrafted on their previous usages, and brought into harmony with those national dispositions on which the execution of laws depends.* The Romans, under Justinian, adopted at least the true principle, if they did not apply it with sufficient freedom and boldness. They considered the multitude of occasional laws, and the still greater mass of usages, opinions, and determinations, as the materials of legislation, not precluding, but demanding a systematic arrangement of the whole by the supreme authority. Had the arrangement been more scientific, had there been a bolder examination and a more free reform of many particular branches, a model would have been offered for liberal imitation by modern lawgivers. It cannot be denied, without injustice and ingratitude, that Mr. Bentham has done more than any other writer to rouse the spirit of juridical reformation, which is now gradually examining every part of law, and, when further progress is facilitated by digesting the present laws, will doubtless proceed to the improvement of all. Greater praise it is given to few to earn. It ought to satisfy Mr. Bentham, for the disappointment of hopes which were not reasonable, that Russia should receive a code from him, or that North America could be brought to renounce the variety of her laws and institutions,

---

* An excellent medium between those who absolutely require new codes, and those who obstinately adhere to ancient usages, has been pointed out by M. Meyer, in his most justly celebrated work, *Institutions Judiciaires des Principaux Pays de l'Europe*, tome i. Introduction, pp. 8, 9. La Haye et Amst. 1819-23, 6 vols. 8vo.

on the single authority of a foreign philosopher, whose opinions had not worked their way either into legislation or into general reception in his own country. It ought also to dispose his followers to do fuller justice to the Romillys and Broughams, without whose prudence and energy, as well as reason and eloquence, the best plans of reformation must have continued a dead letter—for whose sake it might have been fit to reconsider the obloquy heaped on their profession, and to show more general indulgence to all those whose chief offence seems to consist in their doubts whether sudden changes, almost always imposed by violence on a community, be the surest road to lasting improvement.

It is unfortunate that Ethical Theory, with which we are now chiefly concerned, is not the province in which Mr. Bentham has reached the most desirable distinction. It may be remarked, both in ancient and in modern times, that whatever modifications prudent followers may introduce into the system of an innovator, the principles of the Master continue to mould the habitual dispositions, and to influence the practical tendency, of the School. Mr. Bentham preaches the principle of utility with the zeal of a discoverer. Occupied more in reflection than in reading, he knew not, or forgot, how often it had been the basis, and how generally an essential part, of moral systems.* That in which he really differs from others, is in the necessity which he teaches, and the example which he sets, of constantly bringing that principle before us. This peculiarity appears to us to be his radical error. In an attempt of which the constitution of human nature forbids the success, he seems to us to have been led into fundamental errors in moral theory, and to have given to his practical doctrine a dangerous taint.

The confusion of *moral approbation* with the *moral qualities* which are its objects, common to Mr. Bentham with

* See Notes and Illustrations, Note V.

many other philosophers, is much more uniform and prominent in him than in most others. This general error, already mentioned at the opening of this volume, has led him more than others to assume, that because the principle of utility forms a necessary part of every moral theory, it ought therefore to be the chief motive of human conduct. Now it is evident that this assumption, rather tacitly than avowedly made, is wholly gratuitous. No practical conclusion can be deduced from the principle, but that we ought to cultivate those habitual dispositions which are the most effectual motives to useful actions. But before a regard to our own interest, or a desire to promote the welfare of men in general, be allowed to be the exclusive, or even the chief regulators of human conduct, it must be shown that they are the most effectual motives to such useful actions. It is demonstrated by experience that they are not. It is even owned by the most ingenious writers of Mr. Bentham's school, that desires which are pointed to general and distant objects, although they have their proper place and their due value, are commonly very faint and ineffectual inducements to action. A theory founded on utility, therefore, requires that we should cultivate, as excitements to practice, those other habitual dispositions which we know by experience to be generally the source of actions beneficial to ourselves and our fellows; habits of feeling, productive of habits of virtuous conduct, and in their turns strengthened by the reaction of these last. What is the result of experience on the choice of the objects of moral culture? Beyond all dispute, that we should labour to attain that state of mind in which all the social affections are felt with the utmost warmth, giving birth to more comprehensive benevolence, but not supplanted by it; when the moral sentiments most strongly approve what is right and good, without being perplexed by a calculation of consequences, though not incapable of being gradually rectified by reason, whenever they are decisively proved by experience not to correspond in some of their parts to the universal and perpetual effects of conduct. It is a false representation of human nature to affirm that "courage" is only "prudence." * They coincide in their effects, and it is always prudent to be courageous. But a man who fights *because* he thinks it more hazardous to yield, is not brave. He does not become brave till he feels cowardice to be base and painful, and till he is no longer in need of any aid from *prudence*. Even if it were the *interest* of every man to be bold, it is clear that so cold a consideration cannot prevail over the fear of danger. Where it seems to do so, it must be by the unseen power either of the fear of shame, or of some other powerful passion, to which it lends its name. It was long ago, with striking justice, observed by Aristotle, that he who abstains from present gratification, under a distinct apprehension of its painful consequences, is only *prudent*, and that he must acquire a disrelish for excess on its own account, before he deserves the name of a temperate man. It is only when the means are firmly and unalterably converted into ends, that the process of forming the mind is completed. Courage may then seek, instead of avoiding danger. Temperance may prefer abstemiousness to indulgence. Prudence itself may choose an orderly government of conduct, according to certain rules, without regard to the degree in which it promotes welfare. Benevolence must desire the happiness of others, to the exclusion of the consideration how far it is connected with that of the

---

* Mr. Mill's *Analysis of the Human Mind*, vol. ii. p. 237. It would be unjust not to say that this book, partly perhaps from a larger adoption of the principles of Hartley, holds out fairer opportunities of negotiation with natural feelings and the doctrines of former philosophers, than any other production of the same school. But this very assertion about courage clearly shows at least a forgetfulness that courage, even if it were the offspring of prudence, would not for that reason be a species of it.

benevolent agent; and those alone can be accounted just who obey the dictates of justice from having thoroughly learned an habitual veneration for its strict rules and for its larger precepts. In that complete state the mind possesses no power of dissolving the combinations of thought and feeling which impel it to action. Nothing in this argument turns on the difference between implanted and acquired principles. As no man can cease, by any act of his, to *see* distance, though the power of seeing it be universally acknowledged to be an acquisition; so no man has the power to extinguish the affections and the moral sentiments, however much they may be thought to be acquired, any more than that of eradicating the bodily appetites. The best writers of Mr. Bentham's school overlook the indissolubility of these associations, and appear not to bear in mind that their strength and rapid action constitute the perfect state of a moral agent.

The pursuit of our own general welfare, or of that of mankind at large, though from their vagueness and coldness they are unfit habitual motives and unsafe ordinary guides of conduct, yet perform functions of essential importance in the moral system. The former, which we call self-love, preserves the balance of all the active principles which regard ourselves ultimately, and contributes to subject them to the authority of the moral principles.* The latter, which is general benevolence, regulates in like manner the equipoise of the narrower affections; quickens the languid, and checks the encroaching; borrows strength from pity, and even from indignation; receives some compensation, as it enlarges, in the addition of beauty and grandeur, for the weakness which arises from dispersion; enables us to look on all men as brethren, and overflows on every sentient being. The general interest of mankind in truth almost solely affects us through the affections of benevolence and sympathy; for the coincidence of

* See Notes and Illustrations, Note W.

general with individual interest, even where it is certain, is too dimly seen to produce any emotion which can impel to or restrain from action. As a general truth, its value consists in its completing the triumph of morality, by demonstrating the absolute impossibility of forming any theory of human nature which does not preserve the superiority of virtue over vice; a great, though not a directly practical advantage.

The followers of Mr. Bentham have carried to an unusual extent the prevalent fault of the more modern advocates of utility, who have dwelt so exclusively on the outward advantages of virtue as to have lost sight of the delight which is a part of virtuous feeling, and of the beneficial influence of good actions upon the frame of the mind. "Benevolence towards others," says Mr. Mill, "produces a return of benevolence from them."* The fact is true, and ought to be stated. But how unimportant is it in comparison with that which is passed over in silence, the pleasure of the affection itself, which if it could become lasting and intense, would convert the heart into a heaven! No one who has ever felt kindness, if he could accurately recall his feelings, could hesitate about their infinite superiority. The cause of the general neglect of this consideration is, that it is only when a gratification is something distinct from a state of mind, that we can easily learn to consider it as a pleasure. Hence the great error respecting the affections, where the *inherent* delight is not duly estimated, on account of that very peculiarity of being a part of a state of mind, which renders it unspeakably more valuable as independent of every thing without. The social affections are the only principles of human nature which have no direct pains. To have any of these desires is to be in a state of happiness. The malevolent passions have properly no pleasures; for that attainment of their purpose which is improperly so called, consists only in healing or assuaging the torture

* *Analysis of the Human Mind*, vol. ii.

which envy, jealousy, and malice, inflict on the malignant mind. It might with as much propriety be said that the toothache and the stone have pleasures, because their removal is followed by an agreeable feeling. These bodily disorders, indeed, are often cured by the process which removes the suffering; but the mental distempers of envy and revenge are nourished by every act of odious indulgence which for a moment suspends their pain.

The same observation is applicable to every virtuous disposition, though not so obviously as to the benevolent affections. That a brave man is, on the whole, far less exposed to danger than a coward, is not the chief advantage of a courageous temper. Great dangers are rare; but the constant absence of such painful and mortifying sensations as those of fear, and the steady consciousness of superiority to what subdues ordinary men, are the perpetual source of inward enjoyment. No man who has ever been visited by a gleam of magnanimity can place any outward advantage of fortitude in comparison with the feeling of being always able fearlessly to defend a righteous cause.* Even *Humility*, in spite of first appearances, is a remarkable example. It has of late been unwarrantably used to signify that painful consciousness of inferiority which is the first stage of envy.† It is a term consecrated in Christian ethics to denote that disposition which, by inclining towards a modest estimate of our qualities, corrects the prevalent tendency of human nature to overvalue our merits and to overrate our claims. What can be a less

---

* According to Cicero's definition of fortitude, "*Virtus pugnans pro æquitate.*" The remains of the original sense of *Virtus*, Manhood, give a beauty and force to these expressions which cannot be preserved in our language. The Greek Ἀρετή, and the German *Tugend*, originally denoted *Strength*, afterwards *Courage*, and at last *Virtue*. But the happy derivation of *Virtus* from *Vir* gives an energy to the phrase of Cicero, which illustrates the use of etymology in the hands of a skilful writer.

† Mr. Mill's *Analysis of the Human Mind*, vol. ii. p. 222.

doutful or a much more considerable blessing than this constant sedative, which soothes and composes the irritable passions of vanity and pride? What is more conducive to lasting peace of mind than the consciousness of proficiency in that most delicate species of equity which, in the secret tribunal of conscience, labours to be impartial in the comparison of ourselves with others? What can so perfectly assure us of the purity of our moral sense, as the habit of contemplating, not that excellence which we have reached, but that which is still to be pursued;* of not considering how far we may outrun others, but how far we are from the goal?

Virtue has often outward advantages, and always inward delights; but the second, though constant, strong, inaccessible, and inviolable, are not easily considered by the common observer as apart from the virtue with which they are blended. They are so subtile and evanescent as to escape the distinct contemplation of all but the very few who meditate on the acts of mind. The outward advantages, on the other hand, cold, uncertain, dependent, and precarious as they are, yet stand out to the sense and to the memory, may be handled, and counted, and are perfectly on a level with the general apprehension. Hence they have become the almost exclusive theme of all moralists who profess to follow reason. There is room for suspecting that a very general illusion prevails on this subject. Probably the smallest part of the pleasure of virtue, because it is the most palpable, has become the sign and mental representative of the whole. The outward and visible sign suggests insensibly the inward and mental delight. Those who display the external benefits of magnanimity and kindness, would speak with far less fervour, and perhaps less confidence, if their feelings were not unconsciously affected by

* For a description of vanity by a great orator, see the Rev. R. Hall's *Sermon on Modern Infidelity.*

the mental state which they overlook in their statements, though they feel some part of it when they write or speak on it. When they speak of what is *without*, they feel what was *within*, and their words excite the same feeling in others.

Is it not probable that much of our love of praise may be thus ascribed to humane and sociable pleasure in the sympathy of others with us? Praise is the symbol which represents sympathy, and which the mind insensibly substitutes for it in recollection and in language. Does not the desire of posthumous fame, in like manner, manifest an ambition for the fellow-feeling of our race, when it is perfectly unproductive of any advantage to ourselves? In this point of view it may be considered as the passion of which the very existence proves the mighty power of disinterested desire. Every other pleasure from sympathy is confined to the men who are now alive. The love of fame alone seeks the sympathy of unborn generations, and stretches the chain which binds the race of man together, to an extent to which hope sets no bounds. There is a noble, even if unconscious, union of morality with genius in the mind of him who sympathises with the masters who lived twenty centuries before him, in order that he may learn to command the sympathies of the countless generations who are to come.

In the most familiar, as well as in the highest instances, it would seem that the inmost thoughts and sentiments of men are more pure than their language. Those who speak of "a regard to character," if they be serious, generally infuse into that word, unawares, a large portion of that sense in which it denotes the frame of the mind. Those who speak of "honour" very often mean a more refined and delicate sort of conscience, which ought to render the more educated classes of society alive to such smaller wrongs as the laborious and the ignorant can scarcely feel. What heart does not warm at the noble exclamation of the ancient poet: "Who is pleased by false honour, or frightened by lying infamy, but he who is false and depraved!" Every uncorrupted mind feels unmerited praise as a bitter reproach, and regards a consciousness of demerit as a drop of poison in the cup of honour. How different is the applause which truly delights us all, a proof that the consciences of others are in harmony with our own! "What," says Cicero, "is glory but the concurring praise of the good, the unbought approbation of those who judge aright of excellent virtue?" A far greater than Cicero rises from the purest praise of man, to more sublime contemplations.

> Fame is no plant that grows on mortal soil,
> But lives and spreads aloft, by those pure eyes
> And perfect witness of all-judging Jove.

Those who have most inculcated the doctrine of utility have given another notable example of the very vulgar prejudice which treats the unseen as insignificant. Tucker is the only one of them who occasionally considers that most important effect of human conduct which consists in its action on the frame of the mind, by fitting its faculties and sensibilities for their appointed purpose. A razor or a penknife would well enough cut cloth or meat; but if they were often so used, they would be entirely spoiled. The same sort of observation is much more strongly applicable to habitual dispositions, which, if they be spoiled, we have no certain means of replacing or mending. Whatever act, therefore, discomposes the moral machinery of mind, is more injurious to the welfare of the agent than most disasters from without can be, for the latter are commonly limited and temporary; the evil of the former spreads through the whole of life. Health of mind as well as of body is not only productive in itself of a greater sum of enjoyment than arises from other sources, but it is the only condition of our frame in which we are capable of receiving pleasure from without. Hence it appears how incredibly absurd it is to prefer, on grounds of calculation, a present interest to the preservation of those mental habits on which our well-being depends. When they are most moral, they may often prevent us from obtaining advantages. It would be as absurd to desire to lower them for that reason, as it would be to weaken the body, lest its strength should render it more liable to contagious disorders of rare occurrence.

It is, on the other hand, impossible to combine the benefit of the general habit with the advantages of occasional deviation; for every such deviation either produces remorse, or weakens the habit, and prepares the way for its gradual destruction. He who obtains a fortune by the undetected forgery of a will may indeed be honest in his other acts; but if he had such a scorn of fraud before as he must himself allow to be generally useful, he must suffer a severe punishment from contrition; and he will be haunted with the fears of one who has lost his own security for his good conduct. In all cases, if they be well examined, his loss by the distemper of his mental frame will outweigh the profits of his vice.

By repeating the like observation on similar occasions, it will be manifest that the infirmity of recollection, aggravated by the defects of language, gives an appearance of more selfishness to man than truly belongs to his nature; and that the effect of active agents upon the habitual state of mind, one of the considerations to which the epithet "sentimental" has of late been applied in derision, is really among the most serious and reasonable objects of moral philosophy. When the internal pleasures and pains which *accompany* good and bad feelings, or rather form a part of them, and the internal advantages and disadvantages which *follow* good and bad actions, are sufficiently considered, the comparative importance of *outward consequences* will be more and more narrowed; so that the Stoical philosopher may be thought almost excusable for rejecting it altogether, were it not an indispensably necessary consideration for those in whom right habits of feeling are not sufficiently strong. They alone are happy, or even truly virtuous, who have little need of it.

The latter moralists who adopt the principle of utility, have so *misplaced* it, that in their hands it has as great a tendency as any theoretical error can have to lessen the intrinsic pleasure of virtue, and to unfit our habitual feelings for being the most effectual inducements to good conduct. This is the natural tendency of a discipline which brings utility too closely and frequently into contact with action. By this habit, in its best state, an essentially weaker motive is gradually substituted for others which must always be of more force. The frequent appeal to utility as the standard of action tends to introduce an uncertainty with respect to the conduct of other men, which would render all intercourse insupportable. It affords also so fair a disguise for selfish and malignant passions, as often to hide their nature from him who is their prey. Some taint of these mean and evil principles will at least creep in, and by their venom give an animation not its own to the cold desire of utility. The moralists who take an active part in those affairs which often call out unamiable passions, ought to guard with peculiar watchfulness against such self-delusions. The sin that must most easily beset them, is that of sliding from general to particular consequences—that of trying single actions instead of dispositions, habits, and rules, by the standard of utility— that of authorising too great a latitude for discretion and policy in moral conduct—that of readily allowing exceptions to the most important rules—that of too lenient a censure of the use of doubtful means when the end seems to them good —and that of believing unphilosophically, as well as dangerously, that there can be any measure or scheme so useful to the world as the existence of men who would not do a base thing for any public advantage. It was said of Andrew

Fletcher, "he would lose his life to *serve* his country, but would not do a base thing to *save* it." Let those preachers of utility who suppose that such a man sacrifices *ends* to *means*, consider whether the scorn of baseness be not akin to the contempt of danger, and whether a nation composed of such men would not be invincible. But theoretical principles are counteracted by a thousand causes, which confine their mischief as well as circumscribe their benefits. Men are never so good or so bad as their opinions. All that can be with reason apprehended is, that they may always produce some part of their natural evil, and that the mischief will be greatest among the many who seek excuses for these passions. Aristippus found in the Socratic representation of the union of virtue and happiness a pretext for sensuality; and many Epicureans became voluptuaries in spite of the example of their master; easily dropping by degrees the limitations by which he guarded his doctrines. In proportion as a man accustoms himself to be influenced by the utility of particular acts, without regard to rules, he approaches to the casuistry of the Jesuits, and to the practical maxims of Cæsar Borgia.

Injury on this as on other occasions has been suffered by *Ethics*, from its close affinity to *Jurisprudence*. The true and eminent merit of Mr. Bentham is that of a reformer of jurisprudence. He is only a moralist with a view to being a jurist; and he sometimes becomes for a few hurried moments a metaphysician with a view to laying the foundation of both the moral sciences. Both he and his followers have treated Ethics too *juridically*. They do not seem to be aware, or at least they do not bear constantly in mind, that there is an essential difference in the subjects of these two sciences.

The object of law is the prevention of actions injurious to the community. It considers the dispositions from which they flow only *indirectly*, to ascertain the likelihood of their recurrence, and thus to determine the necessity and the means of preventing them. The *direct* object of Ethics is only mental disposition. It considers actions *indirectly* as the signs by which such dispositions are manifested. If it were possible for the mere moralist to see that a moral and amiable temper was the mental source of a bad action, he could not cease to approve and love the temper, as we sometimes presume to suppose may be true of the judgments of the Searcher of Hearts. Religion necessarily coincides with morality in this respect; and it is the peculiar distinction of Christianity that it places the seat of virtue in the heart. Law and Ethics are necessarily so much blended, that in many intricate combinations the distinction becomes obscure. But in all strong cases the difference is evident. Thus law punishes the most sincerely repentant; but wherever the soul of the penitent can be thought to be thoroughly purified, religion and morality receive him with open arms. .

It is needless, after these remarks, to observe, that those whose habitual contemplation is directed to the rules of action are likely to underrate the importance of feeling and disposition; an error of very unfortunate consequences, since the far greater part of human actions flow from these neglected sources; while the law interposes only in cases which may be called exceptions, which are now rare, and ought to be less frequent.

The coincidence of Mr. Bentham's school with the ancient Epicureans in the disregard of the pleasures of taste and of the arts dependent on imagination, is a proof both of the inevitable adherence of much of the popular sense of the words "interest" and "pleasure," to the same words in their philosophical acceptation, and of the pernicious influence of narrowing "utility" to mere visible and tangible objects, to the exclusion of those which form the larger part of human enjoyment.

The mechanical philosophers who, under Descartes and Gassendi, began to reform Physics in the seventeenth century, attempted to explain all the appearances of nature by an immediate reference to the figure of particles of matter impelling each other in various directions, and with unequal force, but in all other points alike. The communication of motion by impulse they conceived to be perfectly simple and intelligible. It never occurred to them, that the movement of one ball when another is driven against it, is a fact of which no explanation can be given which will amount to more than a statement of its constant occurrence. That no body can act where it is not, appeared to them as self-evident as that the whole is equal to all the parts. By this axiom they understood that no body moves another without touching it. They did not perceive that it was only self-evident where it means that no body can act *where it has not the power of acting;* and that if it be understood more largely, it is a mere assumption of the proposition on which their whole system rested. Sir Isaac Newton reformed Physics, not by simplifying that science, but by rendering it much more complicated. He introduced into it the force of attraction, of which he ascertained many laws, but which even he did not dare to represent as being as intelligible and as conceivably ultimate as impulsion itself. It was necessary for Laplace to introduce intermediate laws, and to calculate disturbing forces, before the phenomena of the heavenly bodies could be reconciled even to Newton's more complex theory.* In the present state of physical and chemical knowledge, a man who should attempt to refer all the immense variety of facts to the simple impulse of the Cartesians, would have no chance of serious confutation. The number of laws augments with the progress of knowledge. The speculations of the followers of Mr. Bentham are

* [This does not describe accurately the offices of Newton and Laplace in the history of astronomical theory. Laplace did not introduce new intermediate laws or disturbing forces, but only new *modes of calculating* the effect of the laws and disturbing forces which Newton had discovered.—W. W.]

not unlike the unsuccessful attempt of the Cartesians. Mr. Mill, for example, derives the whole theory of Government* from the single fact, that every man pursues his interest when he knows it; which he assumes to be a sort of self-evident practical principle, if such a phrase be not contradictory. That a man's pursuing the interest of another, or indeed any other object in nature, is just as *conceivable* as that he should pursue his own interest, is a proposition which seems never to have occurred to this acute and ingenious writer. Nothing, however, can be more certain than its truth, if the term "interest" be employed in its proper sense of general well-being, which is the only acceptation in which it can serve the purpose of his arguments. If, indeed, the term be employed to denote the gratification of a predominant desire, his proposition is self-evident, but wholly unserviceable in his argument; for it is clear that individuals and multitudes often desire what they know to be most inconsistent with their general welfare. A nation, as much as an individual, and sometimes more, may not only mistake its interest, but, perceiving it clearly, may prefer the gratification of a strong passion to it.† The whole fabric of his political reasoning seems to be overthrown by this single observation; and instead of attempting to explain the immense variety of political facts by the simple principle of a contest of interests, we are reduced to the necessity of once more referring them to that variety of passions, habits, opinions, and prejudices, which we discover only by experience. Mr. Mill's *Essay on Education*‡ affords another example of the inconvenience of leaping at once from the most general laws to a multiplicity of minute appearances.

* *Essay on Government*, originally printed in the Supplement to the fourth, fifth, and sixth editions of the Encyclopædia Britannica.

† The same mode of reasoning has been adopted by the writer of a late criticism on Mill's *Essay*. [Written by Lord Macaulay.—W. W.] See *Edinburgh Review*, No. 97, March 1829.

‡ In the Supplement to the Encyclopædia Britannica.

Having assumed, or at least inferred from insufficient premises, that the intellectual and moral character is entirely formed by circumstances, he proceeds in the latter part of the essay, as if it were a necessary consequence of that doctrine that we might easily acquire the power of combining and directing circumstances in such a manner as to produce the best possible character. Without disputing for the present the theoretical proposition, let us consider what would be the reasonableness of similar expectations in a more easily intelligible case. The general theory of the winds is pretty well understood; we know that they proceed from the rushing of air from those portions of the atmosphere which are more condensed, into those which are more rarefied; but how great a chasm is there between that simple law and the great variety of facts which experience teaches us respecting winds! The constant winds between the Tropics are large and regular enough to be in some measure capable of explanation; but who can tell why, in variable climates, the wind blows to-day from the east, to-morrow from the west? Who can foretell what its shiftings and variations are to be? Who can account for a tempest on one day, and a calm on another? Even if we could foretell the irregular and infinite variations, how far might we not still be from the power of combining and guiding their causes? No man but the lunatic in the story of Rasselas ever dreamt that he could command the weather. The difficulty plainly consists in the multiplicity and minuteness of the circumstances which act on the atmosphere. Are those which influence the formation of the human character likely to be less minute and multiplied?

The style of Mr. Bentham underwent a more remarkable revolution than perhaps befell that of any other celebrated writer. In his early works, it was clear, free, spirited, often and seasonably eloquent. Many passages of his later writings retain the inimitable stamp of genius; but he seems to have been oppressed by the vastness of his projected works—to have thought that he had no longer more than leisure to preserve the heads of them—to have been impelled by a fruitful mind to new plans before he had completed the old. In this state of things, he gradually ceased to use words for conveying his thoughts to others, but merely employed them as a short-hand, to preserve his meaning for his own purpose. It was no wonder that his language should thus become obscure and repulsive. Though many of his technical terms are in themselves exact and pithy, yet the overflow of his vast nomenclature was enough to darken his whole diction.

It was at this critical period that the arrangement and translation of his manuscripts were undertaken by M. Dumont, a generous disciple, who devoted a genius formed for original and lasting works to diffuse the principles and promote the fame of his master. He whose pen Mirabeau did not disdain to borrow—who in the same school with Romilly had studiously pursued the grace as well as the force of composition—was perfectly qualified to strip of its uncouthness a philosophy which he understood and admired. As he wrote in a general language, he propagated its doctrines throughout Europe, where they were beneficial to jurisprudence, but perhaps injurious to the cause of reformation in government. That they became more popular abroad than at home, is partly to be ascribed to the taste and skill of M. Dumont; partly to that tendency towards free speculation and bold reform which was more prevalent among nations newly freed, or impatiently aspiring to freedom, than in a people long satisfied with the possession of a system of government like that which others were struggling to obtain, and not yet aware of the imperfections and abuses in their laws, to the amendment of which a cautious consideration of Mr. Bentham's works will undoubtedly most materially contribute.

P

DUGALD STEWART.
Born 1753—died 1828.

MANIFOLD are the discouragements, rising up at every step in that part of this Dissertation which extends to very recent times. No sooner does the writer escape from the angry disputes of the living, than he may feel his mind clouded by the name of a departed friend. But there are happily men whose fame is brightened by free discussion, and to whose memory an appearance of belief that they needed tender treatment would be a grosser injury than it could suffer from a respectable antagonist.

Dugald Stewart was the son of Dr. Matthew Stewart, Professor of Mathematics in the University of Edinburgh; a station immediately before filled by Maclaurin, on the recommendation of Newton. Hence the poet spoke of "the philosophic sire and son."[*] He was educated at Edinburgh, and he heard the lectures of Reid at Glasgow. He was early associated with his father in the duties of the Mathematical Professorship; and during the absence of Dr. Adam Ferguson as Secretary to the Commissioners sent to conclude a peace with North America, he occupied the chair of Moral Philosophy. He was appointed to the Professorship on the resignation of Ferguson, not the least distinguished among the modern moralists inclined to the Stoical school.

This office, filled in immediate succession by Ferguson, Stewart, and Brown, received a lustre from their names, which it owed in no degree to its modest exterior, or its limited advantages; and was rendered by them the highest dignity, in the humble, but not obscure, establishments of Scottish literature. The lectures of Mr. Stewart, for a quarter of a century, rendered it famous through every

[*] Burns.

country where the light of reason was allowed to penetrate. Perhaps few men ever lived, who poured into the breasts of youth a more fervid and yet reasonable love of liberty, of truth, and of virtue. How many are still alive, in different countries, and in every rank to which education reaches, who, if they accurately examined their own minds and lives, would ascribe much of whatever goodness and happiness they possess, to the early impressions of his gentle and persuasive eloquence! He lived to see his disciples distinguished among the lights and ornaments of the council and the senate.* He had the consolation to be sure that no words of his promoted the growth of an impure taste, of an exclusive prejudice, of a malevolent passion. Without derogation from his writings, it may be said that his disciples were among his best works.

* As an example of Mr. Stewart's school may be mentioned Francis Horner, a favourite pupil, and, till his last moment, an affectionate friend. The short life of this excellent person is worthy of serious contemplation, by those, more especially, who, in circumstances like his, enter on the slippery path of public affairs. Without the aids of birth or fortune, in an assembly where aristocratical propensities prevail—by his understanding, industry, pure taste, and useful information—still more by modest independence, by steadiness and sincerity, joined to moderation—by the stamp of unbending integrity, and by the conscientious considerateness which breathed through his well-chosen language—he raised himself, at the early age of thirty-six, to a moral *authority* which, without these qualities, no brilliancy of talents or power of reasoning could have acquired. No eminent speaker in Parliament owed so much of his success to his moral *character*. His high place was therefore honourable to his audience and to his country. Regret for his death was expressed with touching unanimity from every part of a divided assembly, unused to manifestations of sensibility, abhorrent from theatrical display, and whose tribute on such an occasion derived its peculiar value from their general coldness and sluggishness. The tears of those to whom he was unknown were shed over him : and at the head of those by whom he was "praised, wept, and honoured," was one, whose commendation would have been more enhanced in the eye of Mr. Horner, by his discernment and veracity, than by the signal proof of the concurrence of all orders, as well as parties, which was afforded by the name of Howard.

He, indeed, who may justly be said to have cultivated an extent of mind which would otherwise have lain barren, and to have contributed to raise virtuous dispositions where the natural growth might have been useless or noxious, is not less a benefactor of mankind, and may *indirectly* be a larger contributor to knowledge, than the author of great works, or even the discoverer of important truths. The system of conveying scientific instruction to a large audience by lectures, from which the English universities have in a great measure departed, renders his qualities as a lecturer a most important part of his merit in a Scottish university, which still adheres to the general method of European education. Probably no modern ever exceeded him in that species of eloquence which springs from sensibility to literary beauty and moral excellence; which neither obscures science by prodigal ornament, nor disturbs the serenity of patient attention; but though it rather calms and soothes the feelings, yet exalts the genius, and insensibly inspires a reasonable enthusiasm for whatever is good and fair.

He embraced the philosophy of Dr. Reid, a patient, modest, and deep thinker,* who, in his first work (*Enquiry*

---

* Those who may doubt the justice of this description will do well to weigh the words of the most competent of judges, who, though candid and even indulgent, was not prodigal of praise. " It is certainly very rare that a piece so *deeply philosophical* is wrote with so much spirit, and affords so much entertainment to the reader. Whenever I enter into your ideas, no man appears to express himself with greater perspicuity. Your style is so correct, and so good English, that I found not any thing worth the remarking. I beg my compliments to my friendly adversaries Dr. Campbell and Dr. Gerard, and also to Dr. Gregory, whom I suspect to be of the same disposition, though he has not openly declared himself such." (*Letter from Mr. Hume to Dr. Reid*: STEWART's *Biographical Memoirs*, p. 417.)

The latter part of the above sentences (written after a perusal of the proof-sheets of Dr. Reid's *Enquiry*, but before its publication) sufficiently shows that Mr. Hume felt no displeasure against Reid and Campbell, undoubtedly his most formidable antagonists, however he

into the Human Mind), deserves a commendation more descriptive of a philosopher than that bestowed by Professor Cousin—of having made "a vigorous protest against scepticism on behalf of common sense." His observations on suggestion, on natural signs, on the connection between what he calls sensation and perception, though perhaps occasioned by Berkeley, whose idealism Reid had once adopted, are marked by the genuine spirit of original observation. As there are too many who seem more wise than they are, so it was the more uncommon fault of Reid to appear less a philosopher than he really was. Indeed his temporary adoption of Berkeleianism is a proof of an unprejudiced and acute mind. Perhaps no man ever rose finally above the seductions of that simple and ingenious system, who had not sometimes tried their full effect by surrendering his whole mind to them.

But it is never with entire impunity that philosophers borrow vague and inappropriate terms from vulgar use. Never did man afford a stronger instance of the danger than Reid, in his two most unfortunate terms, *Common Sense* and *Instinct*. Common Sense is that average portion of understanding, possessed by most men, which, as it is nearly always applied to conduct, has acquired an almost exclusively practical sense. Instinct is the habitual power of producing effects like contrivances of reason, yet so far beyond the intelligence and experience of the agent, as to be utterly inexplicable by reference to them. No man, if he had been in search of improper words, could have discovered any more unfit than these two, for denoting that *law*, or *state*, or *faculty* of mind, which compels us to acknowledge certain simple and very abstract truths, not being identical propositions, to lie at the founda-

might resent the language of Dr. Beattie, an amiable man, an elegant and tender poet, and a good writer on miscellaneous literature in prose, but who, in his *Essay on Truth*—an unfair appeal to the multitude on philosophical questions—indulged himself in the personalities and invectives of a public pamphleteer.

tion of all reasoning, and to be the necessary ground of all belief.

Long after the death of Dr. Reid, his philosophy was taught at Paris by M. Royer Collard,* who, on the restoration of free debate, became the most philosophical orator of his nation, and filled, with impartiality and dignity, the chair of the Chamber of Deputies. His ingenious and eloquent scholar, Professor Cousin, dissatisfied with what he calls "the sage and timid" doctrines of Edinburgh, which he considered as only a vigorous protest, on behalf of common sense, against the scepticism of Hume, sought in Germany for a philosophy of "such a masculine and brilliant character as might command the attention of Europe, and be able to struggle with success on a great theatre, against the genius of the adverse school."† It may be questioned whether he found in Kant more than the same *vigorous protest*, under a more systematic form, with an immense nomenclature, and constituting a philosophical edifice of equal symmetry and vastness. The preference of the more boastful system, over a philosophy thus chiefly blamed for its modest pretensions, does not seem to be entirely justified by its permanent authority in the country which gave it birth: where, however powerful its influence still continues to be, its doctrines do not appear to have now many supporters; and, indeed, the accomplished Professor himself [Cousin] rapidly shot through Kantianism, and appears to rest or to stop at the doctrines of Schelling and Hegel, at a point so high, that it is hard to descry from it any distinction between objects—even that indispensable distinction between *Reality* and *Illusion*. As the works of Reid, and those of Kant, otherwise so different,

---

* Fragments of his lectures have been published in a French translation of Dr. Reid, by M. Jonffroy: *Œuvres Completes de* Thomas Reid, vol. iv. Paris, 1828.

† *Cours de Philosophie*, par M. Cousin, leçon xii. Paris, 1828.

appear to be simultaneous efforts of the conservative power of philosophy to expel the mortal poison of scepticism, so the exertions of M. Royer Collard and M. Cousin, however at variance in metaphysical principles, seem to have been chiefly roused by the desire of delivering Ethics from that fatal taint of personal, and indeed gross interest, which that science had received in France from the followers of Condillac, especially Helvetius, St. Lambert, and Cabanis. The success of these attempts to render Speculative Philosophy once more popular in the country of Descartes has already been considerable. The French youth, whose desire of knowledge and love of liberty afford an auspicious promise of the succeeding age, have eagerly received doctrines, of which the moral part is so much more agreeable to their liberal spirit, than the selfish theory generated in the stagnation of a corrupt, cruel, and dissolute tyranny.

These agreeable prospects bring us easily back to our subject; for though the restoration of Speculative Philosophy in the country of Descartes is due to the precise statement and vigorous logic of M. Royer Collard, the modifications introduced by him into the doctrine of Reid coincide with those of Mr. Stewart, and would have appeared to agree more exactly, if the forms of the French philosopher had not been more dialectical, and the composition of Mr. Stewart had retained less of that oratorical character which belonged to a justly celebrated speaker. Amidst excellences of the highest order, his writings, it must be confessed, leave some room for criticism. He took precautions against offence to the feelings of his contemporaries, more anxious and frequent than the impatient searcher for truth may deem necessary. For the sake of promoting the favourable reception of philosophy itself, he studies perhaps too visibly to avoid whatever might raise up prejudices against it. His gratitude and native modesty dictated a superabundant care in softening and excusing his dissent from those who had been his own instructors, or who were the objects of general reverence. Exposed by his station, both to the assaults of political prejudice, and to the religious animosities of a country where a few sceptics attacked [and had aroused] the slumbering zeal of a Calvinistic people, it would have been wonderful if he had not betrayed more wariness than would have been necessary or becoming in a very different position. The fulness of his literature seduced him too much into multiplied illustrations. Too many of the expedients happily used to allure the young may unnecessarily swell his volumes. Perhaps a successive publication in separate parts made him more voluminous than he would have been if the whole had been at once before his eyes. A peculiar susceptibility and delicacy of taste produced forms of expression, in themselves extremely beautiful, but of which the habitual use is not easily reconcilable with the condensation desirable in works necessarily so extensive. If, however, it must be owned that the caution incident to his temper, his feelings, his philosophy, and his station, has somewhat lengthened his composition, it is not less true, that some of the same circumstances have contributed towards those peculiar beauties which place him at the head of the most adorned writers on philosophy in our language.

Few writers rise with more grace from a plain groundwork to the passages which require greater animation or embellishment. He gives to narrative, according to the precept of Bacon, the colour of the time, by a selection of happy expressions from original writers. Among the secret arts, by which he diffuses elegance over his diction, may be remarked the skill which, by deepening or brightening a shade in a secondary term, by opening partial or preparatory glimpses of a thought to be afterwards unfolded, unobservedly heightens the import of a word, and gives it a new meaning, without any offence against old use. It is in this manner that philosophical originality may be reconciled to purity and stability of speech,—that we may avoid new terms, which are the easy resource of the unskilful or the indolent, and often a characteristic mark of writers who love their language too little to feel its peculiar excellences, or to study the art of calling forth its powers.

He reminds us not unfrequently of the character given by Cicero to one of his contemporaries, "who expressed refined and abstruse thought in soft and transparent diction." His writings are a proof that the mild sentiments have their eloquence as well as the vehement passions. It would be difficult to name works in which so much refined philosophy is joined with so fine a fancy,—so much elegant literature with such a delicate perception of the distinguishing excellences of great writers, and with an estimate in general so just of the services rendered to knowledge by a succession of philosophers. They [his writings] are pervaded by a philosophical benevolence, which keeps up the ardour of his genius without disturbing the serenity of his mind,—which is felt in his reverence for knowledge, in the generosity of his praise, and in the tenderness of his censure. It is still more sensible in the general tone with which he relates the successful progress of the human understanding among many formidable enemies. Those readers are not to be envied who limit their admiration to particular parts, or to excellences merely literary, without being warmed by the glow of that honest triumph in the advancement of knowledge, and of that assured faith in the final prevalence of truth and justice, which breathe through every page of them, and give the unity and dignity of a moral purpose to the whole of these classical works.

He has often quoted poetical passages, of which some throw much light on our mental operations. If he sometimes prized the moral commonplaces of Thomson and the speculative fancy of Akenside more highly than the higher poetry of their betters, it was not to be wondered at that the metaphysician and the moralist should sometimes prevail over the lover of poetry. His natural sensibility was perhaps occasionally cramped by the cold criticism of an unpoetical age; and some of his remarks may be thought to indicate a more constant and exclusive regard to diction than is agreeable to the men of a generation who have been trained by tremendous events to a passion for daring inventions, and to an irregular enthusiasm impatient of minute elegancies and refinement. Many of those beauties which his generous criticism delighted to magnify in the works of his contemporaries, have already faded under the scorching rays of a fiercer sun.

Mr. Stewart employed more skill in contriving, and more care in concealing, his very important reforms of Reid's doctrines, than others exert to maintain their claims to originality. Had his well-chosen language of "laws of human thought or belief" been at first adopted in that school, instead of "instinct" and "common sense," it would have escaped much of the reproach (which Dr. Reid himself did not merit) of shallowness and popularity. Expressions so exact, employed in the opening, could not have failed to influence the whole system, and to have given it, not only in the general estimation, but in the minds of its framers, a more scientific complexion. In those parts of Mr. Stewart's speculations in which he most departed from his general principles, he seems sometimes, as it were, to be suddenly driven back by what he unconsciously shrinks from as ungrateful apostasy; and to be desirous of making amends to his master by more harshness than is otherwise natural to him towards the writers whom he has insensibly approached. Hence, perhaps, the unwonted severity of his language towards Tucker and Hartley. It is thus at the very time when he largely adopts the Principle of Association in his excellent Essay on the

Beautiful,* that he treats most rigidly the latter of these writers, to whom, though neither the discoverer nor the sole advocate of that principle, it surely owes the greatest illustration and support.

In matters of far other importance, causes perhaps somewhat similar may have led to the like mistake. When he absolutely contradicts Dr. Reid, by truly stating that "it is more philosophical to resolve the power of habit into the association of ideas, than to resolve the association of ideas into habit,"† he, in the sequel of the same volume,‡ refuses to go farther than to own that "the theory of Hartley, concerning the *origin* of our affections, and of the moral sense, is a most *ingenious refinement on the selfish system*, and that by means of it the force of many of the common reasonings against that system is *eluded;*" though he somewhat inconsistently allows that "active principles which, arising from circumstances, in which all the situations of mankind must agree, are therefore common to the whole species, at whatever period of life they may appear, are to be regarded as a part of human nature, no less than the instinct of suction ; in the same manner as the acquired perception of distance by the eye, is to be ranked among the perceptive powers of man, no less than the original perceptions of the other senses."§ In another place, also, he makes a remark on mere beauty, which might have led him to a more just conclusion respecting the theory of the origin of the affections and the moral sense: "It is scarcely necessary for me to observe, that, in those instances where association operates in heightening (or he

---

* Stewart's *Philosophical Essays,* part ii. essay i., especially chap. vi. The condensation, if not omission, of the discussion of the theories of Buffier, Reynolds, Burke, and Price, in this essay, would have lessened that temporary appearance which is unsuitable to a scientific work.

† *Elements of the Philosophy of the Human Mind,* vol. i. p. 281, edit. 1792, 4to.   ‡ *Ibid.* p. 383.   § *Ibid.* p. 385.

might have said creates) the pleasures we receive from sight, the pleasing emotion continues still to appear, to our consciousness, simple and uncompounded."* To this remark he might have added, that until all the separate pleasures be melted into one—as long as any of them are discerned and felt as distinct from each other—the associations are incomplete, and the qualities which gratify are not called by the name of beauty. In like manner, as has been repeatedly observed, it is only when all the separate feelings, pleasurable and painful, excited by the contemplation of voluntary action, are lost in the general sentiments of approbation or disapprobation—when these general feelings retain no trace of the various emotions which originally attended different actions—when they are held in a state of perfect fusion by the habitual use of the words used in every language to denote them—that conscience can be said to exist, or that we can be considered as endowed with a moral nature. The theory which thus ascribes the uniform formation of the moral faculty to universal and paramount laws, is not a refinement of the selfish system, nor is it any modification of that hypothesis. The partisans of selfishness maintain that in acts of will the agent must have a view to the pleasure or happiness which he hopes to reap from it. The philosophers who regard the *social affections* and the *moral sentiments* as formed by a process of association, on the other hand contend that these affections and sentiments must work themselves clear from every particle of *self-regard*, before they deserve the names of benevolence and of conscience. In the actual state of *human motives*, the two systems are not to be likened, but to be contrasted to each other. It is remarkable that Mr. Stewart, who admits the "question respecting the *origin* of the affections to be rather curious than important,"† should have held a directly

---

* *Philosophical Essays*, part ii. essay i. chap. vi.
† *Outlines of Moral Philosophy*, p. 93.

contrary opinion respecting the moral sense ;* to which these words, in his sense of them, seem to be equally applicable. His meaning in the former affirmation is, that if the affections be *acquired,* yet they are justly called *natural;* and if their origin be personal, yet their nature may and does *become* disinterested. What circumstance distinguishes the former from the latter case? With respect to the origin of the affections, it must not be overlooked that his language is somewhat contradictory. For if the theory on that subject from which he dissents were merely "a refinement on the selfish system," its truth or falsehood could not be represented as subordinate, since the controversy would continue to relate to the existence of disinterested motives of human conduct.† It may also be observed, that he uniformly represents his opponents as deriving the affections from *self-love,* which, in its proper sense, is not the source to which they refer even avarice ; and which is itself derived from other antecedent principles, some of which are inherent and some acquired. If the objects of this theory of the rise of the most important feelings of human nature were, as our philosopher supposes, "to *elude* objections against the *selfish system,*" it would be at best worthless. Its positive merits are several. It affirms the actual disinterestedness of human motives as strongly as Butler himself. The explanation of the mental law, of which benevolence and conscience are formed habitually, when it is contemplated deeply, impresses on the mind the truth that they not only *are* but *must* be disinterested. It confirms, as

* *Outlines,* p. 117. "This is the most important question that can be stated with respect to the Theory of Morals."

† In the *Philosophy of the Active and Moral Powers of Man* (vol. i. p. 164), Mr. Stewart has done more manifest injustice to the Hartleian theory, by calling it "a doctrine *fundamentally the same with the selfish system,*" and especially by representing Hartley, who ought to be rather classed with Butler and Hume, as agreeing with Gay, Tucker, and Paley.

it were, the testimony of consciousness, by exhibiting to the understanding the means employed to insure the production of disinterestedness. It affords the only effectual answer to the prejudice against the disinterested theory, from the multiplication of ultimate facts and implanted principles, which, under all its other forms, it seems to require. No room is left for this prejudice by a representation of disinterestedness, which *ultimately* traces its formation to principles almost as simple as those of Hobbes himself. Lastly, every step in just generalisation is an advance in philosophy. No one has yet shown, either that man is not actually disinterested, or that he may not have been destined to become so by such a process as has been described: the cause to which the effects are ascribed is a real agent, which seems adequate to the appearance; and if future observation should be found to require that the theory shall be confined within narrower limits, such a limitation will not destroy its value.

The acquiescence of Mr. Stewart in Dr. Reid's general representation of our mental constitution, led him to indulge more freely the natural bent of his understanding, by applying it to theories of character and manners, of life and literature, of taste and the arts, more than to the consideration of those more simple principles which rule over human nature under every form. His chief work, as he frankly owns, is indeed rather a collection of such theories, pointing toward the common end of throwing light on the structure and functions of the mind, than a systematic treatise, such as might be expected from the title of "Elements." It is in essays of this kind that he has most surpassed other cultivators of mental philosophy. His remarks on the effects of casual associations may be quoted as a specimen of the most original and just thoughts, conveyed in the best manner.* In this beautiful passage, he proceeds from their power of confusing speculation,

* *Elements of the Philosophy of the Human Mind*, vol. i. pp. 340-352.

to that of disturbing experience, and of misleading practice; and ends with their extraordinary effect in bestowing on trivial, and even ludicrous circumstances, some portion of the dignity and sanctity of those sublime principles with which they are associated. The style, at first only clear, afterwards admitting the ornaments of a calm and grave elegance, at last rising to as high a strain as philosophy will endure, and of which all the parts (various as their nature is) are held together by an invisible thread of gentle transition, affords a specimen of adaptation of manner to matter which it will be hard to match in any philosophical writer. Another very fine remark, which seems to be as original as it is just, may be quoted as a sample of those beauties with which his writings abound. "The apparent coldness and selfishness of mankind may be traced, in a great measure, to a want of attention and a want of imagination. In the case of those misfortunes which happen to ourselves or our near connections, neither of these powers is necessary to make us acquainted with our situation. But without an uncommon degree of both, it is impossible for any man to comprehend completely the situation of his neighbour, or to have an idea of the greater part of the distress which exists in the world. If we feel more for ourselves than for others, in the former case the facts are more fully before us than they can be in the latter."* Yet several parts of his writings afford the most satisfactory proof that his abstinence from what is commonly called metaphysical speculation arose from no inability to pursue it with signal success. As examples, his observations on *General Terms*, and on *Causation*, may be appealed to with perfect confidence. In the first two Dissertations of the volume bearing the title of *Philosophical Essays*, he, with equal boldness and acuteness, grapples with the most extensive and abstruse questions of mental philosophy, and points out both the sources and the

* *Elements of the Philosophy of the Human Mind,* vol. i. p. 502.

uttermost boundaries of human knowledge with a Verulamean hand. In another part of his writings, he calls what are denominated first principles of experience, "*fundamental laws of human belief, or primary elements of human reason;*"* which last form of expression has so close a resemblance to the language of Kant, that it should have protected the latter from the imputation of writing jargon.

Mr. Stewart's excellent volume entitled *Outlines of Moral Philosophy*,† though composed only as a text-book for the use of his hearers, is one of the most decisive proofs that he was perfectly qualified to unite precision with ease, to be brief with the utmost clearness, and to write with becoming elegance in a style where the meaning is not overladen by ornaments. This volume contains his properly *Ethical Theory*,‡ which is much expanded, but not substantially altered, in his *Philosophy of the Active and Moral Powers*,§—a work almost posthumous, and composed under circumstances which give it a deeper interest than can be inspired by any desert in science. Though, with his usual modesty, he manifests an anxiety to fasten his ethical theory to the kindred speculations of other philosophers of the Intellectual School, especially to those of Cudworth, afterwards clothed in more modern phraseology by Price, yet it still shows that independence and originality which all his aversion from parade could not entirely conceal. *Right, duty, virtue, moral obligation,* and the like, or the opposite forms of expression, represent, according to him, certain thoughts, which arise necessarily and instantaneously in the mind (or in the reason, if we take that word in a large sense in which it denotes all that is not emotive) at the contemplation of actions, and which are utterly incapable of all resolution, consequently of all expla-

---

* *Elements of the Philosophy of the Human Mind*, vol. ii. p. 57.
† Edinburgh, 1794, 8vo.   ‡ Pp. 76-148.
   § Two vols. 8vo. Edinburgh, 1828.

nation, and which can be known only by being experienced. These thoughts or ideas, or by whatever other name they may be called, are followed as inexplicably, but as inevitably, by pleasurable and painful emotions, which suggest the conception of *moral beauty;* a quality of human actions distinct from their *adherence to or deviation from rectitude*, though generally coinciding with it. The question which a reflecting reader will here put is, whether any purpose is served by the introduction of the intermediate mental process between the particular thoughts and the moral emotions. How would the view be darkened or confused, or indeed in any degree changed, by withdrawing that process, or erasing the words which attempt to express it? No advocate of the *intellectual origin of the moral faculty* has yet stated a case in which a mere operation of reason or judgment, unattended by emotion, could, consistently with the universal opinion of mankind, as it is exhibited by the structure of language, be said to have the nature or to produce the effects of Conscience. Such an example would be equivalent to an *experimentum crucis* on the side of that celebrated theory. The failure to produce it, after long challenge, is at least a presumption against it, nearly approaching to that sort of decisively discriminative experiment. It would be vain to re-state what has already been too often repeated, that all the objections to the selfish philosophy turn upon the actual nature, not upon the original source of our principles of action, and that it is by a confusion of these very distinct questions alone that the confutation of Hobbes can be made apparently to involve Hartley. Mr. Stewart appears, like most other metaphysicians, to have blended the inquiry into the nature of our moral sentiments with that other [inquiry] which only seeks a criterion to distinguish moral from immoral habits of feeling and action ; for he considers the appearance of moral sentiment at an early age, before the general tendency of actions could be ascertained, as a decisive objection to the origin of these sentiments in association,—an objection which assumes that if utility be the criterion of morality, associations with utility must be the mode by which the moral sentiments are formed, which no skilful advocate of the theory of association will ever allow. That the main, if not sole, object of conscience is to govern our voluntary exertions, is manifest. But how could it perform this great function if it did not impel the will? and how could it have the latter effect as a mere act of reason, or indeed in any respect otherwise than as it is made up of emotions, by which alone its grand aim could in any degree be attained? Judgment and reason are therefore preparatory to conscience, not properly a part of it. That the exclusion of reason reduces virtue to be a relative quality is another instance of the confusion of the two questions in moral theory; for though a fitness to excite approbation may be only a relation of objects to our susceptibility, yet the proposition that all virtuous actions are beneficial, is a proposition as absolute as any other within the range of our understanding.

A delicate state of health, and an ardent desire to devote himself exclusively to study and composition, induced Mr. Stewart, while in the full blaze of his reputation as a lecturer, to retire, in 1810, from the labour of public instruction. This retirement, as he himself describes it, was that of a quiet but active life. Three quarto and two octavo volumes, besides the magnificent Dissertations prefixed to the Encyclopædia Britannica, were among its happy fruits. These Dissertations are, perhaps, the most profusely ornamented of any of his compositions; a peculiarity which must in part have arisen from a principle of taste, which regarded decoration as more suitable to the history of philosophy than to philosophy itself. But the memorable instances of Cicero, of Milton, and still more those of Dryden and Burke, seem to show that there is some natural tendency in the fire of genius to burn more brightly or to blaze more fiercely in the evening than in the morning of human life. Probably the materials which long experience supplies to the imagination, the boldness with which a more established reputation arms the mind, and the silence of the low but formidable rivals of the higher principles, may concur in producing this unexpected and little observed effect.

It was in the last years of his life, when suffering under the effects of a severe attack of palsy, with which he had been afflicted in 1822, that Mr. Stewart most plentifully reaped the fruits of long virtue and a well-ordered mind. Happily for him, his own cultivation and exercise of every kindly affection had laid up for him a store of that domestic consolation which none who deserve it ever want, and for the loss of which, nothing beyond the threshold can make amends. The same philosophy which he had cultivated from his youth upward employed his dying hand. Aspirations after higher and brighter scenes of excellence, always blended with his elevated morality, became more earnest and deeper as worldly passions died away, and earthly objects vanished from his sight.*

THOMAS BROWN.

Born 1778—died 1820.

A WRITER, as he advances in life, ought to speak with diffidence of systems which he had only begun to consider with care after the age in which it becomes hard for his thoughts

* [For the sake of literary justice I will notice Mr. Hallam's judgment respecting Stewart's attack upon Grotius. "That he should have spoken of a work so distinguished by fame, and so effective, as he himself admits, over the public mind of Europe, in terms of unmingled depreciation, without having done more than glanced at some of its pages, is an extraordinary symptom of that tendency towards prejudices, hasty but inveterate, of which that eminent man seems to have been not a little susceptible."—W. W.]

to flow into new channels. A reader cannot be said practically to understand a theory till he has acquired the power of thinking, at least for a short time, with the theorist. Even a hearer, with all the helps of voice in the instructor, of countenance from him and from fellow-hearers, finds it difficult to perform this necessary process, without either being betrayed into hasty and undistinguishing assent, or falling, while he is in pursuit of an impartial estimate of opinions, into an indifference about their truth. I have felt this difficulty in reconsidering ancient opinions: but it is perhaps more needful to own its power, and to warn the reader against its effects, in the case of a philosopher well known to me, and with whom common friendships stood in the stead of much personal intercourse, as a cement of kindness.

I very early read Brown's *Observations on the Zoonomia* of Dr. Darwin, the perhaps unmatched work of a boy in the eighteenth year of his age.* His first tract on *Causation* appeared to me the finest model of discussion in mental philosophy since Berkeley and Hume; with this superiority over the latter, that its aim is that of a philosopher who seeks to enlarge knowledge, and not that of a sceptic, the most illustrious of whom have no better end than that of displaying their powers in confounding and darkening every truth; so that their very happiest efforts cannot be more leniently described than as brilliant fits of mental debauchery.† From

* Welsh's *Life of Brown*, p. 43; a pleasingly affectionate work, full of analytical spirit and metaphysical reading—of such merit, in short, that I could wish to have found in it no phrenology. Objections *a priori* in a case dependent on facts are indeed inadmissible. Even the allowance of presumptions of that nature would open so wide a door for prejudices, that at most they can be considered only as maxims of logical prudence, which fortify the watchfulness of the individual. The fatal objection to phrenology seems to me to be, that what is new in it, or peculiar to it, has no approach to an adequate foundation in experience.

† " Bayle, a writer who, pervading human nature at his ease, struck into the province of paradox as an exercise for the unwearied vigour of

a diligent perusal of his succeeding works at the time of their publication, I was prevented by pursuits and duties of a very different nature. These causes, together with ill health and growing occupation, hindered me from reading his *Lectures* with due attention, till it has now become a duty to consider with care that part of them which relates to Ethics.

Dr. Brown was born in one of those families of ministers in the Scottish church, who, after a generation or two of an humble life spent in piety and usefulness, with no more than needful knowledge, have more than once sent forth a man of genius from their cool and quiet shade, to make his fellows wiser or better by tongue or pen, by head or hand. Even the scanty endowments and constant residence of that church, by keeping her ministers far from the objects which awaken turbulent passions and disperse the understanding on many pursuits, afforded some of the leisure and calm of monastic life, without the exclusion of the charities of family and kindred. It may be well doubted whether this undissipated retirement, which during the eighteenth century was very general in Scotland, did not make full amends for the loss of curious and ornamental knowledge, by its tendency to qualify men for professional duty, by the cultivation of reason among a considerable number, and by those opportunities for high meditation, and for the unchangeable concentration of mind on worthy objects, to the few who had the natural capacity for such exertions.*

An authentic account of the early exercises of Brown's his mind; who, with a soul superior to the sharpest attacks of fortune, and a heart practised to the best philosophy, had not enough of real greatness to overcome that last foible of superior minds, the temptation of honour which the academic exercise of wit is conceived to bring to its professor." So Warburton (*Divine Legation,* book i. sect. 4), speaking of Bayle, but perhaps in part excusing himself—in a noble strain, of which it would have been more agreeable to find the repetition than the contrast in his language towards Hume.

* See Sir H. Moncreiff's *Life of the Rev. Dr. Erskine.*

mind is preserved by his biographer.* At the age of nineteen he took a part with others, some of whom became the most memorable men of their time, in the foundation of a private society in Edinburgh, under the name of "The Academy of Physics."†

The character of Dr. Brown is very attractive as an example of one in whom the utmost tenderness of affection, and the indulgence of a flowery fancy, were not repressed by the highest cultivation, and by a perhaps excessive refinement of intellect. His mind soared and roamed through every region of philosophy and poetry; but his untravelled heart clung to the hearth of his father, to the children who shared it with him, and after them, first to the other partners of his childish sports, and then almost solely to those companions of his youthful studies who continued to be the friends of his life. Speculation seemed to keep his kindness at home. It is observable, that, though sparkling with fancy, he does

* Welsh's *Life of Brown*, p. 77, and App. p. 498.

† A part of the first day's minutes is here borrowed from Mr. Welsh :—"7th January 1797.—Present, Mr. Erskine, President; Mr. Brougham, Mr. Reddie, Mr. Brown, Mr. Birbeck, Mr. Leyden," etc., who were afterwards joined by Lord Webb Seymour, Messrs. Horner, Jeffrey, Smyth, etc. Mr. Erskine, who thus appears at the head of so remarkable an association, and whom diffidence and untoward circumstances have hitherto withheld from the full manifestation of his powers, continued to be the bosom friend of Brown to the last; and showed the constancy of his friendship for others by converting all his invaluable preparations for a translation of Sultan Baber's *Commentaries* (perhaps the best, certainly the most European work of modern eastern prose) into the means of completing the imperfect attempt of Leyden; with a regard equally generous to the fame of his early friend, and to the comfort of that friend's surviving relations. The review of Baber's *Commentaries*, by M. Silvestre de Sacy, in the *Journal des Savans* for May and June 1829, is perhaps one of the best specimens extant of the value of literary commendation when it is bestowed with conscientious calmness, and without a suspicion of bias, by one of the greatest orientalists, in a case where he pronounces everything to have been done by Mr. Erskine "which could have been performed by the most learned and the most scrupulously conscientious of editors and translators."

not seem to have been deeply or durably touched by those affections which are lighted at its torch, or at least tinged with its colours. His heart sought little abroad, but contentedly dwelt in his family and in his study. He was one of those men of genius who repaid the tender care of a mother by rocking the cradle of her reposing age. He ended a life, spent in searching for truth and exercising love, by desiring that he should be buried in his native parish, with his " dear father and mother." Some of these delightful qualities were perhaps hidden from the casual observer in general society, by the want of that perfect simplicity of manner which is doubtless their natural representative. Manner is a better mark of the state of a mind than those large and deliberate actions which form what is called conduct. It is the constant and insensible transpiration of character. In serious acts a man may display himself. In the thousand nameless acts which compose manner, the mind betrays its habitual bent. But manner is then only an index of disposition, when it is that of men who live at ease in the intimate familiarity of friends and equals. It may be diverted from simplicity by causes which do not reach so deep as the character; by bad models, or by a restless and wearisome anxiety to shine, arising from many circumstances, none of which were probably more common than the unseasonable exertions of a recluse student in society, and the unfortunate attempts of some others to take by violence the admiration of those with whom they do not associate with ease. The association with unlike or superior companions, which least distorts manners, is that which takes place with those classes whose secure dignity generally renders their own manners easy; with whom the art of pleasing or of not displeasing each other in society is a serious concern; who have leisure enough to discover the positive and negative parts of the smaller moralities, and who, being trained to a watchful eye on what is ludicrous, apply the lash of ridicule to affectation, the most ridiculous of faults. The busy in every department of life are too respectably occupied to form these manners or to bestow them. They are the frivolous work of polished idleness; and perhaps their most serious value consists in the war which they wage against affectation; though even there they betray their nature in punishing it, not as a deviation from nature, but as a badge of vulgarity.

The prose of Dr. Brown is brilliant to excess. It must not be denied that its beauty is sometimes womanly; that it too often melts down precision into elegance; that it buries the main idea under a load of illustration, of which every part is expanded and adorned with such a visible labour, as to withdraw the mind from attention to the thoughts which it professes to introduce more easily into the understanding. It is darkened by excessive brightness; it loses ease and liveliness by over-dress; and, in the midst of its luscious sweetness, we wish for the striking and homely illustrations of Tucker, and for the pithy and sinewy sense of Paley, either of whom, by a single short metaphor from a familiar, perhaps a low object, could at one blow set the two worlds of reason and fancy in movement.

It would be unjust to censure severely the declamatory parts of his Lectures; they are excusable in the first warmth of composition. They might even be justifiable allurements in attracting young hearers to abstruse speculations. Had he lived, he would probably have taken his thoughts out of the declamatory forms of spoken address, and given to them the appearance, as well as the reality, of deep and subtile discussion. The habits, indeed, of so successful a lecturer, and the natural luxuriancy of his mind, could not fail to have somewhat tinctured all his compositions; but though he might still have fallen short of simplicity, he certainly would have avoided much of the diffusion, and even commonplace, which hang heavily on original and brilliant thoughts; for it must be owned, that though, as a thinker, he is unusually original, yet when he falls among the declaimers, he is infected by their commonplaces.

In like manner, he would assuredly have shortened or left out many of the poetical quotations which he loved to recite, and which hearers even beyond youth hear with delight. There are two very different sorts of passages of poetry to be found in works on philosophy, which are as far asunder from each other in value as in matter. A philosopher will admit some of those wonderful lines or words which bring to light the infinite varieties of character, the furious bursts or wily workings of passion, the winding approaches of temptation, the slippery path to depravity, the beauty of tenderness, the grandeur of what is awful and holy in man. In every such quotation, the moral philosopher, if he be successful, uses the best materials of his science; for what are they but the results of experiment and observation on the human heart, performed by artists of far other skill and power than his? They are facts which could have only been ascertained by Homer, by Dante, by Shakespeare, by Cervantes, by Milton. Every year of admiration since the unknown period when the Iliad first gave delight, has extorted new proofs of the justness of the picture of human nature, from the responding hearts of the admirers. Every strong feeling which these masters have excited, is a successful repetition of their original experiment, and a continually growing evidence of the greatness of their discoveries. Quotations of this nature may be the most satisfactory, as well as the most delightful proofs of philosophical positions. Others of inferior merit are not to be interdicted: a pointed maxim, especially when familiar, pleases, and is recollected. I cannot entirely conquer my passion for the Roman and Stoical declamation of some passages in Lucan and Akenside. But quotations from those who have written on philosophy in verse, or, in other words, from those who generally are inferior philosophers, and voluntarily deliver their doctrines in the most disadvantageous form, seem to be unreasonable. It is agreeable, no doubt, to the philosopher, still more to the youthful student, to meet his abstruse ideas clothed in the sonorous verse of Akenside. The surprise of the unexpected union of verse with science is a very lawful enjoyment. But such slight and momentary pleasures, though they may tempt the writer to display them, do not excuse a vain effort to obtrude them on the sympathy of the searcher after truth in after times. It is peculiarly unlucky that Dr. Brown should have sought supposed ornament from the moral commonplaces of Thomson, rather than from that illustration of philosophy which is really to be found in his picturesque strokes.

Much more need not be said of Dr. Brown's own poetry, somewhat voluminous as it is, than that it indicates fancy and feeling, and rose at least to the rank of an elegant accomplishment. It may seem a paradox, but it appears to me that he is really most poetical in those poems and passages which have the *most properly metaphysical* character. For every various form of life and nature, when it is habitually contemplated, may inspire feeling; and the just representation of these feelings may be poetical. Dr. Brown observed man, and his wider world, with the eye of a metaphysician; and the dark results of such contemplations, when he reviewed them, often filled his soul with feelings which, being both grand and melancholy, were truly poetical. Unfortunately, however, few readers can be touched with fellow-feeling. He sings to few, and must be content with sometimes moving a string in the soul of the lonely visionary, who, in the day-dreams of youth, has felt as well as meditated on the mysteries of nature. His heart has produced charming passages in all his poems; but, generally speaking, they are only beautiful works of art and imitation. The choice of

Akenside as a favourite and a model may, without derogation from that writer, be considered as no proof of a poetically formed mind.* There is more poetry in many single lines of Cowper than in volumes of sonorous verses such as Akenside's. Philosophical poetry is very different from versified philosophy. The former is the highest exertion of genius, the latter cannot be ranked above the slighter amusements of ingenuity. Dr. Brown's poetry was, it must be owned, composed either of imitations, which, with some exceptions, may be produced and read without feeling, or of effusions of such feelings only as meet a rare and faint echo in the human breast.

A few words only can here be bestowed on the intellectual part of his philosophy. It is an open revolt against the authority of Reid; and, by a curious concurrence, he began to lecture nearly at the moment when the doctrines of that philosopher came to be taught with applause in France. Mr. Stewart had dissented from the language of Reid, and had widely departed from his opinions on several secondary theories. Dr. Brown rejected them entirely. He very justly considered the claim of Reid to the merit of detecting the universal delusion which had betrayed philosophers into the belief that ideas which were the sole objects of knowledge had a separate existence, as a proof of his having mistaken their illustrative language for a metaphysical opinion ;† but he does not do justice to the service which Reid really rendered to mental science, by keeping the attention of all future speculators in a state of more constant watchfulness against the transient influence of such an illusion. His choice

---

* His accomplished friend, Mr. Erskine, confesses that Brown's poems "are not written in the language of plain and gross emotion. The string touched is too delicate for general sympathy. They are in an unknown tongue to one-half" (he might have said nineteen-twentieths) " of the reading part of the community." (Welsh's *Life of Brown*, p. 431.)

† Brown's *Lectures*, vol. ii. pp. 1-49.

of the term *feeling** to denote the operations which we usually refer to the understanding, is evidently too wide a departure from its ordinary use to have any probability of general adoption. No definition can strip so familiar a word of the thoughts and emotions which have so long accompanied it, so as to fit it for a technical term of the highest abstraction. If we can be said to have a feeling "of the equality of the angle of forty-five degrees to half the angle of ninety degrees,"† we may call Geometry and Arithmetic sciences of feeling He has very forcibly stated the necessity of assuming "*the primary universal intuitions of direct belief*," which, in their nature, are incapable of all proof. They seem to be accurately described as notions which cannot be conceived separately, but without which nothing can be conceived. They are not only necessary to reasoning and to belief, but to thought itself. It is equally impossible to prove or to disprove them. He has very justly blamed the school of Reid for "an extravagant and ridiculous" multiplication of those principles which he truly represents as inconsistent with sound philosophy. To philosophise is indeed nothing more than to simplify securely.‡

The substitution of *suggestion* for the former phrase, *association of ideas*, would hardly deserve notice in so cursory a view, if it had not led him to a serious misconception of the doctrines and deserts of other philosophers. The fault of the latter phrase is rather in the narrowness of the

---

* Brown's *Lectures*, vol. i. p. 220, etc.   † *Ibid.* vol. i. p. 222.

‡ Dr. Brown always expresses himself best where he is short and familiar. "An hypothesis is nothing more than a reason for making one experiment or observation rather than another." (*Lectures*, vol. i. p. 170.) In 1812, as the present writer observed to him that Reid and Hume differed more in words than in opinion, he answered, "Yes; Reid bawled out, We must believe an outward world; but added in a whisper, We can give no reason for our belief. Hume cries out, We can give no reason for such a notion; and whispers, I own we cannot get rid of it."

last, than in the inadequacy of the first word. *Association* presents the fact in the light of a *relation* between two mental acts. *Suggestion* denotes rather the *power* of the one to call up the other. But whether we say that the sight of ashes suggests fire, or that the ideas of fire and ashes are associated, we mean to convey the same fact; and, in both cases, an exact thinker means to accompany the fact with no hypothesis. Dr. Brown has supposed the word *association* as intended to affirm that there was some "intermediate process"[*] between the original succession of the mental acts, and the power which they acquired therefrom of calling up each other. This is quite as much to raise up imaginary antagonists for the honour of conquering them, as he justly reprehends Dr. Reid for doing in the treatment of preceding philosophers. He falls into another more important and unaccountable error, in representing his own reduction of Mr. Hume's principles of association (resemblance, contrariety, causation, contiguity in time or place) to the one principle of contiguity, as a discovery of his own, by which his theory is distinguished from "the universal opinion of philosophers."[†] Nothing but too exclusive a consideration of the doctrines of the Scottish school could have led him to speak thus of what was hinted by Aristotle, distinctly laid down by Hobbes, and fully unfolded both by Hartley and Condillac. He has, however, extremely enlarged the proof and the illustration of this law of mind, by the exercise of "a more subtle analysis," and the disclosure of "a finer species of proximity."[‡] As he has thus aided and confirmed, though he did not discover the general law, so he has rendered a new and very important service to mental science, by what he properly calls "secondary laws of suggestion"[§] or association—circumstances which modify the action of the general law, and must be distinctly considered,

---

[*] *Lectures*, vol. ii. pp. 335-347.   [†] *Ibid.* vol. ii. p. 349.
[‡] *Ibid.* vol. ii. p. 218, etc.   [§] *Ibid.* vol. ii. p. 270.

in order to explain its connection with the phenomena. The enumeration and exposition are instructive, and the example is worthy of commendation. For it is in this lower region of science that most remains to be discovered; it is that which rests most on observation, and least tempts to controversy; it is by improvements in that part of knowledge that the foundations are secured and the whole building so repaired as to rest steadily on them. The distinction of common language between the head and the heart, which, as we have seen, is so often overlooked or misapplied by metaphysicians, is, in the system of Brown, signified by the terms "mental states" and "emotions." It is unlucky that no single word could be found for the former, and that the use of "feeling," as the generic term, should disturb its easy comprehension when it is applied more naturally.

In our more proper province he has followed Butler, who appears to have been chiefly known to him through Mr. Stewart, in the theory of the social affections. Their disinterestedness is enforced by the arguments of both these philosophers, as well as of Hutcheson.* It is observable, however, that he applies the principle of suggestion or association boldly to this part of human nature, and seems inclined to refer to it even sympathy itself.† It is hard to understand how, with such a disposition, on the subject of a principle so generally thought ultimate as *Sympathy*, he should, inconsistently with himself, follow Mr. Stewart in representing the theory which derives the affections from association, as "*a modification of the selfish system.*"‡ He mistakes that theory by stating that it derives the affections from our experience that our own interest was connected with that of others; while, in truth, it considers our regard to our own interest as formed from the same original pleasures by association, which,

---

* Brown's *Lectures*, vol. iii. p. 248. † *Ibid.* vol. iii. p. 282.
‡ *Ibid.* vol. iv. p. 82, *et seq.*

by the like process, may and do *directly* generate affections towards others, without passing through the channel of regard to our general happiness. But, says he, this is only an hypothesis, since the formation of these affections is acknowledged to belong to a time of which there is no remembrance ;[*] —an objection fatal to every theory of any mental function— subversive, for example, of Berkeley's discovery of acquired visual perception, and most strangely inconsistent in the mouth of a philosopher whose numerous simplifications of mental theory are and must be founded on occurrences which precede experience. It is in all other cases, and it must be in this, sufficient that the principle of the theory is really existing, that it explains the appearances, that its supposed action *resembles* what we know to be its action in those similar cases of which we have direct experience. Lastly, he in express words admits that, according to the theory to which he objects, we have affections which are at present disinterested.[†] Is it not a direct contradiction in terms to call such a theory "a modification of the selfish system?" His language in the sequel clearly indicates a distrust of his own statement, and a suspicion that he is not only inconsistent but altogether mistaken.[‡]

As we enter more deeply into the territory of Ethics, we at length discover in Brown a distinction, the neglect of which by preceding speculators we have more than once lamented as productive of obscurity and confusion:—"The moral affections," says he, "which I consider at present, I consider rather physiologically" (or, as he elsewhere better expresses it, " psychologically ") " than ethically, *as parts of our mental constitution*, not as involving the *fulfilment or violation of duties.*"[§] He immediately, however, loses sight of this distinction, and reasons inconsistently with it instead of following it to its

---

[*] Brown's *Lectures*, vol. iv. p. 87. [†] *Ibid.* vol. iv. p. 87.
[‡] *Ibid.* vol. iv. pp. 94-97. [§] *Ibid.* vol. iii. p. 231.

proper consequences in his explanation of conscience. Perhaps, indeed (for the words are capable of more than one sense), he meant to distinguish the virtuous affections from those sentiments which have morality exclusively in view, rather than to distinguish the theory of moral sentiment from the attempt to ascertain the characteristic quality of right action. Friendship is conformable in its dictates to morality; but it may and does exist, without any view to it. He who feels the affections and performs the duties of friendship, is the object of that distinct emotion which is called moral approbation.

It is on the subject of conscience, that, in imitation of Mr. Stewart, and with no other arguments than his, he makes his chief stand against the theory which considers the formation of that master faculty itself as probably referable to the necessary and universal operation of those laws of human nature to which he himself ascribes almost every other state of mind. On both sides of this question the supremacy of conscience is held alike to be venerable and absolute. Once more, be it remembered that the question is purely philosophical, and is only, whether, from the impossibility of explaining its formation by more general laws, we are reduced to the necessity of considering it as an original fact in human nature, of which no further account can be given. Let it, however, be also remembered that we are not driven to this supposition by the mere circumstance, that no satisfactory explanation has yet appeared; for there are many analogies in an unexplained state of mind to states already explained, which may justify us in believing that the explanation requires only more accurate observation, and more patient meditation, to be brought to that completeness which it probably will attain.

SECTION VII.

GENERAL REMARKS.

HAVING thus again premised an already often repeated warning, it remains that we should offer a few observations on the questions so understood, which naturally occur on the consideration of Dr. Brown's argument, in support of the proposition, that moral approbation is not only in its mature state independent of, and superior to, any other principle of human nature, regarding which there is no dispute, but that its origin is altogether inexplicable, and that its existence is an ultimate fact in mental science. Though these observations are immediately occasioned by the perusal of Brown, they are yet, in the main, of a general nature, and might have been made without reference to any particular writer.

The term *Suggestion*, which might be inoffensive in describing merely intellectual associations, becomes peculiarly unsuitable when it is applied to those combinations of thought with emotion, and to those unions of feeling, which compose the emotive nature of man. Its common sense of a sign *recalling* the thing signified, always embroils the new sense vainly forced upon it. No one can help owning, that if it were consistently pursued, so as that we were to speak of *suggesting a feeling or passion*, the language would be universally thought absurd. To suggest love or hatred is a mode of expression so manifestly incongruous, that most readers would choose to understand it as suggesting reflections on the subject of these passions. *Suggest* would not be understood by any common reader as synonymous with *revive* or *rekindle*. Defects of the same sort may indeed be found in the parallel

R

phrases of most if not all philosophers, and all of them proceed from the same source—namely, the erroneous but prevalent notion, that the law of association produces only such a close union of a thought and a feeling, as gives one the power of reviving the other; instead of the truth, that it forms them into a new compound, in which the properties of the component parts are no longer discoverable, and which may itself become a substantive principle of human nature. They supposed the condition, produced by its power, to resemble that of material substances in a state of mechanical diffusion; whereas, in reality, it may be better likened to a chemical combination of the same substances, from which a totally new product arises. The language involves a confusion of the question, which relates to the *origin* of the principles of human activity, with the other and far more important question which relates to their *nature;* and as soon as this distinction is hidden, the theorist is either betrayed into the selfish system by a desire of clearness and simplicity, or tempted to the needless multiplication of ultimate facts by mistaken anxiety for what he supposes to be the guards of our social and moral nature. The defect is common to Brown with his predecessors, but in him less excusable; for he saw the truth and recoiled from it.

It is the main defect of the term *association* itself that it does not, without long habit, convey the notion of a perfect union, but rather leads to that of a combination which may be dissolved, if not at pleasure, at least with the help of care and exertion; which [notion] is utterly and dangerously false in the important cases where such unions are considered as constituting the most essential principles of human nature. Men can no more dissolve these unions than they can disuse their habit of judging of distance by the eye, and often by the ear. But *suggestion* implies, that what suggests is separate from what is suggested, and consequently negatives that unity in an active principle which the whole analogy of nature, as well as our own direct consciousness, shows to be perfectly compatible with its origin in composition.

Large concessions are, in the first place, to be remarked, which must be stated, because they very much narrow the matter in dispute. Those who, before Brown, contended against beneficial tendency as the standard of morality, have either shut their eyes on the connection of virtue with general utility ; or carelessly and obscurely allowed, without further remark, a connection which is at least one of the most remarkable and important of ethical facts. He acts more boldly, and avowedly discusses "the relation of virtue to utility." He was compelled by that discussion to make those concessions which so much abridge this controversy. "Utility and virtue are so related, that there is perhaps no action generally felt to be virtuous, which it would not be beneficial that all men in similar circumstances should imitate."* "In every case of benefit or injury, willingly done, there arise certain emotions of moral approbation or disapprobation."† "The intentional produce of evil, as pure evil, is always hated ; and that of good, as pure good, always loved."‡ All virtuous acts are thus admitted to be universally beneficial ; morality and the general benefit are acknowledged always to coincide. It is hard to say, then, why they should not be reciprocally tests of each other, though in a very different way ;—the virtuous feelings, fitted as they are by immediate appearance, by quick and powerful action, being sufficient

---

* *Lectures*, vol. iv. p. 45. The unphilosophical word "perhaps" must be struck out of the proposition, unless the whole be considered as a mere conjecture. It limits no affirmation, but destroys it, by converting it into a guess. See the like concession, vol. iv. p. 33, with some words interlarded, which betray a sort of reluctance and fluctuation, indicative of the difficulty with which Brown struggled to withhold his assent from truths which he unreasonably dreaded.

† *Ibid.* vol. iii. p. 567.   ‡ *Ibid.* vol. iii. p. 621.

tests of morality in the moment of action, and for all practical purposes; while the consideration of tendency to general happiness, a more obscure and slowly discoverable quality, should be applied in general reasoning, as a test of the sentiments and dispositions themselves. It has been thus employed, and no proof has been attempted that it has ever deceived those who used it in the proper place. It has uniformly served to justify our moral constitution, and to show how reasonable it is for us to be guided in action by our higher feelings. At all events, it should be, but has not been considered, that from these concessions alone it follows that beneficial tendency is at least one constant property of virtue. Is not this, in effect, an admission that beneficial tendency does distinguish virtuous acts and dispositions from those which we call vicious? If the criterion be incomplete or delusive, let its faults be specified, and let some other quality be pointed out, which, either singly or in combination with beneficial tendency, may more perfectly indicate the distinction.

But let us not be assailed by arguments which leave untouched its value as a test, and are in truth directed only against its fitness as an *immediate* incentive and guide to right action. To those who contend for its use in the latter character, it must be left to defend, if they can, so untenable a position. But all others must regard as pure sophistry the use of arguments against it as a test, which really show nothing more than its acknowledged unfitness to be a motive.

When voluntary benefit and voluntary injury are pointed out as the main, if not the sole objects of moral approbation and disapprobation—when we are told truly, that the production of good, as good, is always loved, and that of evil, as such, always hated—can we require a more clear, short, and unanswerable proof, that beneficial tendency is an essential quality of virtue? It is indeed an evidently necessary consequence of this statement, that if benevolence be amiable in itself, our affection for it must increase with its extent; and that no man can be in a perfectly right state of mind, who, if he consider general happiness at all, is not ready to acknowledge that a good man must regard it as being in its own nature the most desirable of all objects, however the constitution and circumstances of human nature may render it unfit or impossible to pursue it *directly* as the object of life. It is at the same time apparent that no such man can consider any habitual disposition, clearly discerned to be in its whole result at variance with general happiness, as not unworthy of being cultivated, or as not fit to be rooted out. It is manifest that, if it were otherwise, he would cease to be benevolent. As soon as we conceive the sublime idea of a Being who not only foresees, but commands, all the consequences of the actions of all voluntary agents, this scheme of reasoning appears far more clear. In such a case, if our moral sentiments remain the same, they compel us to attribute his whole government of the world to benevolence. The consequence is as necessary as in any process of reasoning; for if our moral nature be supposed, it will appear self-evident, that it is as much impossible for us to love and revere such a Being, if we ascribe to him a mixed or imperfect benevolence, as to believe the most positive contradiction in terms. Now, as religion consists in that love and reverence, it is evident that it cannot subsist without a belief in benevolence as the sole principle of Divine government. It is nothing to tell us that this is not a process of reasoning, or, to speak more exactly, that the first propositions are assumed. The first propositions in every discussion relating to intellectual operations must likewise be assumed. Conscience is not reason, but it is not less an essential part of human nature than reason. Principles which are essential to all its operations are as much entitled to immediate and implicit assent, as those principles which stand in the same relation to the reasoning faculties. The laws prescribed by a benevolent Being to his creatures must necessarily be founded on the principle of promoting their happiness. It would be singular indeed, if the proofs of the goodness of God, legible in every part of nature, should not, above all others, be most discoverable and conspicuous in the beneficial tendency of His moral laws.

But we are asked, If tendency to general welfare be the standard of virtue, why is it not always present to the contemplation of every man who does or prefers a virtuous action? Must not utility be in that case "the felt essence of virtue?"* Why are other ends, besides general happiness, fit to be morally pursued?

These questions, which are all founded on that confusion of the *theory of actions* with the theory of *sentiments*, against which the reader was so early warned,† might be dismissed with no more than a reference to that distinction from the forgetfulness of which they have arisen. By those advocates of utility, indeed, who hold it to be a necessary part of their system that some glimpse at least of tendency to personal or general well-being is an essential part of the motives which render an action virtuous, these questions cannot be satisfactorily answered. Against such they are arguments of irresistible force; but against the doctrine itself, rightly understood and justly bounded, they are altogether powerless. The reason why there may, and must be, many ends morally more fit to be pursued in practice than general happiness, is plainly to be found in the limited capacity of man. A perfectly good being who foresees and commands all the consequences of action, cannot indeed be conceived by us to have any other end in view than general well-being. Why evil exists under that perfect government is a question towards the solution of which the human understanding can

---

* *Lectures*, vol. iv. p. 38. † See *supra*, pp. 11-15.

scarcely advance a single step. But all who hold the evil to exist only for good, and own their inability to explain why or how, are perfectly exempt from any charge of inconsistency in their obedience to the dictates of their moral nature. The measure of the faculties of man renders it absolutely necessary for him to have many other practical ends ; the pursuit of all of which is moral, when it actually tends to general happiness, though that last end never entered into the contemplation of the agent. It is impossible for us to calculate the effects of a single action, any more than the chances of a single life. But let it not be hastily concluded that the calculation of consequences is impossible in moral subjects. To calculate the general tendency of every sort of human action, is a possible, easy, and common operation. The general good effects of temperance, prudence, fortitude, justice, benevolence, gratitude, veracity, fidelity—of the affections of kindred, and of love for our country—are the subjects of calculations which, taken as generalities, are absolutely unerring. They are founded on a larger and firmer basis of more uniform experience, than any of those ordinary calculations which govern prudent men in the whole business of life. An appeal to these daily and familiar transactions furnishes at once a decisive answer, both to those advocates of utility who represent the consideration of it as a necessary ingredient in virtuous motives, as well as moral approbation, and to those opponents who turn the unwarrantable inferences of unskilful advocates into proofs of the absurdity into which the doctrine leads.

The cultivation of all the habitual sentiments from which the various classes of virtuous actions flow—the constant practice of such actions—the strict observance of rules in all that province of Ethics which can be subjected to rules—the watchful care of all the outworks of every part of duty, of that descending series of useful habits which, being securities to virtue, become themselves virtues—are so many ends which it is absolutely necessary for man to pursue and to seek for their own sake.

"I saw D'Alembert," says a late writer, "congratulate a young man very coldly, who brought him a solution of a problem. The young man said, 'I have done this in order to have a seat in the Academy.' 'Sir,' answered D'Alembert, 'with such dispositions you never will earn one. Science must be loved for its own sake, and not for the advantage to be derived. No other principle will enable a man to make progress in the sciences.'"* It is singular that D'Alembert should not perceive the extensive application of this truth to the whole nature of man. No man can make progress in a virtue who does not seek it for its own sake. No man is a friend, a lover of his country, a kind father, a dutiful son, who does not consider the cultivation of affection and the performance of duty in all these cases respectively as incumbent on him for their own sake, and not for the advantage to be derived from them. Whoever serves another with a view of advantage to himself is universally acknowledged not to act from affection. But the more immediate application of this truth to our purpose is, that in the case of those virtues which are the means of cultivating and preserving other virtues, it is necessary to acquire love and reverence for the secondary virtues for their own sake, without which they never will be effectual means of sheltering and strengthening those intrinsically higher qualities to which they are appointed to minister. Every moral act must be considered as an end, and men must banish from their practice the regard to the most naturally subordinate duty as a means. Those who are perplexed by the supposition that secondary virtues, making up, by the *extent* of their beneficial tendency, for what in each particular instance they may want in *magnitude*, may become of as great

* *Mémoires de Montlosier*, vol. i. p. 50.

importance as the primary virtues themselves, would do well to consider a parallel though very homely case. A house is useful for many purposes: many of these purposes are, in themselves, for the time, more important than shelter. The destruction of the house may, nevertheless, become a greater evil than the defeat of several of these purposes, because it is permanently convenient, and indeed necessary to the execution of most of them. A floor is made for warmth, for dryness —to support tables, chairs, beds, and all the household implements which contribute to accommodation and to pleasure. The floor is valuable only as a means; but, as the only means by which many ends are attained, it may be much more valuable than some of them. The table might be, and generally is, of more valuable timber than the floor; but the workman who should for that reason take more pains in making the table strong than the floor secure would not long be employed by customers of common sense. The connection of that part of morality which regulates the intercourse of the sexes with benevolence, affords the most striking instance of the very great importance which may belong to a virtue, in itself secondary, but on which the general cultivation of the highest virtues permanently depends. Delicacy and modesty may be thought chiefly worthy of cultivation, because they guard purity: but they must be loved for their own sake, without which they cannot flourish. Purity is the sole school of domestic fidelity, and domestic fidelity is the only nursery of the affections between parents and children, from children towards each other, and, through these affections, of all the kindness which renders the world habitable. At each step in the progress, the appropriate end must be loved for its own sake; and it is easy to see how the only means of sowing the seeds of benevolence, in all its forms, may become of far greater importance than many of the modifications and exertions even of benevolence itself. To those who will consider this subject, it will not long seem strange that the sweetest and most gentle affections grow up only under the apparently cold and dark shadow of stern duty. The obligation is strengthened, not weakened, by the consideration that it arises from human imperfection; which only proves it to be founded on the nature of man. It is enough that the pursuit of all these separate ends leads to general well-being, the promotion of which is the final purpose of the creation.

The last and most specious argument against beneficial tendency, even as a test, is conveyed in the question, why moral approbation is not bestowed on every thing beneficial, instead of being confined, as it confessedly is, to voluntary acts? It may plausibly be said, that the establishment of the beneficial tendency of all those voluntary acts which are the objects of moral approbation is not sufficient, since, if such tendency be the standard, it ought to follow, that whatever is useful should also be morally approved. To answer, as has before been done,* that experience gradually limits moral approbation and disapprobation to voluntary acts, by teaching us that they [approbation and disapprobation] influence the will, but are wholly wasted if they be applied to any other object,—though the fact be true, and contributes somewhat to the result,—is certainly not enough. It is at best a partial solution. Perhaps, on reconsideration, it is entitled only to a secondary place. To seek a foundation for universal, ardent, early, and immediate feelings, in processes of an intellectual nature, has, since the origin of philosophy, been the grand error of ethical inquirers into human nature. To seek for such a foundation in association, an early and insensible process, which confessedly mingles itself with the composition of our first and simplest feelings, and which is common to both parts of our nature, is not liable to the same animadversion. If conscience be uniformly produced by the

* See *supra*, pp. 144-5.

regular and harmonious co-operation of many processes of association, the objection is in reality a challenge to produce a complete theory of it, founded on that principle, by exhibiting such a full account of all these processes as may satisfactorily explain why it proceeds thus far and no farther. This would be a very arduous attempt, and perhaps it may be premature. But something may be more modestly tried towards an *outline*, which, though it might leave many particulars unexplained, may justify a reasonable expectation that they are not incapable of explanation; and may even now assign such reasons for the limitation of approbation to voluntary acts, as may convert the objection derived from that fact into a corroboration of the doctrines to which it has been opposed as an insurmountable difficulty. Such an attempt will naturally lead to the close of the present Dissertation. The attempt has indeed been already made,* but not without great apprehensions on the part of the author, that he has not been clear enough, especially in those parts which appeared to himself to owe most to his own reflection. He will now endeavour, at the expense of some repetition, to be more satisfactory.

There must be primary pleasures, pains, and even appetites, which arise from no prior state of mind, and which, if explained at all, can be derived only from bodily organisation; for if there were not, there could be no secondary desires. What the number of the underived principles may be, is a question to which the answers of philosophers have been extremely various, and of which the consideration is not necessary to our present purpose. The rules of philosophising, however, require that causes should not be multiplied without necessity. Of two explanations, therefore, which give an equally satisfactory account of appearances, that theory is manifestly to be preferred which supposes the smaller number

* See *supra*, pp. 120-1, 164-173.

of ultimate and inexplicable principles. This maxim, it is true, is subject to three indispensable conditions. 1. That the principles employed in the explanation should be known really to exist: in which consists the main distinction between hypothesis and theory. Gravity is a principle universally known to exist; ether and a nervous fluid are mere suppositions. 2. That these principles should be known to produce effects *like* those which are ascribed to them in the theory. This is a further distinction between hypothesis and theory; for there are an infinite number of degrees of *likeness*, from the faint resemblances which have led some to fancy that the functions of the nerves depend on electricity, to the remarkable coincidences between the appearances of projectiles on earth and the movements of the heavenly bodies, which constitute the Newtonian system; a theory now perfect, though exclusively founded on analogy, and in which one of the classes of phenomena brought together by it is not the subject of direct experience. 3. That it should correspond, if not with all the facts to be explained, at least with so great a majority of them as to render it highly probable that means will in time be found of reconciling it to all. It is only on this ground that the Newtonian system justly claimed the title of a legitimate theory during that long period when it was unable to explain many celestial appearances, before the labours of a century, and the genius of Laplace, at length completed the theory, by adapting it to all the phenomena. A theory may be just before it is complete.

In the application of these canons to the theory which derives most of the principles of human action from the transfer of a small number of pleasures, perhaps organic, by the law of association, to a vast variety of new objects, it cannot be denied, 1*st*, That it satisfies the first of the above conditions, inasmuch as association is *really* one of the laws of human nature; 2*dly*, That it also satisfies the second, for association certainly produces effects *like* those which are referred to it by this theory, otherwise there would be no secondary desires, no acquired relishes and dislikes ;—facts universally acknowledged, which are and can be explained only by the principle called by Hobbes *mental discourse ;*— by Locke, Hume, Hartley, Condillac, and the majority of speculators, as well as in common speech, *association ;*—by Tucker, *translation ;* and by Brown *suggestion.* The facts generally referred to the principle *resemble* those which are claimed for it by the theory in this important particular, that in both cases equally, pleasure becomes attached to perfectly new things, so that the derivative desires become perfectly independent on the primary. The great dissimilarity of these two classes of passions has been supposed to consist in this, that the former always regards the interest of the individual, while the latter regards the welfare of others. The philosophical world has been almost entirely divided into two sects ; the partisans of selfishness, comprising mostly all the predecessors of Butler, and the greater part of his successors ; and the advocates of benevolence, who have generally contended that the reality of disinterestedness depends on its being a *primary principle.* Enough has been said by Butler against the more fatal heresy of selfishness. Something has already been said against the error of the advocates of disinterestedness, in the progress of this attempt to develop ethical truths historically, in the order in which inquiry and controversy brought them out with increasing brightness. The analogy of the material world is indeed faint, and often delusive ; yet we dare not utterly reject that on which the whole technical language of mental and moral science is necessarily grounded. The whole creation teems with instances where the most powerful agents and the most lasting bodies are the acknowledged results of the composition, sometimes of a few, often of many elements. These compounds often in their turn become the elements of other substances; and it is with them that we are conversant chiefly in the pursuits of knowledge, solely in the concerns of life. No man ever fancied that, because they were compounds, they were therefore less *real*. It is impossible to confound them with any of the separate elements which contribute towards their formation. But a much more close resemblance presents itself. Every secondary desire, or acquired relish, involves in it a transfer of pleasure to something which was before indifferent or disagreeable. Is the new pleasure the less real for being acquired? Is it not often preferred to the original enjoyment? Are not many of these secondary pleasures indestructible? Do not many of them survive primary appetites? Lastly, the important principle of regard to our own general welfare, which disposes us to prefer it to immediate pleasure, unfortunately called self-love (as if, in any intelligible sense of the term *love*, it were possible for a man to love himself), is perfectly intelligible if its origin be ascribed to association, but utterly incomprehensible if it be considered as prior to the appetites and desires, which alone furnish it with materials. As happiness consists of satisfactions, self-love presupposes appetites and desires which are to be satisfied. If the order of time were important, the affections are formed at an earlier period than many self-regarding passions, and they always precede the formation of self-love.

Many of the later advocates of the disinterested system, though recoiling from an apparent approach to the selfishness into which the purest of their antagonists had occasionally fallen, were gradually obliged to make concessions to the derivative system, though clogged with the contradictory assertion, that it was only a refinement of selfishness: and we have seen that Brown, the last and not the least in genius of them, has nearly abandoned the greater, though not indeed the most important part of the territory in dispute, and scarcely contends for any underived principle but the moral faculty.

In this state of opinion among the very small number in Great Britain who still preserve some remains of a taste for such speculations, it is needless here to trace the application of the law of association to the formation of the secondary desires, whether private or social. For our present purposes, the explanation of their origin may be assumed to be satisfactory. In what follows, it must, however, be steadily borne in mind, that this concession involves an admission that the pleasure derived from low objects may be transferred to the most pure; that from a part of a self-regarding appetite such a pleasure may become a portion of a perfectly disinterested desire; and that the disinterested nature and absolute independence of the latter are not in the slightest degree impaired by the consideration that it is formed by one of those grand mental processes to which the formation of the other habitual states of the human mind have been, with great probability, ascribed.

When the social affections are thus formed, they are naturally followed in every instance by the will to do whatever can promote their object. Compassion excites a voluntary determination to do whatever relieves the person pitied. The like process must occur in every case of gratitude, generosity, and affection. Nothing so uniformly follows the kind disposition as the act of will, because it is the only means by which the benevolent desire can be gratified. The result of what Brown justly calls "a finer analysis," shows the mental contiguity of the affection to the volition to be much closer than appears on a coarser examination of this part of our nature. No wonder, then, that the strongest association, the most active power of reciprocal suggestion, should subsist between them. As all the affections are delightful, so the volitions, voluntary acts which are the only means of their gratification, become agreeable objects of contemplation to the mind. The habitual disposition to perform them is felt in ourselves, and observed in others, with satisfaction. As these feelings become more lively, the absence of them may be viewed in ourselves with a pain, in others with an alienaation, capable of indefinite increase. They become entirely independent sentiments; still, however, receiving constant supplies of nourishment from their parent affections, which, in well-balanced minds, reciprocally strengthen each other; unlike the unkind passions, which are constantly engaged in the most angry conflicts of civil war. In this state we desire to experience these *beneficent volitions*, to cultivate a disposition towards them, and to do every correspondent voluntary act. They are for their own sake the objects of desire. They thus constitute a large portion of those emotions, desires, and affections, which regard certain dispositions of the mind and determinations of the will as their sole and ultimate end. These are what are called the moral sense, the moral sentiments, or best, though most simply, by the ancient name of *Conscience;* which has the merit, in our language, of being applied to no other purpose, which peculiarly marks the strong working of these feelings on conduct, and which, from its solemn and sacred character, is well adapted to denote the venerable authority of the highest principle of human nature.

Nor is this all: It has already been seen that not only sympathy with the sufferer, but indignation against the wrong-doer, contributes a large and important share towards the moral feelings. We are angry at those who disappoint our wish for the happiness of others. We make the resentment of the innocent person wronged our own. Our moderate anger approves all well-proportioned punishment of the wrong-doer. We hence approve those dispositions and actions of voluntary agents which promote such suitable punishment, and disapprove those which hinder its infliction or destroy its effect; at the head of which may be placed that excess of punishment beyond the average feelings of good men, which turns the indignation of the calm bystander against the culprit into pity. In this state, when anger is duly moderated,—when it is proportioned to the wrong—when it is detached from personal considerations—when *dispositions and actions are its ultimate objects,*—it becomes a sense of justice, and is so purified as to be fitted to be a new element of conscience. There is no part of morality which is so *directly* aided by a conviction of the necessity of its observance to the general interest as justice. The connection between them is discoverable by the most common understanding. All public deliberations profess the public welfare to be their object; all laws propose it as their end. This calm principle of public utility serves to mediate between the sometimes repugnant feelings which arise in the punishment of criminals, by repressing undue pity on one hand, and reducing resentment to its proper level on the other. Hence the unspeakable importance of criminal laws as a part of the moral education of mankind. Whenever they carefully conform to the moral sentiments of the age and country—when they are withheld from approaching the limits within which the disapprobation of good men would confine punishment, they contribute in the highest degree to increase the ignominy of crimes, to make men recoil from the first suggestions of criminality, and to nourish and mature the sense of justice, which lends new vigour to the conscience with which it has been united.

Other contributary streams present themselves. Qualities which are necessary to virtue, but may be subservient to vice, may, independently of that excellence or of that defect, be in themselves admirable. Courage, energy, decision, are of this nature. In their wild state they are often savage and destructive. When they are tamed by the society of the affections,

S

and trained up in obedience to the moral faculty, they become virtues of the highest order, and, by their name of *magnanimity*, proclaim the general sense of mankind that they are the characteristic qualities of a great soul. They retain whatever was admirable in their unreclaimed state, together with all that they borrow from their new associate and their high ruler. Their nature, it must be owned, is prone to evil; but this propensity does not hinder them from being rendered capable of being ministers of good, in a state where the gentler virtues require to be vigorously guarded against the attacks of daring depravity. It is thus that the strength of the well-educated elephant is sometimes employed in vanquishing the fierceness of the tiger, and sometimes used as a means of defence against the shock of his brethren of the same species. The delightful contemplation, however, of these qualities, when purely applied, becomes one of the sentiments of which the dispositions and actions of voluntary agents are the direct and final object. By this resemblance they are associated with the other moral principles, and with them contribute to form Conscience, which, as the master faculty of the soul, levies such large contributions on every province of human nature.

It is important, in this point of view, to consider also the moral approbation which is undoubtedly bestowed *on those dispositions and actions of voluntary agents* which terminate in their own satisfaction, security, and well-being. They have been called duties to ourselves, as absurdly as a regard to our own greatest happiness is called self-love. But it cannot be reasonably doubted that intemperance, improvidence, timidity, even when considered only in relation to the individual, are not only regretted as imprudent, but blamed as morally wrong. It was excellently observed by Aristotle that a man is not commended as *temperate*, so long as it costs him efforts of *self-denial* to persevere in the practice of temperance, but only when *he prefers that virtue for its own sake*. He is not meek, nor brave, as long as the most vigorous self-command is necessary to bridle his anger or his fear. On the same principle, he may be judicious or prudent, but he is not benevolent, if he confers benefits with a view to his own greatest happiness. In like manner, it is ascertained by experience that all the masters of science and of art—that all those who have successfully pursued truth and knowledge —love them for their own sake, without regard to the generally imaginary power of interest, or even to the dazzling crown which fame may place on their heads.* But it may still be reasonably asked, why these useful qualities are morally improved, and how they become capable of being combined with those public and disinterested sentiments which principally constitute conscience? The answer is, because they are entirely conversant with volitions and voluntary actions, and in that respect resemble the other constituents of conscience, with which they are thereby fitted to mingle and coalesce. Like those other principles, they may be detached from what is personal and outward, and fixed on the dispositions and actions, which are the only means of promoting their ends. The sequence of these principles and acts of will becomes so frequent that the association between

* See the "Pursuit of Knowledge under Difficulties," a discourse forming the first part of the third volume of the *Library of Entertaining Knowledge*, London, 1829. The author of this Essay will by others be placed at the head of those who, in the midst of arduous employments, and surrounded by all the allurements of society, yet find leisure for exerting the unwearied vigour of their minds in every mode of rendering permanent service to the human species; more especially in spreading a love of knowledge, and diffusing useful truth among all classes of men. These voluntary occupations deserve our attention still less as examples of prodigious power than as proofs of an intimate conviction, which binds them by unity of purpose with his public duties, that (to use the almost dying words of an excellent person), "man can neither be happy without virtue, nor actively virtuous without liberty, nor securely free without rational knowledge." (Close of Sir W. Jones' last *Discourse to the Asiatic Society at Calcutta*.)

both may be as firm as in the former cases. All those sentiments of which the final object is a state of the will become thus intimately and inseparably blended; and of that perfect state of solution (if such words may be allowed) the result is *Conscience*—the judge and arbiter of human conduct; which, though it does not supersede *ordinary motives* of virtuous feelings and habits, which are the ordinary motives of good actions, yet exercises a lawful authority even over them, and ought to blend with them. Whatsoever actions and dispositions are approved by conscience acquire the name of virtues or duties; they are pronounced to deserve commendation; and we are justly considered as under a moral *obligation* to practise the actions and cultivate the dispositions.

The coalition of the private and public feelings is very remarkable in two points of view, from which it seems hitherto to have been scarcely observed. *First,* It illustrates very forcibly all that has been here offered to prove, that the peculiar character of the moral sentiments consists in their *exclusive reference to states of will,* and that every feeling which has that quality, when it is purified from all admixture with different objects, becomes capable of being absorbed into Conscience, and of being assimilated to it, so as to become a part of it. For no feelings can be more unlike each other in their object than the private and the social; and yet, as both employ voluntary actions as their sole immediate means, both may be transferred by association to states of the will, in which case they are transmuted into moral sentiments. No example of the coalition of feelings in their general nature less widely asunder, could afford so much support to this position. *Secondly,* By raising qualities useful to ourselves to the rank of virtues, it throws a strong light on the relation of virtue to individual interest; very much as justice illustrates the relation of morality to general interest. The coincidence of morality with individual interest is an important truth in Ethics. It is most manifest in that part of Ethics which we are now considering. A calm regard to our general interest is indeed a faint and unfrequent motive of action. Its chief advantage is, that it is regular, and that its movements may be calculated. In deliberate conduct it may often be relied on, though perhaps never safely without knowledge of the whole temper and character. But in moral reasoning at least, the coincidence is of unspeakable advantage. If there be a miserable man who has cold affections, a weak sense of justice, dim perceptions of right and wrong, and faint feelings of them;—if, still more wretched, his heart be constantly torn and devoured by malevolent passions—the vultures of the soul;—we have one resource still left, even in cases so dreadful. Even *he* still retains a human principle, to which we can speak. He must own that he has some wish for his own lasting welfare. We can prove to him that his state of mind is inconsistent with it. It may be impossible indeed to show, that while the disposition continues the same, he can derive any enjoyment from the practice of virtue. But it may be most clearly shown that every advance in the amendment of that disposition is a step towards even temporal happiness. If he do not amend his character, we may compel him to own that he is at variance with himself, and offends against a principle of which even *he* must recognise the reasonableness.

The formation of conscience from so many elements, and especially the combination of elements so unlike as the private desires and the social affections, early contributes to give it the appearance of that simplicity and independence which in its mature state really distinguish it. It becomes, from these circumstances, more difficult to distinguish its separate principles; and it is impossible to exhibit them in separate action. The affinity of these various passions to each other, which consists in their having no object but *states of the will*, is the only common property which strikes the mind. Hence the facility with which the general terms, first probably limited to the relations between ourselves and others, are gradually extended to all voluntary acts and dispositions. Prudence and temperance become the objects of moral approbation. When imprudence is immediately disapproved by the bystander, without deliberate consideration of its consequences, it is not only displeasing as being pernicious, but it is blamed as *wrong*, though with a censure so much inferior to that bestowed on inhumanity and injustice, as may justify those writers who use the milder term *improper*. At length, when the general words come to signify the objects of moral approbation, and the reverse, they denote merely the power to excite feelings which are as independent as if they were underived, and which coalesce the more perfectly, because they are detached from objects so various and unlike as to render their return to their primitive state very difficult.

The question,* why we do not morally approve the useful qualities of actions which are altogether *involuntary*, may now be shortly and satisfactorily answered: because conscience is in perpetual contact, as it were, with all the dispositions and actions of *voluntary* agents, and is by that means indissolubly associated with them exclusively. It has a direct action on the will, and a constant mental contiguity to it. It has no such mental contiguity to involuntary changes. It has never perhaps been observed that an operation of the conscience precedes all acts deliberate enough to be in the highest sense voluntary, and does so as much when it is defeated as when it prevails. In either case the association is repeated. It extends to the whole of the active man. All passions have a definite outward object to which they tend, and a limited sphere within which they act. But conscience has no object but a state of will; and as an act of will is the sole means of gratifying any passion, conscience is co-extensive with the

* See *supra*, p. 120.

whole man, and without encroachment curbs or aids every feeling, even within the peculiar province of that feeling itself. As will is the universal means, conscience, which regards will, must be a universal principle. As nothing is interposed between conscience and the will when the mind is in its healthy state, the dictate of conscience is followed by the determination of the will, with a promptitude and exactness which very naturally is likened to the obedience of an inferior to the lawful commands of those whom he deems to be rightfully placed over him. It therefore seems clear, that, on the theory which has been attempted, moral approbation must be limited to voluntary operations, and conscience must be universal, independent, and commanding.

One remaining difficulty may perhaps be objected to the general doctrines of this Dissertation, though it does not appear at any time to have been urged against other modifications of the same principle. "If moral approbation," it may be said, "involve no perception of beneficial tendency, whence arises the coincidence between that principle and the moral sentiments?" It may seem at first sight that such a theory rests the foundation of morals upon a coincidence altogether mysterious, and apparently capricious and fantastic. Waiving all other answers, let us at once proceed to that which seems conclusive. It is true that conscience rarely contemplates so distant an object as the welfare of all sentient beings. But to what point is every one of its elements directed? What, for instance, is the aim of all the social affections? Nothing but the production of larger or smaller masses of happiness among those of our fellow-creatures who are the objects of these affections. In every case these affections promote happiness as far as their foresight and their power extend. What can be more conducive, or even necessary, to the being and *well-being* of society than the rules of justice? Are not the angry passions themselves, as far as they are ministers of morality, employed in removing hindrances to the *welfare* of ourselves and others, which is indirectly promoting it? The private passions terminate indeed in the happiness of the individual, which, however, is a part of general happiness, and the part over which we have most power. Every principle of which conscience is composed has some portion of happiness for its object. To that point they all converge. General happiness is not indeed one of the natural objects of conscience, because our voluntary acts are not felt and perceived to affect it. But how small a step is left for reason. It only casts up the items of the account. It has only to discover that the acts of those who labour to promote separate portions of happiness must increase the amount of the whole. It may be truly said, that if observation and experience did not clearly ascertain that beneficial tendency is the constant attendant and mark of all virtuous dispositions and actions, the same great truth would be revealed to us by the voice of conscience. The coincidence, instead of being arbitrary, arises necessarily from the laws of human nature, and the circumstances in which mankind are placed. We perform and approve virtuous actions, partly because conscience regards them as right, partly because we are prompted to them by good affections. All these affections contribute towards general well-being, though it were not necessary, nor would it be fit, that the agent should be distracted by the contemplation of that vast and remote object.

The various relations of conscience to religion we have already been led to consider on the principles of Butler, of Berkeley, of Paley, and especially of Hartley, who was led by his own piety to contemplate as the last and highest stage of virtue and happiness, a sort of self-annihilation, which, however unsuitable to the present condition of mankind, yet places in the strongest light the disinterested character of the system, of which it is a conceivable though perhaps not attainable result. The completeness and rigour acquired by conscience, when all its dictates are revered as the commands of a perfectly wise and good Being, are so obvious, that they cannot be questioned by any reasonable man, however extensive his incredulity may be. It is thus that conscience can add the warmth of an affection to the inflexibility of principle and habit. It is true that, in examining the evidence of the divine original of a religious system, in estimating an imperfect religion, or in comparing the demerits of religions of human origin, conscience must be the standard chiefly applied. But it follows with equal clearness that those who have the happiness to find satisfaction and repose in divine revelation, are bound to consider all those precepts for the government of the will, delivered by it, which are manifestly universal, as the rules to which all their feelings and actions should conform. The true distinction between conscience and a taste for moral beauty has already been pointed out;* a distinction which, notwithstanding its simplicity, has been unobserved by philosophers, perhaps on account of the frequent co-operation and intermixture of the two feelings. Most speculators have either denied the existence of the taste, or kept it out of view in their theory, or exalted it to the place which is rightfully filled only by conscience. Yet it is perfectly obvious that, like all the other feelings called pleasures of imagination, it terminates in delightful contemplation, while the moral faculty always aims exclusively at voluntary action. Nothing can more clearly show that this last quality is the characteristic of conscience, than its being thus found to distinguish that faculty from the sentiments which most nearly resemble it, most frequently attend it, and are most easily blended with it.

Some attempt has now been made to develop the fundamental principles of ethical theory, in that historical order in which meditation and discussion brought them successively into a clearer light. That attempt, as far as it regards Great

* See *supra*, pp. 169-171.

Britain, is at least chronologically complete. The spirit of bold speculation conspicuous among the English of the seventeenth century languished after the earlier part of the eighteenth, and seems, from the time of Hutcheson, to have passed into Scotland, where it produced Hume, the greatest of sceptics, and Smith, the most eloquent of modern moralists; besides giving rise to that sober, modest, perhaps timid Philosophy, which is commonly called Scotch—which has the singular merit of having first strongly and largely inculcated the absolute necessity of admitting certain principles as the foundation of all reasoning, and as being the indispensable conditions of thought itself. In the eye of the moralist, all the philosophers of Scotland, Hume and Smith, as much as Reid, Campbell, and Stewart, have also the merit of having avoided the selfish system; and of having, under whatever variety of representation, alike maintained the disinterested nature of the social affections and the supreme authority of the moral sentiments. Brown reared the standard of revolt against the masters of the Scottish School, and in reality, still more than in words, adopted those very doctrines against which his predecessors, after their war against scepticism, uniformly combated. The law of association, though expressed in other language, became the nearly universal principle of his system; and perhaps it would have been absolutely universal if he had not been restrained rather by respectful feelings than by cogent reasons. With him the love of speculative philosophy, as a pursuit, appears to have expired in Scotland. There are some symptoms, yet, however, very faint, of the revival of a taste for it among the English youth. It was received with approbation in France from M. Royer Collard, the scholar of Stewart more than of Reid, and with enthusiasm from his pupil and successor M. Cousin, who has clothed the doctrines of the Schools of Germany in an unwonted eloquence, which always adorns, but sometimes disguises them.

The history of Political Philosophy, even if its extent and subdivisions were better defined, would, it is manifest, have occupied another Dissertation, at least equal in length to the present. The most valuable parts of it belong to Civil History. It is too often tainted by a turbulent and factious spirit to be easily combined with the calmer history of the progress of science, or even of the revolutions of speculation. In no age of the world were its principles so interwoven with political events, and so deeply imbued with the passions and divisions excited by them, as in the eighteenth century.

It was at one time the purpose, or rather perhaps hope, of the writer, to close this discourse by an account of the ethical systems which have prevailed in Germany during the last half-century; which, maintaining the same spirit amidst great changes of technical language, and even of speculative principle, have now exclusive possession of Europe to the north of the Rhine, have been welcomed by the French youth with open arms, have roused in some measure the languishing genius of Italy, but are still little known and unjustly estimated by the mere English reader. He found himself, however, soon reduced to the necessity of either being superficial, and by consequence uninstructive; or of devoting to that subject a far longer time than he can now spare, and a much larger space than the limits of this work would probably allow. The majority of readers will indeed be more disposed to require an excuse for the extent of what has been done, than for the relinquishment of projected additions. All readers must agree that this is peculiarly a subject on which it is better to be silent than to say too little.*

A very few observations, however, on the German Philo-

* [In the *Philosophy of Discovery*, chap. xxiv., I have given some account of the successive German philosophies of Kant, Fichte, Schelling, and Hegel, so far as the progress of knowledge is concerned: and in the following chapter I have treated of moral progress.—W. W.]

sophy, as far as relates to its ethical bearings and influence, may perhaps be pardoned. These remarks are not so much intended to be applied to the moral doctrines of that school, considered in themselves, as to those apparent defects in the prevailing systems of Ethics throughout Europe, which seem to have suggested the necessity of their adoption. Kant has himself acknowledged that his whole theory of the percipient and intellectual faculty was intended to protect the first principles of human knowledge against the assaults of Hume. In like manner, his ethical system is evidently framed for the purpose of guarding certain principles, either directly governing or powerfully affecting practice, which seemed to him to have been placed on unsafe foundations by their advocates, and which were involved in perplexity and confusion, especially by those who adapted the results of various and sometimes contradictory systems to the taste of multitudes, more eager to know than prepared to be taught. To the theoretical reason he superadded the practical reason, which had peculiar laws and principles of its own, from which all the rules of morals may be deduced. The practical reason cannot be conceived without these laws; therefore they are *inherent.* It perceives them to be *necessary* and *universal.* Hence, by a process not altogether dissimilar, at least in its gross results, to that which was employed for the like purpose by Cudworth and Clarke, by Price, and in some degree by Stewart, he raises the social affections, and still more the moral sentiments, above the sphere of enjoyment, and beyond that series of enjoyments which is called happiness. The performance of duty, not the pursuit of happiness, is in this system the chief end of man. By the same intuition we discover that virtue deserves happiness; and as this desert is not uniformly so requited in the present state of existence, it compels us to believe a moral government of the world, and a future state of existence, in which all the conditions of the practical reason will be realised;—

truths, of which, in the opinion of Kant, the argumentative proofs were at least very defective, but of which the revelations of the practical reason afforded a more conclusive demonstration than any process of reasoning could supply. The understanding, he owned, saw nothing in the connection of motive with *volition* different from what it discovered in every other uniform sequence of a cause and an effect. But as the moral law delivered by the practical reason issues peremptory and inflexible commands, the power of always obeying them is implied in their very nature. All individual objects, all outward things, must indeed be viewed in the relation of cause and effect. They are necessary conditions of all reasoning. But the acts of the faculty which *wills*, of which we are immediately conscious, belong to another province of mind, and are not subject to these laws of the theoretical reason. The mere intellect must still regard them as necessarily connected; but the practical reason distinguishes its own *liberty* from the *necessity* of nature, conceives volition without at the same time conceiving an antecedent to it, and regards all moral beings as the original authors of their own actions.

Even those who are unacquainted with this complicated and comprehensive system will at once see the slightness of the above sketch. Those who understand it will own that so brief an outline could not be otherwise than slight. It will, however, be sufficient for the present purpose, if it render what follows intelligible.

With respect to what is called the practical reason, the Kantian system varies from ours, in treating it as having more resemblance to the intellectual powers than to sentiment and emotion. Enough has already been said on that question. At the next step, however, the difference seems to resolve itself into a misunderstanding. The character and dignity of the human race surely depend, not on the state in which they are born, but on that which they are all destined to attain or to approach. No man would hesitate in assenting to this observation when applied to the intellectual faculties. Thus the human infant comes into the world imbecile and ignorant; but a vast majority acquire some vigour of reason and extent of knowledge. Strictly, the human infant is born neither selfish nor social; but the far greater part acquire some provident regard to their own welfare, and a number, probably not much smaller, feel some sparks of affection towards others. On our principles, therefore, as much as on those of Kant, human nature is capable of disinterested sentiments. For we too allow and contend that our moral faculty is a *necessary* part of human nature—that it *universally* exists in human beings—that we cannot conceive any moral agents without qualities which are either like, or produce the like effects. It is necessarily regarded by us as co-extensive with human, and even with moral nature. In what other sense can *universality* be predicated of any proposition not identical? Why should it be tacitly assumed that all these great characteristics of conscience should necessarily presuppose its being unformed and underived? What contradiction is there between them and the theory of regular and uniform formation?

In this instance it should seem that a general assent to truth is chiefly if not solely obstructed by an inveterate prejudice, arising from the mode in which the questions relating to the affections and the moral faculty have been discussed among ethical philosophers. Generally speaking, those who contend that these parts of the mind are acquired, have also held that they are, in their perfect state, no more than modifications of self-love. On the other hand, philosophers " of purer fire," who felt that conscience is sovereign, and that affection is disinterested, have too hastily fancied that their ground was untenable, without contending that these qualities were inherent or innate, and absolutely underived from any other properties of mind. If a choice were necessary between these two systems as masses of opinion, without any freedom of discrimination and selection, I should unquestionably embrace that doctrine which places in the clearest light the reality of benevolence and the authority of the moral faculty. But it is surely easy to apply a test, which may be applied to our conceptions as effectually as a decisive experiment is applied to material substances. Does not he who, whatever he may think of the origin of these parts of human nature, believes that *actually* conscience is supreme, and affection terminates in its direct object, retain all that for which the partisans of the underived principles value and cling to their system? "But they are made," these philosophers may say, "by this class of our antagonists, to rest on insecure foundations. Unless they are underived, we can see no reason for regarding them as independent." In answer, it may be asked, how is the connection between these two qualities established? It is really assumed. It finds its way easily into the mind under the protection of another coincidence, which is of a totally different nature. The great majority of those speculators who have represented the moral and social feelings as acquired, have also considered them as being mere modifications of self-love, and sometimes as being casually formed and easily eradicated, like local and temporary prejudices. But when the nature of our feelings is thoroughly explored, is it not evident that this coincidence is the result of superficial confusion? The better moralists observed accurately, and reasoned justly, on the province of the moral sense and the feelings in the formed and mature man. They reasoned mistakingly on the origin of these principles. But the Epicureans were by no means right, even on the latter question; and they were totally wrong on the other and far more momentous part of the subject. Their error is more extensive, and infinitely more injurious. But what should now hinder an inquirer after truth from embracing but amending their doctrine where it is partially true, and adopting without any change the just description of the most important principles of human nature which we owe to their more enlightened as well as more generous antagonists?

Though unwilling to abandon the arguments by which, from the earliest times, the existence of the Supreme and Eternal Mind has been established, we, as well as the German philosophers, are entitled to call in the help of our moral nature to lighten the burden of those tremendous difficulties which cloud his moral government. The moral nature is an actual part of man, as much on our scheme as on theirs.

Even the celebrated question of Liberty and Necessity may perhaps be rendered somewhat less perplexing, if we firmly bear in mind that peculiar relation of conscience to will which we have attempted to illustrate. It is impossible for reason to consider occurrences otherwise than as bound together by the connection of cause and effect; and in this circumstance consists the strength of the necessitarian system. But conscience, which is equally a constituent part of the mind, has other laws. It is composed of *emotions and desires, which contemplate only those dispositions which depend on the will.* Now, it is the nature of an emotion to withdraw the mind from the contemplation of every idea but that of the object which excites it. Every desire exclusively looks at the object which it seeks. Every attempt to enlarge the mental vision alters the state of mind, weakens the emotion, or dissipates the desire, and tends to extinguish both. If a man, while he was pleased with the smell of a rose, were to reflect on the chemical combinations from which it arose, the condition of his mind would be changed from an enjoyment of the senses to an exertion of the understanding. If, in the view of a beautiful scene, a man were suddenly to turn his thoughts to the disposition of water, vegetables, and earth, on which its appearance depended, he might enlarge his knowledge of geology, but he must lose the pleasure of the prospect. The anatomy and analysis of the flesh and blood of a beautiful woman necessarily suspend admiration and affection. Many analogies here present themselves. When life is in danger either in a storm or a battle, it is certain that less fear is felt by the commander or the pilot, and even by the private soldier actively engaged, or the common seaman laboriously occupied, than by those who are exposed to the peril, but not employed in the means of guarding against it. The reason is not that the one class believe the danger to be less. They are likely in many instances to perceive it more clearly. But having acquired a habit of instantly turning their thoughts to the means of counteracting the danger, their minds are thrown into a state which excludes the ascendency of fear. Mental fortitude entirely depends on this habit. The timid horseman is haunted by the horrors of a fall. The bold and skilful thinks only about the best way of curbing or supporting his horse. Even when all means are equally unavailable, and his condition appears desperate to the bystander, he still owes to his fortunate habit that he does not suffer the agony of the coward. Many cases have been known where fortitude has reached such strength that the faculties, instead of being confounded by danger, are never raised to their highest activity by a less violent stimulant. The distinction between such men and the coward does not depend on difference of opinion about the reality or extent of the danger, but on a state of mind which renders it more or less accessible to fear. Though it must be owned that the moral sentiments are very different from any other human faculty, yet the above observations seem to be in a great measure applicable to every state of mind. The emotions and desires which compose conscience, while they occupy the mind, must exclude all contemplation of the cause in which the object of these feelings may have

T

originated. To their eye the *voluntary dispositions and actions*, their sole object, must appear to be the first link of a chain. In the view of conscience they have no foreign original. The conscience being so constantly associated with *all volitions*, its view becomes habitual:—being always possessed of some, and capable of intense warmth, it predominates over the habits of thinking of those few who are employed in the analysis of mental occupations. The reader who has in any degree been inclined to adopt the explanations attempted above, of the imperative character of conscience, may be disposed also to believe that they afford some foundation for that conviction of the existence of a power to obey its commands, which (it ought to be granted to the German philosophers) is irresistibly suggested by the commanding tone of all its dictates. If such an explanation should be thought worthy of consideration, it must be very carefully distinguished from that illusive sense by which some writers have laboured to reconcile the feeling of liberty with the reality of necessity.* In this case there is no illusion;—nothing is required but the admission, that every faculty observes its own laws, and that when the action of the one fills the mind, that of every other is suspended. The ear cannot see, nor can the eye hear. Why, then, should not the greater powers of reason and conscience have different habitual modes of contemplating voluntary actions? How strongly do experience and analogy seem to require the arrangement of motive and volition under the class of causes and effects! With what irresistible power, on the other hand, do all our moral sentiments remove extrinsic agency from view, and concentrate all feeling in the agent himself! The one manner of thinking may predominate among the speculative few in their short moments of abstraction; the other will be that of all

---

* Lord Kames in his *Essays on Morality and Natural Religion*, and in his *Sketches of the History of Man*.

other men, and of the speculator himself when he is called upon to act, or when his feelings are powerfully excited by the amiable or odious dispositions of his fellow-men. In these workings of various faculties there is nothing that can be accurately described as contrariety of opinion. An intellectual state, and a feeling, never can be contrary to each other. They are too utterly incapable of comparison to be the subject of contrast. They are agents of a perfectly different nature, acting in different spheres. A feeling can no more be called true or false, than a demonstration, considered simply in itself, can be said to be agreeable or disagreeable. It is true, indeed, that in consequence of the association of all mental acts with each other, emotions and desires may occasion habitual errors of judgment ;—but liability to error belongs to every exercise of human reason ; it arises from a multitude of causes ; it constitutes, therefore, no difficulty peculiar to the case before us. Neither truth nor falsehood can be predicated of the perceptions of the senses, but they lead to false opinions. An object seen through different mediums may by the inexperienced be thought to be no longer the same. All men long concluded falsely, from what they saw, that the earth was stationary, and the sun in perpetual motion around it. The greater part of mankind still adopt the same error. Newton and Laplace used the same language with the ignorant, and conformed (if we may not say to their opinion) at least to their habits of thinking on all ordinary occasions, and during the far greater part of their lives. Nor is this all : The language which represents various states of mind is very vague. The word which denotes a compound state is often taken from its *principal* fact, from that which is most *conspicuous*, most easily *called to mind*, most *warmly felt*, or most *frequently recurring*. It is sometimes borrowed from a separate, but, as it were, neighbouring condition of mind. The grand distinction between thought and feeling is so little observed, that we are peculiarly liable to confusion on this subject. Perhaps when we use language which indicates an opinion concerning the acts of the will, we may mean little more than to express strongly or warmly the moral sentiments which voluntary acts alone call up. It would argue disrespect for the human understanding, vainly employed for so many centuries in reconciling contradictory opinions, to propose such suggestions without peculiar diffidence; but before they are altogether rejected, it may be well to consider, whether the constant success of the advocates of necessity on one ground, and of the partisans of free-will on another, does not seem to indicate that the two parties contemplate the subject from different points of view, that neither habitually sees more than one side of it, and that they look at it through the medium of different states of mind.

It should be remembered that these hints of a possible reconciliation between seemingly repugnant opinions are proposed, not as perfect analogies, but to lead men's minds into the inquiry, whether that which certainly befalls the mind, in many cases on a small scale, may not, under circumstances favourable to its development, occur with greater magnitude and more important consequences. The coward and brave, as has been stated, act differently at the approach of danger, because it produces exertion in the one and fear in the other. But very brave men must, by the terms, be few. They have little aid in their highest acts, therefore, from fellow-feeling. They are often too obscure for the hope of praise, and they have seldom been trained to cultivate courage as a virtue. The very reverse occurs in *the different view taken by understanding and by conscience, of the nature of voluntary actions.* The conscientious view must, in some degree, present itself to all mankind. It is therefore unspeakably strengthened by general sympathy. All men respect themselves for being habitually guided by it. It is the object of general commendation; and moral discipline has no other aim but its cultivation. Whoever does not feel more pain from his crimes than from his misfortunes, is looked on with general aversion. And when it is considered that a Being of perfect wisdom and goodness estimates us according to the degree in which conscience governs our voluntary acts, it is surely no wonder that, in this most important discrepancy between the great faculties of our nature, we should consider the best habitual disposition to be that which the coldest reason shows us to be most conducive to well-doing and well-being.

On every other point, at least, it should seem that, without the multiplied suppositions and immense apparatus of the German School, the authority of morality may be vindicated, the disinterestedness of human nature asserted, the first principles of knowledge secured, and the hopes and consolations of mankind preserved. Ages may yet be necessary to give to ethical theory all the forms and language of science, and to apply it to the multiplied and complicated facts and rules which are within its province. In the meantime, if any statement of the opinions here unfolded or intimated shall be proved to be at variance with the reality of social affections, and with the feeling of moral distinction, the author of this Dissertation will be the first to relinquish a theory which will then show itself inadequate to explain the most indisputable, as well as by far the most important, parts of human nature. If it shall be shown to lower the character of man, to cloud his hopes, or to impair the sense of duty, he will be grateful to those who may point out his error, and deliver him from the poignant regret of adopting opinions which lead to consequences so pernicious.

NOTES AND ILLUSTRATIONS.

NOTES AND ILLUSTRATIONS.

Note A, p. 29.

The remarks of Cicero on the Stoicism of Cato are perhaps the most perfect specimen of that refined raillery which attains the object of the orator without general injustice to the person whose authority is for the moment to be abated.

"Accessit his doctrina non moderata, nec mitis, sed, ut mihi videtur, paulo asperior et durior quam aut veritas aut natura patiatur." After an enumeration of the Stoical paradoxes, he adds, "Hæc homo ingeniosissimus M. Cato arripuit, neque disputandi causa, ut magna pars, sed ita vivendi. Nostri autem illi (fatebor enim me quoque in adolescentia diffisum ingenio meo quæsisse adjumenta doctrinæ) nostri, inquam, illi a Platone atque Aristotele moderati homines et temperati aiunt apud sapientem valere aliquando gratiam; viri boni esse misereri; . . . . . omnes virtutes mediocritate quadam moderatas. Hos ad magistros si qua te fortuna, Cato, cum ista natura detulisset, non tu quidem vir melior esses, nec fortior, nec temperantior, nec justior (neque enim esse posses), sed paulo ad lenitatem propensior."—(Cicero *pro Murœna.*)

Note B, p. 36.

The greater part of the following extract from Grotius' *History of the Netherlands* is inserted as the best abridgment of the ancient history of these still subsisting controversies known in our time. I extract also the introduction as a model of the manner in which an historian may state a religious dispute which has influenced political affairs; but far more because it is an unparalleled example of equity and forbearance in the narrative of a contest of which the historian was himself a victim.

"Habuit hic annus (1608) haud spernendi quoque mali semina, vix ut arma desierant, exorto publicæ religionis dissidio, latentibus initiis, sed ut paulatim in majus erumperet. Lugduni sacras literas docebant viri eruditione præstantes Gomarus et Arminius, quorum ille æterna Dei lege fixum memorabat, cui hominum salus destinaretur, quis in exitium tenderet; inde alios ad pietatem trahi, et tractos custodiri ne elabantur; relinqui alios communi humanitatis vitio et suis criminibus involutos: hic vero contra integrum judicem, sed eundem optimum patrem, id reorum fecisse discrimen, ut peccandi pertæsis fiduciamque in Christum reponentibus veniam ac vitam daret, contumacibus pœnam; Deoque gratum, ut omnes resipiscant, ac meliora edocti retineant; sed cogi neminem. Accusabantque invicem; Arminius Gomarum, quod peccandi causas Deo ascriberet, ac fati persuasione teneret immobiles animos; Gomarus Arminium, quod longius ipsis Romanensium scitis hominem arrogantia impleret, *nec pateretur soli Deo acceptam ferri, rem maximam, bonam mentem.* Constat his queis cura legere veterum libros, antiquos Christianorum tribuisse hominum voluntati vim liberam, tam in acceptanda, quam in retinenda disciplina; unde sua præmiis ac suppliciis æquitas. Neque iidem tamen omisere cuncta divinam ad bonitatem referre, cujus munere salutare semen ad nos pervenisset, ac cujus singulari auxilio pericula nostra indigerent. Primus omnium Augustinus, ex quo ipsi cum Pelagio et eum secutis certamen (*nam ante aliter et ipse senserat*), acer disputandi, ita libertatis vocem relinquere, ut ei decreta quædam Dei præponeret, quæ vim ipsam destruere viderentur. At per Græciam quidem Asiamque retenta vetus illa ac simplicior sententia. Per occidentem magnum Augustini nomen multos traxit in consensum, repertis tamen per Galliam et alibi que se opponerent. Posterioribus sæculis, cum schola non alio magis quam Augustino doctore uteretur, quis ipsi sensus, quis dexter pugnare visa conciliandi modus, diu inter Francisci et Dominici familiam disputato, doctissimi Jesuitarum, cum exactiori subtilitate nodum solvere laborassent, Romæ accusati ægre damnationem effugere. At Protestantium princeps, Lutherus, egressus monasterio quod Augustini ut nomen, ita sensus sequebatur, parte Augustini arrepta, id quod is reliquerat, libertatis nomen, cœpit exscindere; quod tam grave Erasmo visum, ut cum cætera ipsius aut probaret aut silentio transmitteret, hic objiciat sese; cujus, argumentis motus Philippus Melanchthon, Lutheri adjutor, quæ prius scripserat immutavit, auctorque fuit Luthero, quod multi volunt, certe quod constat Lutheranis, deserendi decreta rigida et conditionem respuentia; sic tamen ut libertatis vocabulum quam rem magis perhorrescerent. At in altera Protestantium parte dux Calvinus, primis Lutheri dictis in hac controversia inhærescens, novis ea fulsit præsidiis, *addiditque intactum Augustino, veram ac salutarem fidem rem esse perpetuam et amitti nesciam :* cujus proinde qui sibi essent conscii, eos æternæ felicitatis jam nunc certos esse, quos interim in crimina, quantumvis gravia, prolabi posse non diffitebatur. Auxit sententiæ rigorem Genevæ Beza, per Germaniam Zanchius, Ursinus, Piscator, sæpe eo usque provecti, ut, quod alii anxie vitaverant, apertius nonnunquam traderent, etiam peccandi necessitatem a prima causa pendere : quæ ampla Lutheranis criminandi materia."—(H. GROTII *Hist.* lib. xvii. p. 552.)

Note C, p. 37.

The Calvinism, or rather Augustinianism, of Aquinas, is placed beyond all doubt by the following passages :—

" Prædestinatio est causa gratiæ et gloriæ."—(*Opera*, vii. 356, edit. Paris, 1664.)

" Numerus prædestinatorum certus est."—(*Ibid.* 363.)

" Præscientia meritorum nullo modo est causa prædestinationis divinæ."—(*Ibid.* 370.)

" Liberum arbitrium est facultas qua bonum eligitur, gratia assistente, vel malum, eadem desistente."—(*Ibid.* viii. 222.)

" Deus inclinat ad bonum administrando virtutem agendi et monendo ad bonum. Sed ad malum dicitur inclinare in quantum gratiam non præbet, per quam aliquis a malo retraheretur."—(*Ibid.* 364.)

On the other side :—

" Accipitur fides pro eo quo creditur, et est virtus, et pro eo quod creditur, et non est virtus. Fides qua creditur, si cum caritate sit, virtus est."—(*Ibid.* ix. 236.)

" Divina bonitas est primum principium communicationis totius quam Deus creaturis largitur."

" Quamvis omne quod Deus vult justum sit, non tamen ex hoc justum dicitur quod Deus illud vult."—(*Ibid.* 697.)

Note D, p. 38.

The Augustinian doctrine is, with some hesitation and reluctance, acquiesced in by Scotus, in that milder form which ascribes election to an express decree, and considers the rest of mankind as only left to the deserved penalties of their transgressions. " In hujus quæstionis solutione mallem alios audire quam docere."—(Scoti *Opera*, v. 1329, Ludg. 1639.) This modesty and prudence is foreign from the dogmatical genius of a Schoolman; and these qualities are still more apparent in the very remarkable language which he applies to the tremendous doctrine of reprobation:—" Eorum autem non misereatur (scil. Deus) *quibus gratiam non præbendam esse æquitate occultissima et ab humanis sensibus remotissima judicat.*"—(*Ibid.* 1329.) In the commentary on Scotus which follows, it appears that his acute disciple Ockham disputed very freely against the opinions of his master. "*Mala fieri bonum est*" is a startling paradox, quoted by Scotus from Augustin.—(*Ibid.* 1381.) It appears that Ockham saw no difference between election and reprobation, and considered those who embraced only the former as at variance with themselves.—(*Ibid.* 1313.)

Scotus, at great length, contends that our thoughts (consequently our opinions) are not subject to the will (iv. 1054-1056). One step more would have led him to acknowledge that all erroneous judgment is involuntary, and therefore inculpable and unpunishable, however pernicious.

His attempt to reconcile foreknowledge with contingency (v. 1300-1327), is a remarkable example of the power of human subtlety to keep up the appearance of a struggle where it is impossible to make one real effort.

But the most dangerous of all the deviations of Scotus from the system of Aquinas is, that he opened the way to the opinion that the distinction of right and wrong depends on the mere will of the Eternal mind. The absolute power of the Deity, according to him, extends to all but contradictions. His regular power (*ordinata*) is exercised conformably to an order established by himself; "SI PLACET VOLUNTATI, sub qua libera est, RECTA EST LEX."—(SCOT. V. 1368, *et seq.*)

Note E, p. 38.

Αλλα ημιν ψυχην γε ισμεν ακουσαν πασαν παν αγνοουσαν.
(Plat. *Soph.* edit. Bip. II. 224.)

Πασαν ακουσιον αμαθιανειναι. (*Ibid.* 227.)

Plato is quoted on this subject by Marcus Aurelius, in a manner which shows, if there had been any doubt, the meaning to be, that all *error* is involuntary.

Πασα ψυχη ακουσα, φησιν (Πλατων) στερεται αληθειας.
Every mind is unwillingly led from truth.
(EPICT. lib. i. cap. xxviii.)

Augustin closes the long line of ancient testimony to the involuntary character of error : " Quis est qui velit decipi ? Fallere nolunt boni ; falli autem nec boni volunt nec mali."—(AUG. *Serm. de Verbo.*)

NOTE F, p. 38.

From a long, able, and instructive dissertation by the commentator on Scotus, it appears that this immoral dogma was propounded in terms more bold and startling by Ockham, who openly affirmed that "moral evil was only evil because it was prohibited." " Ochamus, qui putat quod nihil posset esse malum sine voluntate prohibitiva Dei, hancque voluntatem esse liberam ; sic ut posset eam non habere, et consequenter ut posset fieri quod nulla prorsus essent mala."—(SCOT. vii. p. 859.) But, says the commentator, " Dico primo legem naturalem non consistere in jussione ulla quæ sit actus voluntatis Dei. Hæc est communissima theologorum sententia."—(SCOT. vii. p. 858.) And indeed the reason urged against Ockham completely justifies this approach to unanimity. "For," he asks, "why is it right to obey the will of God ? Is it because our moral faculties perceive it to be right ? But they equally perceive and feel the authority of all the primary principles of morality ; and if this answer be made, it is obvious that those who make it do in effect admit the independence of moral distinctions on the will of God."

"If God," said Ockham, "had commanded his creatures to hate himself, hatred of God would have been praiseworthy."—(DOMIN. SOTO *de Justitia et Jure*, lib. ii. quæst. 3, " *Utrum præcepta Decalogi sint dispensabilia ;*" a book dedicated to Don Carlos, the son of Philip II.) Suarez, the last Scholastic philosopher, rejected the Ockhamical doctrine, but allowed will to be a *part* of the foundation of morality. " Voluntas Dei *non est tota* ratio bonitatis aut malitiæ."—(SUAREZ *de Legibus*, lib. ii. 66, p. 71, edit. Lond. 1679.)

As the great majority of the Schoolmen supported their opinion of this subject by the consideration of eternal and immutable ideas of right and wrong in the divine intellect, it was natural that the Nominalists, of whom Ockham was the founder, who rejected all general ideas, should also have rejected those moral distinctions which were then supposed to originate in such ideas. Gerson was a celebrated Nominalist; and he was the more disposed to follow the opinions of his master, because they agreed in maintaining the independence of the State on the Church, and the superiority of the Church over the Pope.

Note G, p. 40.

It must be premised that *Charitas* among the ancient divines corresponded with Ἔρως of the Platonists, and with the Φιλία of later philosophers, as comprehending the love of all that is loveworthy in the Creator or his creatures. It is the theological virtue of charity, and corresponds with no term in use among modern moralists. "Cum objectum amoris sit bonum, dupliciter potest aliquis tendere in bonum alicujus rei; uno modo, quod bonum *illius rei ad alterum referat,* sicut amat quis vinum in quantum dulcedinem vini peroptat; et hic amor vocatur a quibusdam amor concupiscentiæ, *Amor autem iste non terminatur ad rem quæ dicitur amari, sed reflectitur ad rem illam cui optatur bonum illius rei.* Alio modo amor fortior in bonum alicujus rei, *ita quod ad rem ipsam* TERMINATUR; et hic est amor benevolentiæ. Qua bonum nostrum in Deo perfectum est, sicut in causa universali bonorum; ideo bonum *in ipso esse magis naturaliter complacet* quam in nobis *ipsis:* et ideo etiam amore amicitiæ *naturaliter Deus* ab homine plus seipso deligitur."

The above quotations from Aquinas will probably be sufficient for those who are acquainted with these questions, and they will certainly be thought too large by those who are not. In the next question he inquires, whether in the love of God there can be any view to reward. He appears to consider himself as bound by authority to answer in the affirmative; and he employs much ingenuity in reconciling a certain expectation of reward with the disinterested character ascribed by him to piety in common with all the affections which terminate in other beings. "*Nihil aliud est merces nostra quam perfrui Deo.* Ergo charitas non solum non excludit sed etiam facit habere oculum ad mercedem." In this answer he seems to have anticipated the representations of Jeremy Taylor (*Sermon on Growth in Grace*); of Lord Shaftesbury (*Inquiry concerning Virtue*, book i. part iii. sect. 3); of Mr. T. Erskine (*Freeness of the Gospel*, Edin. 1828); and more especially of Mr. John Smith (*Discourses*, Lond. 1660). No extracts could convey a just conception of the observations which follow, unless they were accompanied by a longer examination of the technical language of the Schoolmen than would be warranted on this occasion. It is clear that he distinguishes well the affection of piety from the happy fruits, which, as he cautiously expresses it, "are in the nature of a reward," just as the consideration of the pleasures and advantages of friendship may enter into the affection and strengthen it, though they are not its objects, and never could inspire such a feeling. It seems to me also that he had a dimmer view of another doctrine, by which we are taught, that, though our own happiness be not the end which we pursue in loving others, yet it may be the final cause of the insertion of disinterested affections into the nature of man. "Ponere mercedem aliquam finem amoris ex parte amati, est contra rationem amicitiæ. Sed ponere mercedem esse finem amoris ex parte amantis, non tamen ultimum, prout scilicet ipse amor est quædam operatio amantis, non est contra rationem amicitiæ. Possum operationem amoris amare propter aliquid aliud, salva amicitia. Potest habeas *charitatem habere oculum ad mercedem, uti ponat beatitudinem creatam finem amoris, non autem finem amati.*" Upon the last words my interpretation chiefly depends. The immediately preceding sentence must be owned to have been founded on a distinction between viewing the good fruits of our own affections as enhancing their intrinsic pleasures, and feeling love for another on account of the advantage to be derived from him; which last is inconceivable.

Note H, p. 40.

"Potestas spiritualis et secularis utraque deducitur a potestate divina; ideo in tantum secularis est sub spirituali, in quantum est a Deo supposita; scilicet, in his quæ ad salutem animæ pertinent. In his autem quæ ad bonum civile spectant, est magis obediendum potestati seculari; sicut illud Matthæi, 'Reddite quæ sunt Cæsaris Cæsari.'" What follows is more doubtful. "Nisi *forte* potestati spirituali etiam potestas secularis conjungatur, ut in Papa, qui utriusque potestatis apicem tenet." —(viii. 435.) "Here," says the French editor, "it may be doubted whether Aquinas means the Pope's temporal power in his own dominions, or a secular authority indirectly extending over all for the sake of religion." My reasons for adopting the more national construction are shortly these:—1. The text of Matthew is so plain an assertion of the independence of both owners, that it would be the height of extravagance to quote it as an *authority* for the dependence of the State. At most it could only be represented as *reconcilable* with such dependence in one case. 2. The word *forte* seems manifestly to refer to the territorial sovereignty acquired by the Popes. If they have a general power in secular affairs, it must be because it is necessary to their spiritual authority; and in that case to call it fortuitous would be to ascribe to it an adjunct destructive of its nature. 3. His former reasoning on the same question seems to be decisive. " The power of the Pope over bishops," he says, "is not founded merely in his superior nature, but in their authority being altogether derived from his, as the proconsular power from the imperial." Therefore he infers that this case is not analogous to the relation between the civil and spiritual power, which are alike derived from God. 4. Had an Italian monk of the twelfth century really intended to affirm the Pope's temporal authority, he probably would have laid it down in terms more explicit and more acceptable at Rome. Hesitation and ambiguity are here indications of unbelief. Mere veneration for the apostolical see might present a more precise determination against it, as it caused the quotation which follows, respecting the primacy of Peter.—(AQUIN. *Opera*, viii. 434, 435.)

A mere abridgment of these very curious passages might excite a suspicion that I had tinctured Aquinas unconsciously with a colour of my own opinions. Extracts are very difficult, from the scholastic method of stating objections and answers, as well as from the mixture of theological authorities with philosophical reasons.

Note I, p. 43.

The debates in the first assembly of the Council of Trent (1546), between the Dominicans who adhered to Aquinas, and the Franciscans who followed Scotus on original sin, justification, and grace, are to be found in Fra Paolo, *Istoria del Concilio Tridentino*, lib. ii. They show how much metaphysical controversy is hid in a theological form, how many disputes of our times are of no very ancient origin, and how strongly the whole Western church, through all the divisions into which it has been separated, has manifested the same unwillingness to avow the Augustinian system, and the same fear of contradicting it. To his admirably clear and short statement of these abstruse controversies, must be added that of his accomplished opponent Cardinal Pallavicino (lib. vii. and viii.), who shows still more evidently the strength of the Augustinian party, and the disposition of the Council to tolerate opinions almost Lutheran, if not accompanied by revolt from the Church. A little more compromising disposition in the Reformers might have betrayed reason to a prolonged thraldom. We must esteem Erasmus and Melanchthon, but we should reserve our gratitude for Luther and Calvin. The Scotists maintained their doctrine of merit of congruity, waived by the Council and soon after condemned by the Church of England; by which they meant that they who had good dispositions always received the divine grace, not indeed as a reward of which they were worthy, but as aid which they were fit and willing to receive. The Franciscans denied that belief was in the power of man. "I Francescani lo negavano seguendo Scoto, qual vuole che siccome dalle dimostrazioni per necessità nasce la scienza, così dalle persuasioni nasca la fede; e ch'essa é nell' intelletto, il quale é agente naturale, e mosso naturalmente dall'oggetto. Allegavano l'esperienza, che nessuno può credere che vuole, ma quello che gli par vero."—(FRA PAOLO, *Istoria del Concilio Tridentino*, i. 193; edit. Helmstadt, 1763, 4to.)

Cardinal Sforza Pallavicino, a learned and very able Jesuit, was appointed, according to his own account, in 1651, many years after the death of Fra Paolo, to write a true history of the Council of Trent, as a corrective of the misrepresentations of the celebrated Venetian. Algernon Sidney, who knew this court historian at Rome, and who may be believed when he speaks well of a Jesuit and a Cardinal, commends the work in a letter to his father, Lord Leicester. At the end of Pallavicino's work is a list of three hundred and sixty errors in matters of fact, which the papal party pretend to have detected in the independent historian, whom they charge with heresy or infidelity, and, in either case, with hypocrisy.

Note K, p. 48.

"Hoc tempore, Ferdinando et Isabella regnantibus, in academia Salmantina jacta sunt robustioris theologiæ semina; ingentis enim famæ vir Franciscus de Victoria, non tam lucubrationibus editis, quamvis hæc non magnæ molis at magni pretii sint, sed doctissimorum theologorum educatione, quamdiu fuerit sacræ scientiæ honos inter mortales, vehementer laudabitur."—(ANTONII *Bibl. Hisp. Nova*, Præf. iv. Madrid, 1783.) "Si ad morum instructores respicias, Sotus iterum nominabitur."—(*Ibid.*)

Note L, p. 49.

The title of the published account of the conference at Valladolid is, "The controversy between the Bishop of Chiapa and Dr. Sepulveda; in which the Doctor contended that the conquest of the Indies from the natives was lawful, and the Bishop maintained that it was unlawful, tyrannical, and unjust, in the presence of many theologians, lawyers, and other learned men assembled by his majesty."—(ANTONII *Bibl. Hisp. Nova*, tom. i. p. 192.)

Las Casas died in 1566, in the 92d year of his age; Sepulveda died in 1571, in his 82d year.

Sepulveda was the scholar of Pomponatius, and a friend of Erasmus, Cardinal Pole, Aldus Manutius, etc. In his book *De Justis Belli Causis contra Indos suscepti*, he contended only that the king might justly "ad ditionem Indos, non herilem sed regiam et civilem, lege belli redigere."—(ANTONIUS in voce *Sepulveda: Bibl. Hisp. Nova*, tom. i. p. 703.)

But this smooth and specious language covered a poison. Had it entirely prevailed, the cruel consequence of the defeat of the advocate of the oppressed would alone have remained; the limitations and softenings employed by their opponent to obtain success would have been speedily disregarded and forgotten.

Covarruvias, another eminent Jurist, was sent by Philip II. to the Council of Trent, at its renewal in 1560, and, with Cardinal Buoncampagni, drew up the decrees of reformation. Francis Sanchez, the father of philosophical grammar, published his *Minerva* at Salamanca in 1587; so active was the cultivation of Philosophy in Spain in the age of Cervantes.

Note M, p. 79.

"Alors en repassant dans mon esprit les diverses opinions qui m'avoient tour-à-tour entraîné depuis ma naissance, je vis que bien qu'aucune d'elles ne fût assez évidente pour produire immédiatement la conviction, elles avoient divers degrés de vraisemblance, et que l'assentiment intérieur s'y prêtoit ou s'y refusoit à différentes mesures. Sur cette première observation, comparant entr' elles toutes ces différentes idées dans le silence des préjugés, je trouvai que la première, et la plus commune, étoit aussi la plus simple et la plus raisonnable; et qu'il ne lui manquoit, pour réunir tous les suffrages, que d'avoir été proposée la dernière. Imaginez tous vos philosophes anciens et modernes, ayant d'abord épuisé leur bizarres systêmes de forces, de chances, de fatalité, de nécessité, d'atomes, de monde animé, de matiere vivante, de matérialisme de toute espèce ; et après eux tous l'illustre Clarke, éclairant le monde annonçant enfin l'Etre des êtres, et le dispensateur des choses. Avec quelle universelle admiration, avec quel applaudissement unanime n'eût point été reçu ce nouveau systême si grand, si consolant, si sublime, si propre à élever l'ame à donner une base à la vertu, et en même tems si frappant, si lumineux, si simple, et, ce me semble, offrant moins de choses incompréhensibles à l'esprit humain, qu'il n'en trouve d'absurdes en tout autre systême ! Je me disois, les objections insolubles sont communes à tous, parceque l'esprit de l'homme est trop borné pour les résoudre : elles ne prouvent donc rien contre aucun par préférence, mais quelle différence entre les preuves directes."—(*Emile*, tome iii. livre iv. p. 25.)

NOTE N, pp. 102, 103.

" Est autem *jus* quædam potentia moralis, et obligatio necessitas moralis. *Moralem* autem intelligo, quæ apud virum bonum æquipollet naturali : Nam ut præclare jurisconsultus Romanus ait, *quæ contra bonos mores sunt, ea nec facere nos posse credendum est. Vir bonus* autem est, qui amat omnes, quantum ratio permittit. *Justitiam* igitur, quæ virtus est hujus affectus rectrix, quem Φιλανθρωπιαν Græci vocant, commodissime, ni fallor, definiemus caritatem sapientis, hoc est, sequentem sapientiæ dictata. Itaque, quod *Carneades* dixisse, fertur, justitiam esse summam stultitiam, quia alienis utilitatibus consuli jubeat, neglectis propriis, ex ignorata ejus definitione natum est. *Caritas* est benevolentia universalis, et *benevolentia* amandi sive diligendi habitus. *Amare* autem sive diligere est felicitate alterius delectari, vel quod eodem redit, felicitatem alienam adsciscere in suam. Unde difficilis nodus solvitur, magni etiam in Theologia momenti, quomodo amor non mercenarius detur, qui sit a spe metuque et omni utilitatis respectu separatus ; scilicet, quorum utilitas delectat, eorum felicitas nostram ingreditur, nam quæ delectant per se expetuntur. Et uti pulchrorum contemplatio ipsa jucunda est, pictaque tabula *Raphaelis* intelligentem afficit, etsi nullos census ferat, adeo ut in oculis deliciisque feratur, quodam simulacro amoris ; ita quum res pulchra simul etiam felicitatis est capax, transit affectus in verum amorem. Superat autem *divinus amor* alios amores, quos Deus cum maximo successu amare potest, quando Deo simul et felicius nihil est, et nihil pulchrius felicitateque dignius intelligi potest. Et quum idem sit potentiæ sapientiæque summæ, felicitas ejus non tantum ingreditur nostram (si sapimus, id est, ipsum amamus), sed et facit. Quia autem sapientia caritatem dirigere debet, hujus quoque definitione opus erit. Arbitror autem notioni hominum optime satisfieri, si *sapientiam* nihil aliud esse dicamus, quam ipsam scientiam felicitatis."—(LEIBNITII *Opera*, tom. iv. pars iii. p. 294.)

"Et jus quidem merum sive strictum nascitur ex principio servandæ pacis; æquitas sive caritas ad majus aliquid contendit, ut, dum quisque alteri prodest quantum potest, felicitatem suam augeat in aliena; et, ut verbo dicam, jus strictum miseriam vitat, jus superius ad felicitatem tendet, sed qualis in hanc mortalitatem cadit. Quod vero ipsam vitam, et quicquid hanc vitam expetendam facit, magno commodo alieno posthabere debeamus, ita ut maximos etiam dolores in aliorum gratiam præferre oporteat; magis pulchre præcipitur a philosophis quam solide demonstratur. Nam decus et gloriam, et animi sui virtute gaudentis sensum, ad quæ sub honestatis nomine provocant, cogitationis sive mentis bona esse constat, magna quidem, sed non omnibus nec omni malorum acerbitati prævalitura, quando non omnes æque imaginando afficiuntur; præsertim quos neque educatio liberalis, neque consuetudo vivendi ingenua, vel vitæ sectæve disciplina ad honoris æstimationem, vel animi bona sentienda assuefecit. Ut vero universali demonstratione conficiatur, omne honestum esse utile, et omne turpe damnosum, assumenda est immortalitas animæ, et rector universi Deus. Ita fit ut omnes in civitate perfectissima vivere intelligamur, sub monarcha, qui nec ob sapientiam falli, nec ob potentiam vitari potest; idemque tam amabilis est, ut felicitas sit tali domino servire. Huic igitur qui animam impendit, Christo docente, eam lucratur. Hujus potentia providentiaque efficitur, ut omne jus in factum transeat, ut nemo lædatur nisi a se ipso, ut nihil recte gestum sine præmio sit, nullum peccatum sine pœna."—(*Ibid.* p. 296.)

NOTE O, p. 107.

The writer of this Discourse was led, on a former occasion, by a generally prevalent notion, too nearly to confound the theological doctrine of predestination with the philosophical opinion which supposed the determination of the will to be, like other events, produced by adequate causes. (See a criticism on Mr. Stewart's Dissertation, *Edinb. Review*, xxxvi. 255.) More careful reflection has corrected a confusion common to him with most writers on the subject. What is called *Sublapsarian Calvinism*, which was the doctrine of the most eminent men, including Augustin and Calvin himself, ascribed to God, and to man before the Fall, what is called free-will, which they even own still to exist in all the ordinary acts of life, though it be lost with respect to religious morality. The decree of election, on this scheme, arises from God's foreknowledge that man was to fall, and that all men became thereby with justice liable to eternal punishment. The election of some to salvation was an act of divine goodness, and the preterition of the rest was an exercise of holiness and justice.

This sublapsarian predestination is evidently irreconcilable with the doctrine of necessity, which considers free-will or volitions not caused by motives as absolutely inconsistent with the definition of an intelligent being, which is, that he acts from a motive, or, in other words, with a purpose.

The supralapsarian scheme, which represents the Fall itself as fore-ordained, may indeed be built on necessitarian principles. But on that scheme original sin seems wholly to lose that importance which the former system gives it as a revolution in the state of the world, requiring an interposition of divine power to remedy a part of its fatal effects. It becomes no more than the first link in the chain of predestined offences. Yet both Catholic and Protestant predestinarians have borrowed the arguments and distinctions of philosophical necessitarians. One of the propositions of Jansenius, condemned by the bull of Innocent X. in 1653, is, that "to merit or demerit in a state of lapsed nature, it is not necessary that there should be in man a liberty free from necessity. It is sufficient that there be a liberty free from constraint."—(DUPIN, *Histoire de l'Eglise en abrégé*, siècle xvii. livre iv. chap. viii. p. 193.) Luther, in his once famous treatise *de Servo Arbitrio* against Erasmus (printed in 1526), expresses himself as follows:—" Hic est fidei summus gradus, credere illum esse clementem qui tam paucos salvat, tam multos damnat ; credere justum qui sua voluntate nos necessario damnabiles facit, ut videatur, ut Erasmus refert, delectari cruciatibus miserorum, et odio potius quam amore dignus." My copy of this stern and abusive book is not paged. In another passage, he states the distinction between coaction and necessity as familiar a hundred and thirty years before it was proposed by Hobbes, or condemned in the Jansenists. "Necessario dico, non coacte, sed, ut illi dicunt, necessitate immutabilitatis, non coactionis; hoc est homo, cum vocat Spiritus Dei, non quidem violentia, velut raptus obtorto collo, nolens facit malum, quemadmodum fur aut latro nolens ad pœnam ducitur, sed sponte et libera voluntate facit." He uses also the illustration of Hobbes, from the difference between a stream *forced* out of its course and *freely* flowing in its channel.

Note P, p. 134.

Though some parts of the substance of the following letter have already appeared in various forms, perhaps the account of Mr. Hume's illness, in the words of his friend and physician Dr. Cullen, will be acceptable to many readers. I owe it to the kindness of Mrs. Baillie, who had the goodness to copy it from the original, in the collection of her late learned and excellent husband, Dr. Baillie. Some portion of what has been formerly published I do not think it necessary to reprint.

From Dr. Cullen to Dr. Hunter.

"My dear Friend—I was favoured with yours by Mr. Halket on Sunday, and have answered some part of it by a gentleman whom I was otherwise obliged to write by; but as I was not certain how soon that might come to your hand, I did not answer your postscript; in doing which, if I can oblige you, a part of the merit must be that of the information being early, and I therefore give it you as soon as I possibly could. You desire an account of Mr. Hume's last days, and I give it you with some pleasure; for though I could not look upon him in his illness without much concern, yet the tranquillity and pleasantry which he constantly discovered did even then give me satisfaction, and, now that the curtain is dropped, allows me to indulge the less allayed reflection. He was truly an example *des grands hommes qui sont morts en plaisantant*. . . . . . . For many weeks before his death he was very sensible of his gradual decay; and his answer to inquiries after his health was, several times, that he was going as fast as enemies could wish, and as easily as his friends could desire. He was not, however, without a frequent recurrence of pain and uneasiness; but he past most part of the day in his drawing-room, admitted the visits of his friends, and, with his usual spirit, conversed with them upon literature, politics, or whatever else was accidentally started. In conversation he seemed to be perfectly at ease, and to the last abounded with that pleasantry, and those curious and entertaining anecdotes, which ever distinguished him. This, however, I always considered rather as an effort to be agreeable; and he at length acknowledged that it became too much for his strength. For a few days before his death he became more averse to receive visits; speaking became more and more difficult for him, and for twelve hours before his death his speech failed altogether. His senses and judgment did not fail till the last hour of his life. He constantly discovered a strong sensibility to the attention and care of his friends; and, amidst great uneasiness and languor, never betrayed any peevishness or impatience. This is a general account of his last days; but a particular fact or two may perhaps convey to you a still better idea of them.

*   *   *   *   *

"About a fortnight before his death he added a codicil to his will, in which he fully discovered his attention to his friends, as well as his own pleasantry. What little wine he himself drank was generally port, a wine for which his friend the poet [John Home] had ever declared the strongest aversion. David bequeathes to his friend John one bottle of port; and, upon condition of his drinking this at two even down-sittings, bestows upon him twelve dozen of his best claret. He pleasantly adds, that this subject of wine was the only one upon which they had ever differed. In the codicil there are several other strokes of raillery and pleasantry, highly expressive of the cheerfulness which he then enjoyed. He even turned his attention to some of the simple amusements with which he had been formerly pleased. In the neighbourhood of his brother's house in Berwickshire is a brook, by which the access in time of floods is frequently interrupted. Mr. Hume bequeathes £100 for building a bridge over this brook, but upon the express condition that none of the stones for that purpose shall be taken from a quarry in the neighbourhood, which forms part of a romantic scene in which, in his earlier days, Mr. Hume took particular delight. Otherwise the money to go to the poor of the parish.

"These are a few particulars which may perhaps appear trifling; but to me no particulars seem trifling that relate to so great a man. It is perhaps from trifles that we can best distinguish the tranquillity and cheerfulness of the philosopher at a time when the most part of mankind are under disquiet, anxiety, and sometimes even horror. ... I had gone so far when I was called to the country ; and I have returned only so long before the post as to say that I am most affectionately yours,

"William Cullen.

"*Edinburgh, 17th September 1776.*"

Note Q, p. 136.

Pyrrho was charged with carrying his scepticism so far as not to avoid a carriage if it was driven against him. Ænesidemus, the most famous of ancient sceptics, with great probability vindicates the more ancient doubter from such lunacy, of which indeed his having lived to the age of ninety seems sufficient to acquit him. ʽΑινεσίδημος δε φησι φιλοσοφειν μεν αυτον κατα τον της εποχης λογον, μη μεντοι γε απροορατως εκαστα πραττειν. —(Diog. Laert. lib. ix. sect. 62.)

Brief and imperfect as our accounts of ancient scepticism are, it does appear that their reasoning on the subject of causation had some resemblance to that of Mr. Hume. Αναιρουσι δε το αιτιον ὡδε το αιτιον των προς τι εστι, προς γαρ τῳ αιτιατῳ εστι· τα δε προς τι επινοειται μονον ὑπαρχει δε ου· και το αιτιον ουν επινοοιτο αν μονον.—(*Ibid.* ix. sect. 97.) It is perhaps impossible to translate the important technical expression τα προς τι. It comprehends two or more things as related to each other—both the relative and correlative taken together as such. Fire considered as having the power of burning wood is το προς τι. The words of Laertius may therefore be nearly rendered into the language of modern philosophy as follows : " Causation they take away thus. A cause is so only in relation to an effect. What is relative is only conceived, but does not exist. Therefore cause is a mere conception."

The first attempt to prove the necessity of belief in a divine revelation, by demonstrating that natural reason leads to universal scepticism, was made by Algazel, a professor at Bagdad, in the beginning of the twelfth century of our era ; whose work, entitled *The Destruction of the Philosophers,* is known to us only by the answer of Averroes, called *Destruction of the Destruction.* He denied a necessary connection between cause and effect ; for of two separate things, the affirmation of the existence of one does not necessarily contain the affirmation of the existence of the other ; and the same may be said of denial. It is curious enough that this argument was more especially pointed against those Arabian philosophers who, from the necessary connection of causes and effects, reasoned against the possibility of miracles; thus anticipating one doctrine of Mr. Hume to impugn another. —(TENNEMAN, *Gesh. der Phil.* viii. 387.)

The same attempt was made by the learned but unphilosophical Huet, bishop of Avranches (*Quæstiones Alnetanæ*, Caen, 1690, and *Traité de la Foiblesse de l'Esprit Humain*, Amsterdam, 1723). A similar motive urged Berkeley to his attack on Fluxions. The attempt of Huet has been lately renewed by the Abbé Lamennais, in his treatise on *Religious Indifference;* a fine writer, whose apparent reasonings amount to little more than well-varied assertions, and well-disguised assumptions of the points to be proved.

To build religion upon scepticism is the most extravagant of all attempts; for it destroys the proofs of a divine mission, and leaves no natural means of distinguishing between revelation and imposture. The Abbé Lamennais represents authority as the sole ground of belief. Why? If any reason can be given, the proposition must be false; if none, it is obviously a mere groundless assertion.

NOTE R, p. 143.

Casanova, a Venetian doomed to solitary imprisonment in the dungeons at Venice in 1755, thus speaks of the only books which for a time he was allowed to read. The title of the first was *Lé Cité Mystique de Sœur Marie de Jesus, appellée d'Agrada.*

"J'y lus tout ce que peut enfanter l'imagination exaltée d'une vierge Espagnole extravagamment dévote, cloitrée, mélancholique, ayant des directeurs de conscience, ignorans, faux, et dévots. Amoureuse et amie très intime de la Sainte Vierge, elle avait reçu ordre de Dieu même d'écrire la vie de sa divine mère. Les instructions nécessaires lui avaient été fournies par le Saint Esprit. Elle commençoit la vie de Marie, non pas du jour de sa naissance, mais du moment de son immaculée conception dans la sein de sa mère Anne. Après avoir narré en détail tout ce que sa divine héroïne fit les neuf mois qu'elle a passé dans la sein maternel, elle nous apprend qu'à l'âge de trois ans elle balayoit la maison, aidée par neuf cents domestiques, touts anges, commandés par leur propre Prince Michel. Ce qui frappe dans ce livre est l'assurance que tout est dit de bonne foi. Ce sont les visions d'un esprit sublime, qui, sans aucune ombre d'orgueil, ivre de

Dieu, croit ne révéler que ce que l'Esprit Saint lui inspire."—(*Mémoires de Casanova*, iv. 343. Leipsic, 1827.)

A week's confinement to this volume produced such an effect on the author, who, though an unbeliever and a debauchee, was then enfeebled by melancholy, bad air, and bad food, that his sleep was haunted, and his waking hours disturbed by its horrible visions. Many years after, passing through Agrada, in Old Castille, he charmed the old priest of that village by speaking of the biographer of the Virgin. The priest showed him all the spots which were consecrated by her presence, and bitterly lamented that the Court of Rome had refused to canonise her. It is the natural reflection of the writer, that the book was well qualified to turn a solitary prisoner mad, or to make a man at large an atheist. It ought not to be forgotten that the inquisitors of state at Venice, who proscribed this book, were probably of the latter persuasion. It is a striking instance of the infatuation of those who, in their eagerness to rivet the bigotry of the ignorant, use means which infallibly tend to spread utter unbelief among the educated. The book is a disgusting, but in its general outline seemingly faithful, picture of the dissolute manners spread over the Continent of Europe in the middle of the eighteenth century.

Note S, p. 147.

"The Treatise on the Law of War and Peace, the Essay on Human Understanding, the Spirit of Laws, and the Inquiry into the Causes of the Wealth of Nations, are the works which have most directly influenced the general opinion of Europe during the last two centuries. They are also the most conspicuous landmarks in the progress of the sciences to which they relate. It is remarkable that the defects of all these great works are very similar. The leading notions of none of them can, in the strictest sense, be said to be original, though Locke and Smith in that respect surpass their illustrious rivals. All of them employ great care in ascertaining those laws which are immediately deduced from experience, or directly applicable to practice; but apply metaphysical and abstract principles with considerable negligence. None pursues the order of science, beginning with first elements and advancing to more and more complicated conclusions; though Locke is perhaps less defective in method than the rest. All admit digressions which, though often intrinsically excellent, distract attention, and break the chain of thought.

None of them is happy in the choice, or constant in the use, of technical terms ; and in none do we find much of that rigorous precision which is the first beauty of philosophical language. Grotius and Montesquieu were imitators of Tacitus,—the first with more gravity, the second with more vivacity ; but both were tempted to forsake the simple diction of science in pursuit of the poignant brevity which that great historian has carried to a vicious excess. Locke and Smith chose an easy, clear, and free, but somewhat loose and verbose style—more concise in Locke— more elegant in Smith,—in both exempt from pedantry, but not void of ambiguity and repetition. Perhaps all these apparent defects contributed in some degree to the specific usefulness of these great works ; and, by rendering their contents more accessible and acceptable to the majority of readers, have more completely blended their principles with the common opinions of mankind."—(*Edinburgh Review*, vol. xxxvi. p. 244.)

Note T, p. 159.

Δει δ' ούτως, ώσπερ εν γραμματειῳ ᾡ μηδεν ὑπαρχει εντελεχειᾳ γεγραμμενον· ὁπερ συμβαινει επι του νου.—(ARIST. *de Anima*, lib. iii. cap. v. *Opera*, tom. ii. p. 50. Paris, 1639.)

A little before, in the same treatise, appears a great part of the substance of the famous maxim, *Nil est in intellectu quod non prius fuit in sensu.* ʹ Ηδε φαντασια κινησις τις δοκει ειναι, και ουκ ανευ αισθησεως γιγνεσθαι.—(*Ibid.* 47.)

In the tract on *Memory and Reminiscence* we find his enumeration of the principles of association. Διο και το εφεξης θηρευομεν, νοησαντες απο του νυν η αλλου τινος, και αφ' ὁμοιου η εναντιου, η του συνεγγυς.—(*Ibid.* ii. 86.) If the latter word be applied to time as well as space, and considered as comprehending causation, the enumeration will coincide with that of Hume. The term θηρευω is as significant as if it had been chosen by Hobbes. But it is to be observed that these principles are applied only to explain memory.

Something has been said on the subject, and something on the present writer, by Mr. Coleridge, in his unfortunately unfinished work called *Biographia Literaria*, chap. v., which seems to justify, if not to require, a few remarks.* That learned gentleman seems

---

* Coleridge, *Biographia Literaria*, chapter v. *On the Law of Association. Its history traced from Aristotle to Hartley.* "Sir James

to have been guilty of an oversight in quoting as a distinct work the *Parva Naturalia*, which is the collective name given by the scholastic translators to those treatises of Aristotle which form the second volume of Duval's edition of his works, published at Paris in 1639. I have already acknowledged the striking resemblance of Mr. Hume's principles of association to those of Aristotle. In answer, however, to a remark of Mr. Coleridge, I must add, that the manuscript of a part of Aquinas which I bought many years ago (on the faith of a bookseller's catalogue) as being written by Mr. Hume, was not a copy of the Commentary on the *Parva Naturalia*, but of Aquinas' own *Secunda Secundæ;* and that, on examination, it proves not to be the handwriting of Mr. Hume, and to contain nothing written by him. It is certain that, in the passages immediately preceding the quotation, Aristotle explains recollection as depending on a general law—that the idea of an object will remind us of the objects which immediately preceded or followed when originally perceived. But what Mr. Coleridge has not told us is, that the Stagyrite confines the application of this law *exclusively to the phenomena of recollection alone,* without any glimpse of a more general operation extending to all connections of thought and feeling—a wonderful proof, indeed, even so limited, of the sagacity of the great philosopher, but which for many ages continued barren of further consequences. The illustrations of Aquinas throw light on the original doctrine, and show that it was unenlarged in his time. "When we recollect Socrates, the thought of Plato occurs 'as like him.' When we re-

---

Mackintosh . . . affirmed in the Lectures delivered by him in Lincoln's Inn Hall, that the law of association, as established in the contemporaneity of the original impressions, formed the basis of all true psychology, etc. Of this prolific truth, of this great fundamental law, he declared Hobbes to have been the original discoverer, while its full application to the whole intellectual system is due to Hartley, etc.

"Of the former clause of this assertion . . . this is not the place to speak. So wide indeed is the chasm between Sir James Mackintosh's philosophical creed and mine, that so far from being able to join hands, we could scarcely make our views intelligible to each other: and to bridge it over would require more time, skill, and power, than I believe myself to possess. But the latter part involves for the greater part a mere question of fact and history. . . .

"First, then, I deny Hobbes' claim *in toto;* for he had been anticipated by *Descartes,* whose work *De Methodo* preceded Hobbes' *De Natura Humana* by more than a year."

member Hector, the thought of Achilles occurs 'as contrary.' The idea of a father is followed by that of a son 'as near.'"—(AQUIN. *Opera*, i. pars ii. p. 62, *et seq.*) Those of Ludovicus Vives, as quoted by Mr. Coleridge, extend no farther.

But if Mr. Coleridge will compare the parts of Hobbes on *Human Nature* which relate to this subject, with those which explain general terms, he will perceive that the philosopher of Malmesbury builds on these two foundations a general theory of the human understanding, of which reasoning is only a particular case. In consequence of the assertion of Mr. Coleridge that Hobbes was anticipated by Descartes in his excellent and interesting discourse on *Method*, I have twice reperused that work in quest of this remarkable anticipation, though, as I thought, well acquainted by my old studies with the writings of that great philosopher. My labour has, however, been in vain. I have discovered no trace of that or of any similar speculation. My edition is in Latin by Elzevir, at Amsterdam, in 1650, the year of Descartes' death. I am obliged, therefore, to conjecture that Mr. Coleridge, having mislaid his references, has, by mistake, quoted the discourse on *Method*, instead of another work; which would affect his inference from the priority of Descartes to Hobbes. It is not to be denied, that the opinion of Aristotle, repeated by so many commentators, may have found its way into the mind of Hobbes, and also of Hume; though neither might be aware of its source, or even conscious that it was not originally his own. Yet the very narrow view of association by Locke, his apparently treating it as a novelty, and the silence of common books respecting it, afford a presumption that the Peripatetic doctrine was so little known that it might have escaped the notice of these philosophers, one of whom boasted that he was unread,* and the other is not liable to the suspicion of unacknowledged borrowing.

To Mr. Coleridge, who distrusts his own power of building a bridge by which his ideas may pass into a mind so differently trained as mine, I venture to suggest, with that sense of his genius which no circumstance has hindered me from seizing every fit occasion to manifest, that more of my early years were employed in contemplations of an abstract nature, than of those of the majority of his readers; that there are not, even now, many of them less likely to be repelled from doctrines by singularity or uncouthness; more willing to allow that every

* [*i.e.* Unversed in books.—W. W.]

system has caught an advantageous glimpse of some side or corner of the truth; more desirous of exhibiting this dispersion of the fragments of wisdom by attempts to translate the doctrine of one school into the language of another;—who, when he cannot discover a reason for an opinion, considers it as important to discover the causes of its adoption by the philosopher; believing, in the most unfavourable cases, that one of the most arduous and useful researches of mental philosophy is to explore the subtile illusions which enable great minds to satisfy themselves by mere words, before they deceive others by payment in the same counterfeit coin. These habits, together with the natural influence of my age and avocations, lead me to suspect that in speculative philosophy I am nearer to indifference than to an exclusive spirit. I hope that it can neither be thought presumptuous nor offensive in me to doubt whether the circumstances of its being found difficult to convey a metaphysical doctrine to a person who, at one part of his life, made such studies his chief pursuit, may not imply either error in the opinion, or defect in the mode of communication.

Note V, p. 193.

A very late writer, who seems to speak for Mr. Bentham with authority, tells us that " the first time the phrase of ' the principle of utility' was brought decidedly into notice, was in the ' Essays, by David Hume,' published about the year 1742. In that work it is *mentioned* as the *name* of a principle which *might* be made the foundation of a system of morals, in *opposition to a system then in vogue, which was founded on what was called the 'moral sense.'* The ideas, however, there attached to it, are *vague, and defective in practical application.*"—(*Westminster Review*, No. xxi.) If these few sentences were scrutinised with the severity and minuteness of Bentham's *Fragment on Government*, they would be found to contain almost as many misremembrances as assertions. Utility is not " *mentioned*," but fully discussed, in Mr. Hume's Discourse. It is seldom spoken of by " name." Instead of charging it with " *vagueness*," it would be more just to admire the precision which it combines with beauty. Instead of being " *defective in practical application*," perhaps the desire of rendering it popular has crowded it with examples and illustrations taken from life. To the assertion that " *it was opposed to the moral sense*," no reply can be needful but the following words extracted from the Discourse itself:—" I am apt to suspect that reason and *sentiment* concur in almost all moral determinations and conclusions. *The final sentence which pronounces characters and actions amiable or odious probably depends on some internal sense or feeling, which nature has made universal in the whole species."—(An Inquiry concerning the Principles of Morals*, sect. i.) The phrase " made universal," which is here used instead of the more obvious and common word " implanted," shows the anxious and perfect precision of language, by which a philosopher avoids the needless decision of a controversy not at the moment before him.

Note W, p. 196.

A writer of consummate ability, who has failed in little but the respect due to the abilities and character of his opponents, has given too much countenance to the abuse and confusion of language exemplified in the well-known verse of Pope,

> Modes of self-love the Passions we may call.

" We know," says he, " no universal proposition respecting human nature which is true but one—that men always act from self-interest."—(*Edinburgh Review*, March 1829.) It is manifest from the sequel that the writer is not the dupe of the confusion ; but many of his readers may be so. If, indeed, the word *self-interest* could with propriety be used for the gratification of every prevalent desire, he has clearly shown that this change in the signification of terms would be of no advantage to the doctrine which he controverts. It would make as many sorts of self-interest as there are appetites, and it is irreconcilably at variance with the system of association embraced by Mr. Mill. To the word *self-love* Hartley properly assigns two significations :—1. Gross self-love, which consists in the pursuit of the greatest pleasures, from all those desires which look to individual gratification ; or, 2. Refined self-love, which seeks the greatest pleasure which can arise from all the desires of human nature—the latter of which is an invaluable, though inferior principle.

The admirable writer whose language has occasioned this illustration, who at an early age has mastered every species of composition, will doubtless hold fast to simplicity, which survives all the fashions of deviation from it, and which a man of a genius so fertile has few temptations to forsake.

[The reference here is to an article by Macaulay in the *Edinburgh Review*. This article, published in March 1829, produced a reply in the *Westminster Review ;* to which Macaulay replied in June of the same year ; and a further reply in the *Westminster Review* was answered by Macaulay in the *Edinburgh* in October. This exchange of shots between the two belligerents was thus rapid and lively.

Macaulay certainly speaks of the school against which he argued—the Utilitarians, or Benthamites, as they were then called—as shallow and unphilosophical, arrogant and conceited. He says this of the followers of Mr. Bentham, while he expresses great respect for that philosopher himself. I think that any one who has read much of those writers will think that the above character was not ascribed to them without good grounds. That Mr. Bentham himself was open to remark as arrogant and unfair, I have, I think, shown in my Lectures on the History of Moral Philosophy in England.

Macaulay's "universal proposition," that "men always act from self-interest," is, as Mackintosh says, sufficiently shown by himself to be frivolous or false. The following passage contains his illustrations.

"This mission the Utilitarians proclaim with as much pride as if it were new, and as much zeal as if it were important. But in fact, when explained, it means only that men, if they can, will do as they choose. When we see the actions of a man we know with certainty what he thinks his interest to be. But it is impossible to reason with certainty from what *we* take to be his interest to his actions. One man goes without a dinner that he may add a shilling to a hundred thousand pounds ; another man runs in debt to give balls and masquerades. One man volunteers on a forlorn hope ; another is drummed out of a regiment for cowardice. Each of these men has no doubt acted from self-interest. But we gain nothing by knowing this, except the pleasure, if it be one, of multiplying useless words."

We may add, however, as appears to me, that words so employed are not only useless, but mischievous ; since they interfere with any precise use of language on such subjects. In the *Elements of Morality*, Art. 447, I have further discussed this phraseology.

Mackintosh was a veteran man of letters when he wrote this ; and in the expressions which conclude the note, wished to encourage Macaulay, who was then entering upon his distinguished literary career.—W. W.]

INDEX.

AFFECTATION, 232.
Affections (preface), xv; social, 70; benevolent, 116.
African slave trade, first condemned by Soto, 49.
Akenside, 235.
Anselm, Archbishop of Canterbury, 37.
Antisthenes, 17.
Aquinas, 37-40; Calvinism of (note), 283.
Aristippus, 17.
Aristotle, 20.
Association of ideas, 146, 159; (Brown), 237; term, 242; (preface), xxxix.
Atheism, the doctrine of Ockham, 39.
Augustin, Bishop of Hippo, 36.
Augustinian doctrine of election (note), 283.

BAYLE (note), 228.
Beattie, Dr. (note), 213.
Bell's Animal Mechanics, 181.
Benevolent affections, xv, 116.
BENTHAM, 187; (preface), xxv.
BERKELEY, 128.
Berkeley's Minute Philosopher (note), 89.
Blackstone, 186-189.
Boethius, 32.
Bonnet (note), 158.
BOSSUET, 96.
Bradwardine, Archbishop of Canterbury, 38.
Brougham, 193.
BROWN, 227.
BUFFIER, 110.
BUTLER, 113.
Butler's Analogy, 180.

CALVINISM of Aquinas (note), 283.

Cartesians, 206.
Casanova (note), 297.
Celibacy, clerical, 41.
Characteristics, by Lord Shaftesbury, 89.
"Charitas" of ancient divines (note), 286.
Christianity, peculiar distinction of, 205.
Chrysippus, 25.
Cicero, 24.
CLARKE, Dr. Samuel, 78.
Clement and Origen, 32.
Coleridge's Biographia Literaria (note), 299.
Collard's Lectures, 214.
Common Sense and Instinct, 213.
Condillac (note), 157, 160.
Conscience, 120, 169, 170, 240, 264; (preface), xxiii; Theory of, xlii.
Courage, 198.
Cousin's Cours de Philosophie, 214.
CUDWORTH, 73.
CUMBERLAND, Richard, 70.

D'ALEMBERT, anecdote of, 248.
Darwin's Zoonomia, 228.
Declamatory style, 232.
Delicacy and Modesty, 249.
Deontology, etc., from the MSS. of Jeremy Bentham (preface), xxvi.
Duty, 167, 170; (preface), xxiv.

ECLECTIC philosophy, 31.
Edinburgh Academy of Physics (note), 230.
Education, Mill's Essay on, 207.
EDWARDS, Jonathan, 107.
Election, doctrine of (note D), 283.
Epicurus, 22.
Epicureans, coincidence with Bentham school, 205.

x

Erskine's Unconditional Freeness of the Gospel (note), 96.
Ethics, Ancient, 16; Scholastic, 33; Modern, 52; injury to, by affinity to jurisprudence, 204; direct object of, 205.

FAME, love of, 200.
Feeling, 236.
FÉNÉLON, 96.
Ferguson, Dr. Adam, 210.
Fletcher, Andrew, 204.
Fortitude, Cicero's definition (note), 198.
Freethinkers, sect of (Nominalists), 45.
Freewill question, 272; (preface), xlvi.

GENTILI, Alberico, 51.
German philosophy, 267.
Gerson, 39.
Government (note), 186, 207.
Greece, short review of its practical philosophy, 17-32.
Grotius, 52 (note), 227; *History of the Netherlands* (extract from note), 281.
Guyon, Madame, 97.

HABEAS CORPUS ACT secured to England by Warburton, 89.
Hall's Sermon on Modern Infidelity (note), 199.
HARTLEY, 156.
Health of mind, 201.
HOBBES, 54; (preface), xxi.
Honour, 184.
Horner, Francis (note), 211.
HUME, 133; *on the Passions*, 152.
Humility, 198.
HUTCHESON, 124.
Hypothesis, illustration of (note), 236.

INSTINCT, 213.

JURISPRUDENCE, 190.
Justice, sense of, 167.
Justinian, 32.

KAMES, Lord (note), 164.
Kames' Essays on Morality and Natural Religion, etc., 274.

Kant, 268.

LANGUAGE, penury and laxity of, 3.
Laplace, 206.
Lardner's credibility of Gospel History, 180.
Las Casas, 49.
Latitudinarian party, 73.
Law, object of, 204.
LEIBNITZ, 100.
Leighton, Bishop of Dunblane (note), 73.
Lens, late Mr. (note), 190.
Louis XIV. 97.
Love, 115; (Charitas) note, 286. *See* Self-love.
Lowman on the unity and perfections of God, 81.
Luther a Nominalist, 45.

MALEBRANCHE, 105.
Manners, 231.
Mathematical forms and terms, 81.
Metaphysics, faults of the term, 3.
Middle age, progress made during, 33, 34.
Mill's Analysis of the Human Mind, 195; *theory of government*, 207.
Molinos, 97.
Moncreiff's Life of Erskine, 229.
Moral faculties, controversies concerning, 70; (preface), xxiii, xliv; affections, 239; theory of, 10; approbation, 241; judgment, 8; sentiments, xli, 148, 246.
Moralists, the, by Lord Shaftesbury, 92.
More, Henry (note), 96.
Motives, right, as represented by Zeno, 24.
Mystics, 41.

NEWTON, Sir Isaac, 206.
Nominalists, sect of freethinkers founded by Ockham, 39; controversy with Realists, 44.
NORRIS, 106.

OCKHAM, WILLIAM of, 38.
Ockham's doctrines (note), 285.

PALEY, 179; (preface), xxviii.
Perception and Emotion distinct, 84.
Perhaps, word (note), 243.

Peripatetics, doctrine of, 21.
Philo, 31.
Physics, reformation of, 206.
Plato, 17.
Pleasure, 178.
Pleasures of imagination, 170.
Plotinus and Porphyry, 32.
Political Economy, faults of term, 4.
Pope's authority (note), 287.
Praise, love of, 200.
Predestination, defence of, by Bradwardine, Archbishop of Canterbury, 38.
PRICE, 155.
Purity, 249.
Pursuit of Knowledge under difficulties (note), 259.
Pyrrho, 296.

REALISTS, 44.
Reason, 81-87.
Reformatory punishment, 190.
Reid's Enquiry into the Human Mind, 212.
Religion defined, 245.
Religion and Morality, relation of, 95 ; (preface), xlvi.
Right and wrong, 8 ; (Duty, xxiv).
"Righteousness of Scribes and Pharisees," 168.
Roman Patriciate, 27.
Romilly on Codification (note), 191.

SACCAS, 31.
Scepticism, universal, 137 ; ancient, 296.
Schoolmen, the, 36 ; their system, 40.
Science, primary object of, 248.
Scotch metaphysics, 127.
Scottish Church, 229.
Scotists, the, 43.
Scotus, Duns, 38 ; acquiescence in the Augustinian doctrine of election (note), 283 ; quot., 285.
Self-love, 115 ; (note), 303 ; (preface), xv.
Selfish, term (preface), xvii, xix ; System, 219.

"Sense of Justice," quot., 167.
Sepulveda, 49.
Sextus (note), 136.
SHAFTESBURY, EARL OF, 88 ; his *Characteristics*, 89 ; *Inquiry concerning Virtue*, 93.
SMITH, ADAM, 146 ; his *Wealth of Nations*, 146 ; *Theory of Moral Sentiments*, 147, 13.
Smith of Cambridge on Happiness and Holiness (note), 95.
Socrates, 17.
Soto, Dominic, 48.
Spain, and cultivation of speculative theology, 48.
Stahl (note), 157.
STEWART, DUGALD, 210.
Stoics, 24 ; doctrine (note), 113.
Stoicism of Cato (note), 281.
Suarez, Francis, 50.
Suggestion, 236 ; term, 241.
Supremacy, use of term (preface), xxx.
Sympathy, 148.

TAYLOR, JEREMY (note), 73 ; his growth in grace (note), 95.
TUCKER, 174.

UTILITY, 12 ; principle of, 193 ; (note) 302.

VANITY, 199.
Victoria, Francis, of Valladolid, 48.
Virtue represented by Epicurus, 23, 168, 170, 183 ; pleasures of, 199.

WARBURTON'S controversial zeal (note), 89.
Ward's Life of Henry More (note), 96.
Welsh's Life of Brown (note), 228.
Whewell's remarks on Mackintosh's Philosophy (preface), xiii.
Wilson, George, friend of Bentham (note), 190.
Wollaston's system (note), 88.

ZENO, 24.

Printed by R. CLARK, *Edinburgh.*

www.ingramcontent.com/pod-product-compliance
Lightning Source LLC
Chambersburg PA
CBHW020246240426
43672CB00006B/656